FORD FOCUS
WRC

THE **AUTO-BIOGRAPHY**
OF A **RALLY CHAMPION**

Graham Robson

Great Cars
Austin-Healey – A celebration of the fabulous 'Big' Healey (Piggott)
Jaguar E-type (Thorley)
Jaguar Mark 1 & 2 (Thorley)
Triumph TR – TR2 to 6: The last of the traditional sports cars (Piggott)

Truckmakers
DAF Trucks since 1949 (Peck)
Mercedes-Benz Trucks (Peck)

Auto-Graphics Series
Fiat-based Abarths (Sparrow)
Jaguar MKI & II Saloons (Sparrow)
Lambretta Li Series Scooters (Sparrow)

Rally Giants Series
Audi Quattro (Robson)
Austin Healey 100-6 & 3000 (Robson)
Fiat 131 Abarth (Robson)
Ford Escort MkI (Robson)
Ford Escort RS Cosworth & World Rally Car (Robson)
Ford Escort RS1800 (Robson)
Lancia Delta 4WD/Integrale (Robson)
Lancia Stratos (Robson)
Mini Cooper/Mini Cooper S (Robson)
Peugeot 205 T16 (Robson)
Saab 96 & V4 (Robson)
Subaru Impreza (Robson)
Toyota Celica GT4 (Robson)

WSC Giants
Audi R8 (Wagstaff)
Ferrari 312P & 312PB (Collins & McDonough)
Gulf-Mirage 1967 to 1982 (McDonough)
Matra Sports Cars – MS620, 630, 650, 660 & 670 – 1966 to 1974 (McDonough)

Biographies
A Chequered Life – Graham Warner and the Chequered Flag (Hesletine)
A Life Awheel – The 'auto' biography of W de Forte (Skelton)
Amédée Gordini … a true racing legend (Smith)
André Lefebvre, and the cars he created at Voisin and Citroën (Beck)
Chris Carter at Large – Stories from a lifetime in motorcycle racing (Carter & Skelton)
Cliff Allison, The Official Biography of – From the Fells to Ferrari (Gauld)
Edward Turner – The Man Behind the Motorcycles (Clew)
Driven by Desire – The Desiré Wilson Story
First Principles – The Official Biography of Keith Duckworth (Burr)
Inspired to Design – F1 cars, Indycars & racing tyres: the autobiography of Nigel Bennett (Bennett)
Jack Sears, The Official Biography of – Gentleman Jack (Gauld)
Jim Redman – 6 Times World Motorcycle Champion: The Autobiography (Redman)
John Chatham – 'Mr Big Healey' – The Official Biography (Burr)
The Lee Noble Story (Wilkins)
Mason's Motoring Mayhem – Tony Mason's hectic life in motorsport and television (Mason)
Raymond Mays' Magnificent Obsession (Apps)
Pat Moss Carlsson Story, The – Harnessing Horsepower (Turner)
'Sox' – Gary Hocking – the forgotten World Motorcycle Champion (Hughes)
Tony Robinson – The biography of a race mechanic (Wagstaff)
Virgil Exner – Visioneer: The Official Biography of Virgil M Exner Designer Extraordinaire (Grist)

General
1½-litre GP Racing 1961-1965 (Whitelock)
AC Two-litre Saloons & Buckland Sportscars (Archibald)
Alfa Romeo 155/156/147 Competition Touring Cars (Collins)
Alfa Romeo Giulia Coupé GT & GTA (Tipler)
Alfa Romeo Montreal – The dream car that came true (Taylor)
Alfa Romeo Montreal – The Essential Companion (Classic Reprint of 500 copies) (Taylor)
Alfa Tipo 33 (McDonough & Collins)
Alpine & Renault – The Development of the Revolutionary Turbo F1 Car 1968 to 1979 (Smith)
Alpine & Renault – The Sports Prototypes 1963 to 1969 (Smith)
Alpine & Renault – The Sports Prototypes 1973 to 1978 (Smith)
Anatomy of the Classic Mini (Huthert & Ely)
Anatomy of the Works Minis (Moylan)
Armstrong-Siddeley (Smith)
Art Deco and British Car Design (Down)
Autodrome (Collins & Ireland)
Automotive A-Z, Lane's Dictionary of Automotive Terms (Lane)
Automotive Mascots (Kay & Springate)
Bahamas Speed Weeks, The (O'Neil)
Bentley Continental, Corniche and Azure (Bennett)
Bentley MkVI, Rolls-Royce Silver Wraith, Dawn & Cloud/Bentley R & S-Series (Nutland)
Bluebird CN7 (Stevens)
BMC Competitions Department Secrets (Turner, Chambers & Browning)
BMW 5-Series (Cranswick)
BMW Z-Cars (Taylor)
BMW Boxer Twins 1970-1995 Bible, The (Falloon)
BMW Cafe Racers (Cloesen)
BMW Classic 5 Series 1972 to 2003 (Cranswick)
BMW Custom Motorcycles – Choppers, Cruisers, Bobbers, Trikes & Quads (Cloesen)
BMW – The Power of M (Vivian)
Bonjour – Is this Italy? (Turner)
British 250cc Racing Motorcycles (Pereira)
British at Indianapolis, The (Wagstaff)
British Café Racers (Cloesen)
British Cars, The Complete Catalogue of, 1895-1975 (Culshaw & Horrobin)
British Custom Motorcycles – The Brit Chop – choppers, cruisers, bobbers & trikes (Cloesen)
BRM – A Mechanic's Tale (Salmon)
BRM V16 (Ludvigsen)
BSA Bantam Bible, The (Henshaw)
BSA Motorcycles – the final evolution (Jones)
Bugatti – The 8-cylinder Touring Cars 1920-34 (Price & Arbey)
Bugatti Type 40 (Price)
Bugatti 46/50 Updated Edition (Price & Arbey)
Bugatti T44 & T49 (Price & Arbey)
Bugatti 57 2nd Edition (Price)
Bugatti Type 57 Grand Prix – A Celebration (Tomlinson)
Caravan, Improve & Modify Your (Porter)
Caravans, The Illustrated History 1919-1959 (Jenkinson)
Caravans, The Illustrated History From 1960 (Jenkinson)
Carrera Panamericana, La (Tipler)
Car-tastrophes – 80 automotive atrocities from the past 20 years (Honest John, Fowler)
Chrysler 300 – America's Most Powerful Car 2nd Edition (Ackerson)
Chrysler PT Cruiser (Ackerson)
Citroën DS (Bobbitt)
Classic British Car Electrical Systems (Astley)
Cobra – The Real Thing! (Legate)
Competition Car Aerodynamics 3rd Edition (McBeath)
Competition Car Composites A Practical Handbook (Revised 2nd Edition) (McBeath)
Concept Cars, How to illustrate and design – New 2nd Edition (Dewey)
Cortina – Ford's Bestseller (Robson)
Cosworth – The Search for Power (6th edition) (Robson)
Coventry Climax Racing Engines (Hammill)
Daily Mirror 1970 World Cup Rally 40, The (Robson)
Daimler SP250 New Edition (Long)
Datsun Fairlady Roadster to 280ZX – The Z-Car Story (Long)
Dino – The V6 Ferrari (Long)
Dodge Challenger & Plymouth Barracuda (Grist)
Dodge Charger – Enduring Thunder (Ackerson)
Dodge Dynamite! (Grist)
Dorset from the Sea – The Jurassic Coast from Lyme Regis to Old Harry Rocks photographed from its best viewpoint (also Souvenir Edition) (Belasco)
Draw & Paint Cars – How to (Gardiner)
Drive on the Wild Side, A – 20 Extreme Driving Adventures From Around the World (Weaver)
Ducati 750 Bible, The (Falloon)
Ducati 750 SS 'round-case' 1974, The Book of the (Falloon)
Ducati 860, 900 and Mille Bible, The (Falloon)
Ducati Monster Bible (New Updated & Revised Edition), The (Falloon)
Ducati 916 (updated edition) (Falloon)
Dune Buggy, Building A – The Essential Manual (Shakespeare)
Dune Buggy Files (Hale)
Dune Buggy Handbook (Hale)
East German Motor Vehicles in Pictures (Suhr/Weinreich)
Fast Ladies – Female Racing Drivers 1888 to 1970 (Bouzanquet)
Fate of the Sleeping Beauties, The (op de Weegh/Hottendorff/op de Weegh)
Ferrari 288 GTO, The Book of the (Sackey)
Ferrari 333 SP (O'Neil)
Fiat & Abarth 124 Spider & Coupé (Tipler)
Fiat & Abarth 500 & 600 – 2nd Edition (Bobbitt)
Fiats, Great Small (Ward)
Fine Art of the Motorcycle Engine, The (Peirce)
Ford Cleveland 335-Series V8 engine 1970 to 1982 – The Essential Source Book (Hammill)
Ford F100/F150 Pick-up 1948-1996 (Ackerson)
Ford F150 Pick-up 1997-2005 (Ackerson)
Ford Focus WRC (Robson)
Ford GT – Then, and Now (Streather)
Ford GT40 (Legate)
Ford Midsize Muscle – Fairlane, Torino & Ranchero (Cranswick)
Ford Model Y (Roberts)
Ford Small Block V8 Racing Engines 1962-1970 – The Essential Source Book (Hammill)
Ford Thunderbird From 1954, The Book of the (Long)
Formula One - The Real Score? (Harvey)
Formula 5000 Motor Racing, Back then … and back now (Lawson)
Forza Minardi! (Vigar)
France: the essential guide for car enthusiasts – 200 things for the car enthusiast to see and do (Parish)
From Crystal Palace to Red Square – A Hapless Biker's Road to Russia (Turner)
Funky Mopeds (Skelton)
Grand Prix Ferrari – The Years of Enzo Ferrari's Power, 1948-1980 (Pritchard)
Grand Prix Ford – DFV-powered Formula 1 Cars (Robson)
GT – The World's Best GT Cars 1953-73 (Dawson)
Hillclimbing & Sprinting – The Essential Manual (Short & Wilkinson)
Honda NSX (Long)
Inside the Rolls-Royce & Bentley Styling Department – 1971 to 2001 (Hull)
Intermeccanica – The Story of the Prancing Bull (McCredie & Reisner)
Italian Cafe Racers (Cloesen)
Italian Custom Motorcycles (Cloesen)
Jaguar, The Rise of (Price)
Jaguar XJ 220 – The Inside Story (Moreton)
Jaguar XJ-S, The Book of the (Long)
Japanese Custom Motorcycles – The Nippon Chop – Chopper, Cruiser, Bobber, Trikes and Quads (Cloesen)
Jeep CJ (Ackerson)
Jeep Wrangler (Ackerson)
The Jowett Jupiter – The car that leaped to fame (Nankivell)
Karmann-Ghia Coupé & Convertible (Bobbitt)
Kawasaki Triples Bible, The (Walker)
Kawasaki Z1 Story, The (Sheehan)
Kris Meeke – Intercontinental Rally Challenge Champion (McBride)
Lamborghini Miura Bible, The (Sackey)
Lamborghini Urraco, The Book of the (Landsem)
Lambretta Bible, The (Davies)
Lancia 037 (Collins)
Lancia Delta HF Integrale (Blaettel & Wagner)
Land Rover Series III Reborn (Porter)
Land Rover, The Half-ton Military (Cook)
Laverda Twins & Triples Bible 1968-1986 (Falloon)
Lea-Francis Story, The (Price)
Le Mans Panoramic (Ireland)
Lexus Story, The (Long)
Little book of microcars, the (Quellin)
Little book of smart, the – New Edition (Jackson)
Little book of trikes, the (Quellin)
Lola – The Illustrated History (1957-1977) (Starkey)
Lola – All the Sports Racing & Single-seater Racing Cars 1978-1997 (Starkey)
Lola T70 – The Racing History & Individual Chassis Record – 4th Edition (Starkey)
Lotus 18 Colin Chapman's U-turn (Whitelock)
Lotus 49 (Oliver)
Marketingmobiles, The Wonderful Wacky World of (Hale)
Maserati 250F In Focus (Pritchard)
Mazda MX-5/Miata 1.6 Enthusiast's Workshop Manual (Grainger & Shoemark)
Mazda MX-5/Miata 1.8 Enthusiast's Workshop Manual (Grainger & Shoemark)
Mazda MX-5 Miata, The book of the – The 'Mk1' NA-series 1988 to 1997 (Long)
Mazda MX-5 Miata Roadster (Long)
Mazda Rotary-engined Cars (Cranswick)
Maximum Mini (Booij)
Meet the English (Bowie)
Mercedes-Benz SL – R230 series 2001 to 2011 (Long)
Mercedes-Benz SL – W113-series 1963-1971 (Long)
Mercedes-Benz SL & SLC – 107-series 1971-1989 (Long)
Mercedes-Benz SLK – R170 series 1996-2004 (Long)
Mercedes-Benz SLK – R171 series 2004-2011 (Long)
Mercedes-Benz W123-series – All models 1976 to 1986 (Long)
Mercedes G-Wagen (Long)
MGA (Price Williams)
MGB & MGB GT– Expert Guide (Auto-doc Series) (Williams)
MGB Electrical Systems Updated & Revised Edition (Astley)
Micro Caravans (Jenkinson)
Micro Trucks (Mort)
Microcars at Large! (Quellin)
Mini Cooper – The Real Thing! (Tipler)
Mini Minor to Asia Minor (West)
Mitsubishi Lancer Evo, The Road Car & WRC Story (Long)
Montlhéry, The Story of the Paris Autodrome (Boddy)
Morgan Maverick (Lawrence)
Morgan 3 Wheeler – back to the future!, The (Dron)
Morris Minor, 60 Years on the Road (Newell)
Moto Guzzi Sport & Le Mans Bible, The (Falloon)
Motor Movies – The Posters! (Veysey)
Motor Racing – Reflections of a Lost Era (Carter)
Motor Racing – The Pursuit of Victory 1930-1962 (Carter)
Motor Racing – The Pursuit of Victory 1963-1972 (Wyatt/Sears)
Motor Racing Heroes – The Stories of 100 Greats (Newman)
Motorcycle Apprentice (Cakebread)
Motorcycle GP Racing in the 1960s (Pereira)
Motorcycle Road & Racing Chassis Designs (Noakes)
Motorcycling in the '50s (Clew)
Motorhomes, The Illustrated History (Jenkinson)
Motorsport In colour, 1950s (Wainwright)
MV Agusta Fours, The book of the classic (Falloon)
N.A.R.T. – A concise history of the North American Racing Team 1957 to 1983 (O'Neil)
Nissan 300ZX & 350Z – The Z-Car Story (Long)
Nissan GT-R Supercar: Born to race (Gorodji)
Northeast American Sports Car Races 1950-1959 (O'Neil)
Norton Commando Bible – All models 1968 to 1978 (Henshaw)
Nothing Runs – Misadventures in the Classic, Collectable & Exotic Car Biz (Slutsky)
Off-Road Giants! (Volume 1) – Heroes of 1960s Motorcycle Sport (Westlake)
Off-Road Giants! (Volume 2) – Heroes of 1960s Motorcycle Sport (Westlake)
Off-Road Giants! (volume 3) – Heroes of 1960s Motorcycle Sport (Westlake)
Pass the Theory and Practical Driving Tests (Gibson & Hoole)
Peking to Paris 2007 (Young)
Pontiac Firebird – New 3rd Edition (Cranswick)
Porsche Boxster (Long)
Porsche 356 (2nd Edition) (Long)
Porsche 908 (Födisch, Neßhöver, Roßbach, Schwarz & Roßbach)
Porsche 911 Carrera – The Last of the Evolution (Corlett)
Porsche 911R, RS & RSR, 4th Edition (Starkey)
Porsche 911, The Book of the (Long)
Porsche 911 – The Definitive History 2004-2012 (Long)
Porsche – The Racing 914s (Smith)
Porsche 911SC 'Super Carrera' – The Essential Companion (Streather)
Porsche 914 & 914-6: The Definitive History of the Road & Competition Cars (Long)
Porsche 924 (Long)
The Porsche 924 Carreras – evolution to excellence (Smith)
Porsche 928 (Long)
Porsche 944 (Long)
Porsche 964, 993 & 996 Data Plate Code Breaker (Streather)
Porsche 993 'King Of Porsche' – The Essential Companion (Streather)
Porsche 996 'Supreme Porsche' – The Essential Companion (Streather)
Porsche 997 2004-2012 – Porsche Excellence (Streather)
Porsche Racing Cars – 1953 to 1975 (Long)
Porsche Racing Cars – 1976 to 2005 (Long)
Porsche – The Rally Story (Meredith)
Porsche: Three Generations of Genius (Meredith)
Preston Tucker & Others (Linde)
RAC Rally Action! (Gardiner)
Racing Colours – Motor Racing Compositions 1908-2009 (Newman)
Racing Line – British motorcycle racing in the golden age of the big single (Guntrip)
Rallye Sport Fords: The Inside Story (Moreton)
Renewable Energy Home Handbook, The (Porter)
Roads with a View – England's greatest views and how to find them by road (Corfield)
Rolls-Royce Silver Shadow/Bentley T Series Corniche & Camargue – Revised & Enlarged Edition (Bobbitt)
Rolls-Royce Silver Spirit, Silver Spur & Bentley Mulsanne 2nd Edition (Bobbitt)
Rootes Cars of the 50s, 60s & 70s – Hillman, Humber, Singer, Sunbeam & Talbot (Rowe)
Rover P4 (Bobbitt)
Runways & Racers (O'Neil)
Russian Motor Vehicles – Soviet Limousines 1930-2003 (Kelly)
Russian Motor Vehicles – The Czarist Period 1784 to 1917 (Kelly)
RX-7 – Mazda's Rotary Engine Sportscar (Updated & Revised New Edition) (Long)
Scooters & Microcars, The A-Z of Popular (Dan)
Scooter Lifestyle (Grainger)
SCOOTER MANIA! – Recollections of the Isle of Man International Scooter Rally (Jackson)
Singer Story: Cars, Commercial Vehicles, Bicycles & Motorcycle (Atkinson)
Sleeping Beauties USA – abandoned classic cars & trucks (Marek)
SM – Citroën's Maserati-engined Supercar (Long & Claverol)
Speedway – Auto racing's ghost tracks (Collins & Ireland)
Sprite Caravans, The Story of (Jenkinson)
Standard Motor Company, The Book of the (Robson)
Steve Hole's Kit Car Cornucopia – Cars, Companies, Stories, Facts & Figures: the UK's kit car scene since 1949 (Hole)
Subaru Impreza: The Road Car And WRC Story (Long)
Supercar, How to Build your own (Thompson)
Tales from the Toolbox (Oliver)
Tatra – The Legacy of Hans Ledwinka, Updated & Enlarged Collector's Edition of 1500 copies (Margolius & Henry)
Taxi! The Story of the 'London' Taxicab (Bobbitt)
To Boldly Go – twenty six vehicle designs that dared to be different (Hull)
Toleman Story, The (Hilton)
Toyota Celica & Supra, The Book of Toyota's Sports Coupés (Long)
Toyota MR2 Coupés & Spyders (Long)
Triumph Bonneville Bible (59-83) (Henshaw)
Triumph Bonneville!, Save the – The inside story of the Meriden Workers' Co-op (Rosamond)
Triumph Motorcycles & the Meriden Factory (Hancox)
Triumph Speed Twin & Thunderbird Bible (Woolridge)
Triumph Tiger Cub Bible (Estall)
Triumph Trophy Bible (Woolridge)
Triumph TR6 (Kimberley)
TT Talking – The TT's most exciting era – As seen by Manx Radio TT's lead commentator 2004-2012 (Lambert)
Two Summers – The Mercedes-Benz W196R Racing Car (Ackerson)
TWR Story, The – Group A (Hughes & Scott)
Unraced (Collins)
Velocette Motorcycles – MSS to Thruxton – New Third Edition (Burris)
Vespa – The Story of a Cult Classic in Pictures (Uhlig)
Vincent Motorcycles: The Untold Story since 1946 (Guyony & Parker)
Volkswagen Bus Book, The (Bobbitt)
Volkswagen Bus or Van to Camper, How to Convert (Porter)
Volkswagens of the World (Glen)
VW Beetle Cabriolet – The full story of the convertible Beetle (Bobbitt)
VW Beetle – The Car of the 20th Century (Copping)
VW Bus – 40 Years of Splitties, Bays & Wedges (Copping)
VW Bus Book, The (Bobbitt)
VW Golf: Five Generations of Fun (Copping & Cservenka)
VW – The Air-cooled Era (Copping)
VW T5 Camper Conversion Manual (Porter)
VW Campers (Copping)
Volkswagen Type 3, The book of the – Concept, Design, International Production Models & Development (Glen)
Volvo Estate, The (Hollebone)
You & Your Jaguar XK8/XKR – Buying, Enjoying, Maintaining, Modifying – New Edition (Thorley)
Which Oil? – Choosing the right oils & greases for your antique, vintage, veteran, classic or collector car (Michell)
Wolseley Cars 1948 to 1975 (Rowe)
Works Minis, The Last (Purves & Brenchley)
Works Rally Mechanic (Moylan)

www.veloce.co.uk

First published in September 2017 by Veloce Publishing Limited, Veloce House, Parkway Farm Business Park, Middle Farm Way, Poundbury, Dorchester DT1 3AR, England. Fax 01305 250479 / e-mail info@veloce.co.uk / web www.veloce.co.uk or www.velocebooks.com.
ISBN: 978-1-787110-20-5 UPC: 6-36847-01020-1.

Readers with ideas for automotive books, or books on other transport or related hobby subjects, are invited to write to the editorial director of Veloce Publishing at the above address. British Library Cataloguing in Publication Data – A catalogue record for this book is available from the British Library. Typesetting, design and page make-up all by Veloce Publishing Ltd on Apple Mac. Printed in India by Parksons Graphics.

FORD FOCUS WRC

THE **AUTO-BIOGRAPHY** OF A **RALLY CHAMPION**

Graham Robson

Contents

Foreword by Malcolm Wilson

When I look back at the rallying career of the Ford Focus World Rally Car, I am proud to recall just how much this car meant to me, to Ford, and to all of the team who backed it for more than 12 years.

M-Sport was granted the contract to run Ford's FIA World Rally Championship campaign in 1997, and the Focus was our first original product. From then on, I think it's fair to say that the Focus was involved in almost every hour of my life. While the Championship may have progressed since then, the Focus will always have a fond place in my memory.

Reading this book, you will soon note that between 1998 and 2010 M-Sport built no fewer than 97 Focus World Rally Cars. Not only did it manage to win 44 rallies outright on the world stage, it was also able to win the Manufacturers' Championship twice – in 2006 and 2007.

As the Focus gained success and notoriety, so did M-Sport. We moved from small premises at my family home in Cumbria to a purpose-built HQ a few miles away, and our workforce grew from a team of 18 to more than 200. Now, we design, engineer and develop almost everything in-house – something that would never have been possible without the Focus era.

Back in 1998, when Ford and M-Sport first began planning the Focus WRC project, it really was a case of starting from a clean piece or paper.

The relationship between Ford and M-Sport was a true partnership. Ford supplied an invaluable amount of technical information, and we have been lucky enough to have some brilliant technical minds in our team, such as Guenther Steiner and Christian Loriaux. In addition to this, we enjoyed vital assistance from companies and partners such, as Cosworth, Pipo Moteurs, Xtrac, Ricardo, and other expert suppliers and consultants.

It wasn't just the technical side which allowed us to excel. Ford's marketing team was fully onboard and we were also lucky enough to receive very generous support from the likes of Martini, BP-Castrol and the Abu Dhabi Tourism Authority.

Many people had an input on the success that we enjoyed with the Focus, and it was always obvious to me that little could have been achieved without the total commitment of everyone involved – the drivers, co-drivers, partners and staff who never let me down.

There were times when an occasional big crash would result in a tremendous amount of hard work, but my team always knuckled under and made up for the disappointment in a matter of days.

Then, there were occasions when we could step back and think on what we had achieved: enjoying the winner's champagne, or wearing a t-shirt commemorating our latest championship successes or how many victories we had claimed.

The project was a 24-hour-a-day operation, but I received a huge amount of help from my team and my family. My wife Elaine has been a constant support, and managed to travel to many of the events. My son Matthew started rallying as soon as he could, and brought some great results to the Stobart team, which mirrored what the front-line team was always trying to do.

I hope you enjoy reading the Focus story, which was such a significant chapter in the lives of myself, my team and my family.

Today, we're tackling new projects and hope to secure more victories with the new Ford Fiesta WRC.

MALCOLM WILSON
Founder of M-Sport

Introduction

Although the Focus World Rally Car occupied only 12 years in Ford's illustrious motor sporting history, it left behind a peerless record of achievement, ambition, technical innovation, and success. No other European Ford has ever achieved 44 outright victories in the World Rally Championship, and no other was as competitive over such a lengthy period. For all Ford motorsport fanatics – and naturally this includes the author – it was important to set down the complete story of all these cars and their careers.

Over 12 tumultuous years – 1999 to 2010 – the ever-developing pedigree of works Focus WRCs formed the spearhead of a continuous and high-profile programme at Ford, turning a privately-engineered 'why don't we…?' vision into an enterprise that produced one of the most formidably successful rally cars in the world. Not only that, but the cars that were built and operated during this time were all controlled by M-Sport of Cumbria – a private concern that was almost completely independent of Ford itself. Without M-Sport, the Focus WRC might never have been conceived, and without both of them Ford might not have sustained such a laudable public image.

Although books have already been written about many aspects of the most prominent Focus WRCs, no previous author has ever had the opportunity, facilities, or freedom to go into such great detail on the topic. Now, we are finally able to explore the individual histories of each car, Ford's corporate evolution (and resulting financial implications), and especially some of the surrounding myths and legends.

This book covers each and every one of the WRC events that this great car actually contended. I feel honoured that I was always assisted by Malcolm Wilson and his staff at M-Sport, along with reassurances and (occasional) corrections from rallying guru Martin Holmes. As such, I hope this is the very first time that I have been able to list every WRC event tackled by every one of the works cars, and to list (and often illustrate) the different paint jobs, sponsors' deals, and programmes applied to each example.

I should emphasise, here and now, that this is not a story that found space to detail the ever-developing record of all the other teams and individuals that used Focus WRC cars. That being said, I have tried to emphasise the praiseworthy efforts of the Stobart operation, which based itself at Dovenby Hall, and within which Malcolm Wilson's son, Matthew, was a prominent character. In all humility, however, and within the space I had available, I think I can claim that the story of the Focus WRC is all here. To achieve that, and to do so competently, I tried to find as many of the surviving characters from the period as possible, and to find out exactly what and who did which and what. There is no space here for speculation and rumour, which is why I have always steered clear of so-called recreations and replicas.

I don't believe that anything like the full story of the works Focus WRCs has ever previously been told. Now here it is.

Acknowledgements

Many people have helped me to recollect the glittering career of the Focus WRC. Their help was invaluable in bringing back the exciting period in Cumbria when all Focus WRCs began their careers there, as well as the saga of their development and the way in which the M-Sport team operated. Without these people I would never have been able to tap into the character – and charm – of this increasingly successful operation, nor understand why the Focus WRC developed in the manner that it did. As the years passed, too, I managed to interview almost all the important players, whose insight made the compilation of this story so much easier.

These are the people whose personal, face-to-face, interviews and (I am proud to say) whose friendships have all helped enormously: Mark Deans, Cliff Hawkins, Christian Loriaux, David Mountain, Anna Rudd, Dick Scammell, Simon Shaw, Phil Short, Ray Stokoe, John Taylor, Malcolm Tyrrell, Martin Whitaker, and of course Malcolm Wilson himself.

Special thanks go to my good friend – and amazingly knowledgeable character – Martin Holmes, whose WRC annuals were, and still are, vital to the understanding of this exciting period. In addition, I could not have completed the detail of the job without the help of my son Hamish, who was not only in the original Focus WRC design team, but also retains an encyclopaedic knowledge of the entire pedigree.

Hamish cheerfully read what I had to say on this subject, commented on it, helped me flesh out the story by finding several of the characters and the cars, and put me right on several points which would otherwise have been published incorrect.

It would also have been impossible to get everything right if I had not met, talked to, and gotten to know some of the Focus WRC drivers and co-drivers of the period. In particular I would like to mention Nicky Grist, Colin McRae and Carlos Sainz, along with Steve Rockingham, who bought an ex-McRae winning car from M-Sport and took the brave decision to use it in Slowly Sideways events. All their reminiscences were a great help.

Finally, I want to thank all those wonderful people who helped me amass the pictures that do so much to make this book memorable. Almost all of the images used come from Ford's own photographic archive, whose staff know just how many hours were needed to dig out the special images. Finally, therefore, I want to thank Dave Hill and Steve Roots for their patience, assistance, and great service. Unhappily, the service they provided cannot now be repeated for later models; the archive has now closed down, which makes me feel doubly blessed to have obtained the images used in these pages.

GRAHAM ROBSON

CHAPTER ONE
Four-wheel drive Fords before the Focus

Right from the start, it was obvious that any new-generation Ford World Rally Championship contender would need a totally new type of four-wheel drive transmission system. Even so, one must never forget that in 1998 (when design engineering on the new Focus began) Ford's works motorsport operation had already been involved with four-wheel drive systems for nearly 30 years, using several different layouts.

Because each and every one of those systems was unique, in its own way, it is appropriate that we give a summary of how they performed, and how they influenced what would eventually be engineered for the new Focus.

First of all, there was the four-wheel drive Capri in 1969, which astonished the world of British rallycross when it appeared at the beginning of that year - not only because of its transmission layout, but because by rallycross standards it was such a large and heavy machine.

It was Boreham's then team manager, Henry Taylor, who was the inspiration for the car. While four-wheel drive was still specifically banned from rallies at this time, rallycross was different. In that sport, which millions of people were currently watching via TV's *World of Sport* series, there were no restrictions at all.

"I'm not a qualified engineer," Henry once told me, "but I was 'Mr. Fixit', always trying to get things done. One of my bright ideas was to put the Essex V6 3-litre engine into a Capri, and another was to try out the Ferguson four-wheel drive system."

Well before the end of 1968, Taylor somehow got his hands on a preproduction Capri 1600 GT (this new model was not due to be launched until January 1969, and sales would not begin for weeks after that) and set to work on it:

"I knew Tony Rolt very well – he was the managing director of Harry Ferguson Research – so I arranged for the Capri to be sent to him, in Coventry. Although we knew his four-wheel drive system, with Dunlop Maxaret anti-lock braking, was bulky and too heavy, we wanted to see what it would do."

Ford's original 4WD competition car was the Capri rallycross machine of 1969.

By this time, Harry Ferguson Research had already built about 30 Zephyrs with a 4WD conversion, and had also supplied Ford's R&D centre at Dunton with two prototype Capris, complete with V6 engines and 4WD (at a piece price, reputedly, of around £2000 for the conversion job). During the winter of 1968/1969, therefore, the very first competition Capri took shape in Coventry, being returned to Boreham in January.

There, the ever-resourceful mechanics completed preparation of a 3-litre car specifically for rallycross, having Weslake-modified cylinder heads, and producing about 160bhp. Behind the main Capri gearbox was the HFR transfer gearbox that split the torque, with one propeller shaft being aligned forwards and alongside the engine sump, a front differential ahead of it, and with modified Ford Taunus (front-wheel drive) suspension hardware adapted to allow driveshafts to reach the wheels.

On 8 February 1969 – just days after the new Capri range had been unveiled – Boreham sent Roger Clark to contest a rallycross meeting at Croft, near Darlington. Quite simply, this outing caused a sensation. The Clark/Capri/4WD combination won all three races that it started, and set the fastest time of the day overall. Specification details included Goodyear tyres on 7.0in wide Minilite wheels, plastic side and rear window 'glass,' a glass fibre bonnet, plus Taunus front struts.

After those results, everything went very quiet. Taylor soon discovered that performance of the much-vaunted Maxaret anti-lock braking system could easily be beaten by skilled drivers – and went on to personally prove the point on the

Dunlop skidpan in Erdington, Birmingham, when driving his own Ford USA Mustang Shelby Cobra. In any case, time was against him. Rallycross was a bad weather, winter activity, which meant that this advanced Capri would only have the chance to shine again towards the end of 1970. By then Taylor had gone, and the World Cup Rally had taken every priority (and most of the budget) at Boreham …

It was not until then that the four-wheel drive project was revived, with Boreham deciding that the original Capri 4WD rallycross car would be dug out of storage, and be joined by two other newly-built examples. During the winter of 1970/1971, all three works four-wheel drive Capris were further developed for use in the ITV/Castrol rallycross season. All three had further race-tuned Essex V6 engines; Stan Clark and Rod Chapman each received a 212bhp engine, while Roger Clark's machine boasted a rorty 250bhp (as well as Lucas fuel injection).

The ever-resourceful chief mechanic/rally engineer Mick Jones would eventually have many very rude things to say about these cars (particularly about their weight, and the extra friction that seemed to be built-in to the four-wheel drive system). Nevertheless, his team did a great job with what was still a very crude four-wheel drive installation, now allied to a ZF five-speed main gearbox. Interestingly enough, these were apparently the first systems ever to use an FF Developments (previously known as Harry Ferguson Research) viscous coupling limited-slip device in the centre torque-splitting differential, because it was still a top secret project. Nothing was said (or printed) about this at the time, but it would eventually mature at Boreham in the 1980s. These, by the way, were the first works cars from Boreham ever to use Dunlop competition tyres, as the rally team's principal contract with Goodyear was still in force.

The records show that the cars did what they were asked to do and won the series, but as Roger Clark later wrote :

"Basically, we ditched them because they were an enormous amount of trouble; not just in reliability, which was dreadful enough, but because they were absolute pigs to handle …"

In addition, they were heavy and there was a lot of friction in the transmission system, meaning they were not as fast as the original forecasts had suggested. Monsters? Oh yes … and like most monsters, they became extinct.

For the next decade, Boreham put all thoughts of developing a better four-wheel drive system behind it, notably because World Rally Championship regulations continued to put a blanket ban on the subject. Finally, though, came the change of heart from the FIA (Fédération Internationale de l'Automobile), which 'legalised' four-wheel drive from the opening of the 1979 season (even though there were no obvious aspirants to go rallying at that moment). What few knew, however, was that Audi had been doing much of the behind-the-scenes lobbying that encouraged this change of regulation, and that it would shortly launch the all-new four-wheel drive Quattro.

As the world of rallying now acknowledges, it was the Quattro that, in 1981, sparked off the revolution that quickly led to the launch of many other four-wheel drive cars, and indirectly encouraged the arrival of the 1982-1986 Group B formula. As many engineers now agree, in hindsight the Quattro was a success because of its ultra-powerful turbocharged engine, and because of the superstar drivers the works team chose to employ (Hannu Mikkola, Michèle Mouton, Stig Blomqvist and Walter Röhrl in particular), rather than the supremacy of the four-wheel drive system, but it certainly made the important difference.

Although Ford Motorsport was already developing a new rally car at the time – the Escort RS1700T – it proved to be the wrong car for the wrong period, sporting only rear-wheel drive. Internal memos originating from Boreham at the time suggested that "the success of the Audi Quattro has proved that even a relatively bad four-wheel drive configuration can be made to work acceptably … the

The Ghia-styled RS200 was the basis of the Group B 4WD rally car, revealed in 1984, and rallied in 1986.

four-wheel drive option is an essential backup for a large company involved seriously in motorsports." Despite this, requests to be allowed to develop a four-wheel drive version of the RS1700T were refused, and the entire project was scrapped in 1983.

This, though, was to be the dark before the dawn. Within weeks, work on a new four-wheel drive rally car began, and by the autumn of 1983 detail design work was under way. The very first of a new series of Group B cars - the RS200 - was completed in March 1984. This top secret machine was unveiled to the public in November 1984, production (of 200 examples) began in the autumn of 1985, and sporting homologation was duly achieved early in 1986.

The RS200 was a technically advanced and startlingly beautiful mid-engined two-seater car, powered by a 1.8-litre turbocharged version of the famous BDA power unit (this was actually coded the BDT). On top of this, it had an all-new four-wheel drive system engineered for Ford by FF Developments. Although it would have no technical connection with the system eventually developed for the late-1990s Focus WRC, the RS200 established many principles the Focus would later share – particularly regarding operational flexibility – that Ford would find extremely valuable in the future.

In the RS200, the engine was mounted behind the seats, and drove forward to the main transmission, located between the driver's and co-driver's legs. The main transmission was a massive casing that enclosed the main gearbox, the torque-splitting differential, the front-wheel differential, and the outlet for a rear propeller shaft that took the drive for the rear wheels

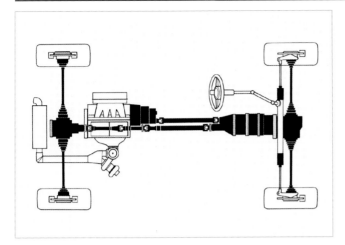

The RS200's four-wheel drive installation was, of course, totally different from that of the still-in-the-future Focus WRC. The engine was behind the seats, and the main transmission was up front, between the driver's and co-driver's legs.

Ford put the Sierra XR4x4 on sale in 1985, before beginning to evolve the transmission for motorsport. Stig Blomqvist drove the works rally cars with great determination in 1987 and 1988.

The RS200's career was cut short when the authorities cancelled Group B in mid-1986, by which time it had already become a front-runner in WRC rallies.

to a differential mounted immediately behind the engine. Finally, it also granted the ability to select rear- or four-wheel drive as required by the driver.

Unfortunately, the entire project was cancelled at the close of 1986, due to the FIA's decision to ban Group B cars from the World Rally Championship in future years (this decision having been hastened by a series of horrifying accidents involving Group B cars that year). The RS200 had already been building up a phenomenal reputation, and it was clear that Ford was rapidly coming to terms with four-wheel drive technology. 200 such cars were built and sold, and the author had the

pleasure of using four such examples of road cars for daily use over the next four years.

By this time, too, Ford's product planners had concluded that there was a mainstream future for four-wheel drive models of road cars, not only as an option in a model range, but perhaps even as a stand-alone car that would appeal to the more sporting motorist. Originally, this FF-inspired system was revealed on the 1985 Sierra XR4x4, but the same basic system would be further developed, improved, and evolved over time. The system was present on cars as varied as the Scorpio four-wheel drive, the Sierra Cosworth four-wheel drive (from 1990) and – this being the most important evolution as far as Ford's motorsport future was concerned – the 1992-1997 Escort RS Cosworth.

Although this all-wheel drive layout was not to figure in the Focus WRC programme that followed, its presence was philosophically important in the long-term scheme of things. In the beginning – 1969, that is – a forerunner system had appeared on the works rallycross Capri 4WDs, and in the end a much-developed version was a vital part of Ford's original World Rally Car, the 1997-1998 Escort WRC.

In the 30 years between the two cars, the ever-increasing sophistication of such engineering meant that every detail of the layout, every component, had been transformed. This lengthy time span also allowed the advantages, installation

Boreham developed the Sierra Cosworth 4x4 into a formidable rally car in 1992; this example being François Delecour's in the 1992 Rallye Sanremo.

The Escort RS Cosworth, introduced in 1993, started winning World Rally Championship events almost at once; its victories including this win in the 1994 Monte Carlo rally, driven by François Delecour.

possibilities, and (yes, there were some) problems of a high-performance four-wheel drive layout to become known. There was, though, one very basic difference between what was central to this layout, and what M-Sport's engineers might decide on for a new Focus WRC layout. The existing system was built around a 'north-south' engine installation, a main gearbox between the front passengers' legs, two propeller shafts, and a sturdy front differential casing bolted to the side of the engine sump.

Thousands of Ford road cars with four-wheel drive installations were manufactured before thoughts once again turned to the idea of building a 4WD works rally car. Boreham's original project was to turn the Sierra Cosworth four-wheel drive road car into a dedicated rally machine, this not only featuring a 300bhp+ turbocharged Cosworth YB power unit, but a newly-engineered 'dog box' seven-speed main gearbox (Ford Motorsport coded it MS90), allied to enlarged front and rear differentials.

The original 1990-1991 works Sierra Cosworth four-wheel drive was something of a disappointment: not only was it too heavy and too cumbersome, but on top it was originally none too reliable. It was not until 1992 that it matured as a *nearly successful* rally car, with several World Rally Championship podium finishes (including second in Portugal for Miki Biasion, second in the Tour de Corse for François Delecour, and third in both the Acropolis and Sanremo events).

Then, for 1993, a new, smaller, and lighter car took centre stage (and one, as we would eventually discover, that was to be a true predecessor of the Focus WRC). The Escort RS Cosworth had been 'invented' at Boreham as early as 1988/1989, when motorsport director Stuart Turner startled a planning meeting by saying, "Why don't we see if we can take a platform and running gear from a Sierra Cosworth four-wheel drive, cut it and shut it, and then see if the new Escort body can be fitted on it …?"

The result was that the very first Escort RS Cosworth rally car appeared in 1990, promptly won a minor event in Spain, achieved sporting homologation on 1 January 1993, and immediately started winning World Rally Championships. With five WRC victories in 1993, and victory for François Delecour in the 1994 Rallye Automobile Monte Carlo, it became a pace-setting icon that Ford would have to match, or supplant, later in the decade.

Along the way, the already-proven Sierra Cosworth four-wheel drive running gear was persistently improved. Changes were continually being introduced to the YB engine, including new turbo anti-lag strategy, and the (compulsory, due to regulation changes) use of a 34mm diameter turbocharger restrictor. Alongside this, the transmission was updated by a reversion to six forward speeds (and all attempts to develop a sequential change abandoned), not to mention wider track suspension and other chassis changes.

The only important motorsport failings were that the car was still very sturdy but slightly overweight (to quote one-time Motorsport Director Peter Ashcroft, "All our works cars were always too heavy"), and that the performance of the semi-trailing link rear suspension was by no means ideal. Operations Manager John Taylor once commented sourly that "At the back end there was always a war going on …"

In 1996 the Escort RS Cosworth had already just peaked, but there had been a boost to morale when the charismatic Spaniard, Carlos Sainz, returned to the scene. That season saw Escorts win two WRC rallies (one for privateer Patrick Bernadini, in Monte Carlo), with Sainz also taking second place three times and placing third twice,

Although this became a real golden recovery period for the works team, there was despondency all around. The sport's organising body was about to impose new World Rally Car regulations, coming into force in 1997. To meet those new regulations, Ford Motorsport would need a new model, as the existing Escort RS Cosworth would no longer be eligible. The new rules were straightforward enough to meet, if only a suitable base car was available.

Although only 20 qualifying kits of parts (of which one was to be a fully-assembled vehicle) had to be built in one season (none for use as road cars), they had to be based on models of which at least 25,000 examples (such as – in this case – front-wheel drive Escorts) were being manufactured in that same year. However, almost every major modification was allowed; conversion from front-wheel drive to four-wheel drive was authorised, as were turbocharged engines of no more than 2-litres in capacity.

Because of the radical nature of the technical changes specified, the original breed of World Rally Car regulations were to be applied with certain exceptions. It was those exceptions, and the opportunities they presented, that caught Ford's attention. One big change from the past was that, in future, World Rally Cars would never be allowed to be reshelled. If a shell had to be written-off, so did the identity of that car. Suddenly, as far as the enthusiasts were concerned, it made number plate spotting worth doing again!

Boreham's works rally engineers, led by Philip Dunabin, soon realised that a WRC could become very specialised. For Ford, the big problem was that WRCs had to be based on a current 25,000/year model; the old Escort RS Cosworth had never even approached these levels, and in any case it was about to drop out of production. There was no obvious alternative Ford model that could be used, as the Fiesta was considered to be too small, and the Escort's mainstream replacement – to be badged 'Focus' – would not be launched until 1998.

As one of the stalwarts of WRC rallying, Ford was able to call the FIA's bluff. Ford said that designing and building an all-new WRC was out of the question at that time, but also offered a potential solution. If the FIA would allow the first-generation WRC to be based on the Escort RS Cosworth – as

Ford's very first World Rally Car was the Escort WRC, developed in a hurry at Boreham in 1996, then rallied in 1997 and 1998. This was the front view ...

a once-only concession, to which rival teams would have to agree – then works Fords could be on the starting line for the Rallye Automobile Monte Carlo in January 1997.

The FIA agreed to this, and the rush to get a competitive Escort WRC ready really began. Boreham did all the design and original development work, though Malcolm Wilson's M-Sport team was contracted to run the cars. Concept work began at Boreham in June 1996, and the first prototype ran on 13 October. Launch came on 3 November, with homologation inspection of the 20 kits of parts completed on 19 December! Boreham only built two prototype test cars, both originally being works Group A Escort RS Cosworth team cars. It was an extremely rapid programme, and one that resulted the Escort WRC going from 'good idea' to homologation in just six months!

Engineering Manager Philip Dunabin commented:

"Our request to the FIA to base the World Rally Car on the existing Escort four-wheel drive allowed us to build a long-term plan for the existing and future Escort models ... the decision to base the World Rally Car on the current Escort was never really questioned."

Using the obsolete Escort RS Cosworth as a base, Motorsport made many improvements to the Escort WRC, some of which (philosophically, at least) would help the engineers' thinking when an all-new World Rally Car came along in 1998/1999:

Engine: New (smaller, to suit a 34mm diameter inlet restrictor) IHI turbocharger, different exhaust manifold, and fuel-injection changes (with eight instead of four active injectors). This delivered 310bhp at 5500rpm, with a very solid torque curve.

… and this the rear, of an interim car, designed to make the most of the existing Escort RS Cosworth, while design work on a new Focus could begin.

Cooling: Improved airflow through larger front bodywork apertures, with relocated intercooler and water radiators.

Rear suspension: Lighter and stronger tubular subframe, with a new MacPherson strut/links system, using geometry rather like that of the contemporary Mondeo.

Aerodynamics: New front bumper profile to suit the radiator/intercooler relocation. Smaller/reshaped rear aerofoil to generate more downforce with less drag, and to meet WRC regulations.

Layout: Idealised, with an 80-litre fuel tank, spare wheel, and 40-litre water reservoir (for cooling sprays of intercooler and brakes) positioned in the rear compartment where the seats had been removed.

Aerodynamics: These were improved with testing at the Ford wind tunnel at Merkenich, resulting in increased downforce. The new rear aerofoil was needed to meet the

regulations, as the established RS Cosworth style was too large.

The water radiator was 33 per cent larger, and the turbo intercooler increased by 50 per cent (it was also cooled by water spray from the reservoir). The intercooler was placed ahead, rather than on top, of the radiator.

From 1 January 1997, and for the very first time, Ford's works cars were to be run by an outside agency. On that date, Malcolm Wilson's M-Sport team – based more than 300 miles north of Boreham, in Cumbria – took over. Although Boreham designed and initially developed the Escort WRC, as well as sourcing all 20 of the first sets of components, it was M-Sport that would always run the cars.

Back at Boreham, Operations Manager John Taylor (most unfairly, according to the stories that later circulated) was

*Boreham's John Taylor (left) was probably Carlos Sainz's biggest fan. It was
John who introduced him to the works Ford product in 1987.*

made redundant, after more than 20 years involvement with the works team. Going forward, the team was to be run by Malcolm Wilson, with Marc Amblard as his senior engineer.

Carlos Sainz led the driving team, and continued to be a real inspiration. At the start of the 1997 programme he was joined by the German driver Armin Schwarz. Unhappily, Schwarz's promised sponsorship funds never arrived, leading to Ford dropping him in mid-1997. As a replacement, it brought in four-times World Rally Champion Juha Kankkunen.

It's worth noting that at this time there were those who suggested that M-Sport would simply be unable to get the job done. As it turned out, these doubts were unfounded; by the middle of 1997, the construction of new cars at M-Sport was almost a batch production business. By the end of the season,

no fewer than 29 Escort WRCs existed, with ten of them actually being converted Group A machines of 1995 or 1996 vintage.

Somehow, M-Sport got two new cars (P6 FMC and P7 FMC) to the start line in Monte Carlo, Sweden and Portugal. In organisational terms the rest of the season was a race against time, but the team managed it using only nine cars over the course of the year. Technical advances in 1997 included differential changes (with an Xtrac sequential gear change transmission), and Hi-Tech dampers replacing Dynamic types from mid-season.

In 1997 Ford finished second in the World Rally Championship for Manufacturers, while the charismatic Carlos Sainz took third place in the Championship for Drivers. Carlos won two individual rallies – in Greece and Indonesia – along with placing second in Monte Carlo, Sweden, Corsica, and

This stunning little show car – for it was no more than that – of the Ford Puma 4WD Concept, was shown in 1998, and hid Escort RS Cosworth/WRC running gear under the skin. Some assumed that the new WRC car would be like this …

New Zealand. Even the second place results were close calls; in Corsica he fell short by just eight seconds, in New Zealand by 13 seconds, and in Sweden by 16 seconds! With his Escort WRCs breaking down in the Safari, Portugal, Argentina, Finland, and Australia rallies, it was no wonder that Carlos knew – in his heart of hearts – that he could have won the Championship.

After being hired as Schwarz's replacement, Juha Kankkunen was immediately on the pace. In half a season he recorded four second place results, two of them close behind team-mate Sainz.

In 1998 everyone, it seemed, knew that the Escort WRC was already technically obsolete. In conditions of great secrecy (as we shall see), M-Sport started working on the new Focus WRC in February/March 1998. There was little time, and no funds, to develop the Escort WRC any further.

Despite this, the team started the season with a different turbocharger housing, and more power. As well as this, the cars were now so light that they needed additional ballast to run at the regulation minimum weight. Electronic engine launch control was also available.

There were important driver changes too. Everyone at Ford was sorry to see Carlos Sainz leave the team at the end of 1997 – when he went off to renew his love affair with Toyota – and Juha Kankkunen stepped in to become team leader. For its second driver Ford rehired Bruno Thiry, who had already driven many works Escort RS Cosworths in previous years.

1998, though, would be a relatively quiet year for Ford. With all efforts being directed to the still-secret new Focus WRC, no technical novelties were available for the old Escort.

Recalled from semi-retirement, Ari Vatanen drove this Escort WRC with great spirit in the 1998 East African Safari, which was one of the last appearances for this charismatic duo.

In November 1998, as a taster, Ford produced this picture of the last of the Escort WRCs, posed with the first (incomplete, as it transpired) Focus WRC.

In this final season, the Escorts would finish fourth in the World Rally Championship.

Although there were no outright victories, there were many fine performances and podium positions. Juha Kankkunen placed second three times (all of them in the season's most high profile events, Monte Carlo, Safari, and Wales Rally GB), and came third an additional four times. Bruno Thiry, not as explosively successful as his team-mate, recorded just one third place on the Wales Rally GB.

These understated results were offset by a happy and nostalgic occasion, when Ari Vatanen was invited to compete in the Safari (Bruno Thiry had broken his ribs in a bizarre accident during practice). It had been 21 years since Ari's first Safari, and even ten years since his most recent one. Equally as rapid as Kankkunen throughout, he eventually finished third, just 25 seconds behind his fellow Finn. Ari also took fifth in Portugal, before handing his seat back to Bruno.

It was fitting – but above all sad – that the works Escort team should start its last event on home ground. It was almost like old times, as in a consistent (though not extremely fast) display, Juha and Bruno finished second and third overall in the Rally of Great Britain.

On the eve of the 1998 Rally of Great Britain, where the Escort WRC was scheduled to appear for the last time, Ford threw a magnificent dinner party at Sudeley Castle, Gloucestershire, to say farewell and to preview the arrival of the Focus WRC. The car was a mock-up, but every other personality in shot was real. No fewer than six previous World Rally Champions were in attendance: Juha Kankkunen, Tommi Mäkinen, Hannu Mikkola, Carlos Sainz, Björn Waldegård, and Ari Vatanen. The event was of course hosted by Walter Hayes, who had always done so much to support Ford's rallying efforts over the years.

None of the experienced reporters missed this, as it was the absolute best that could be expected of an ageing design, especially one that had received no ongoing development for a year. Sebastian Lindholm (in a privately sponsored, but newly built, Escort WRC) took fifth place, while Armin Schwarz finished seventh in a 1997 car that had been prepared by the Lancashire-based concern, RED.

No fewer than 19 Escort WRCs appeared in the 1998 World Rally Championship season, of which only four had previously featured in 1997, and only nine different cars were used as official M-Sport entries. When a number of private conversions, which appeared in lesser events throughout the season, are added in to the total, this brings the total of

Escort WRCs built in two years to well over 40. Not bad for a stopgap design …

Immediately before the Rally of Great Britain, Ford chose to celebrate the imminent retirement of the works Escorts, hosting a glittering celebratory dinner for every important Ford Motorsport personality who could be persuaded to attend. The star of the evening – apart from the drivers themselves – was the infamous blue Focus WRC mock-up that had already been shown at recent Motor Shows (at that time, presented as no more than a potential indication of what was already brewing behind the scenes).

In an occasion that has never been matched by any other team, Ford attracted no fewer than six previous World Rally

The Escort WRC's last appearance as a works car took place in Sweden in February 1999,
when Petter Solberg took a plucky 11th place.

Champions to attend: Björn Waldegård, Ari Vatanen, Hannu Mikkola, Juha Kankkunen, Carlos Sainz, and Tommi Mäkinen. Alongside them, Timo Mäkinen (a triple Escort rally winner in the Wales Rally GB), Ove Andersson, David Richards, Malcolm Wilson and Andrew Cowan were also in attendance. Walter Hayes, Stuart Turner, Martin Whitaker, Bill Barnett, and many others joined them, and there was great regret that long-time manager Peter Ashcroft (who, by this time, had retired to live in the United States) could not be there.

It was an honour for all of us to be present, but there was an additional special pleasure for the author, who received a framed picture of a group of personalities, all having signed their names around the margins. It was an unforgettable evening.

Even after the fitting send-off, the career of the Escort WRC was not quite over. In Sweden, February 1999, the works team's new 'apprentice' – Petter Solberg – finished 11th overall in an M-Sport car (R6 FMC, Kankkunen's car in the Rally of

Great Britain). That really was all, though; Ford's future lay with the Focus. Just two weeks later, Colin McRae would take the Focus WRC to its first ever victory, in the Safari.

It was in Sweden, therefore, that the rallying career of the works Escorts was brought proudly to a close, almost 31 years after it had begun in Sanremo, Italy, in March 1968. This was a period in which countless – tens of thousands, certainly – rallies, rallysprints, and rallycross events had been won by a member of the Escort family. It was a breed of car that had brought success, sparkle, excitement, and glamour to motorsport all over the world, and in most people's opinion no other rally car has ever been as successful.

Ford, Malcolm Wilson, and M-Sport, however, had an eye to the future, as they knew just how much work had already gone into preparing the Focus WRC to be better than any Escort had ever been. The story of how, where, and when the new model took shape starts here.

The germ of the idea for the Focus WRC must have originated in mid-1994, when Boreham's then director of motorsport, Colin Dobinson, took early retirement. His replacement, the Australian-born Peter Gillitzer, was internally promoted from the company's promotion/marketing area within Ford of Europe.

Brutal as it may seem, one must comment that from that moment on, morale at Boreham gradually ebbed away. Although the works Escort RS Cosworth was seen as being at its peak – just beginning the gradual slide from the front of the pack – Gillitzer was neither as charismatic, nor as popular as his more famous predecessors, particularly Stuart Turner and Peter Ashcroft.

Even today it is not widely known that Ford management considered – and even came within sight of – abandoning its long-running World Rally Championship programme at the end of 1995. The Escort RS Cosworth was clearly past its best, and Gillitzer was clearly more interested in, and more familiar with, saloon car racing than rallying. In slightly different circumstances, therefore, the Focus WRC programme might never even have been born.

To keep the pot boiling, as it were, in 1995 Boreham had set up a rather cumbersome partnership with RAS, the Belgium-based tuning organisation. The result of this partnership was the use of rather undistinguished-looking Escorts (no more striking Mobil sponsorship, for instance), not a single outright win to boast of, and a distinct sagging of flair from Boreham itself. It was an arrangement that was to be speedily abandoned at the end of the year.

This, though, was only part of the story. Martin Whitaker, who arrived as Ford's director of motorsport communications during 1995, now takes up the narrative:

"I think it was generally agreed within the company that the Escort RS Cosworth had not been properly developed, and I think matters came to a head when Ford was even considering pulling out of the World Rally Championship at the end of 1995.

"At the time, Toyota had just been banned from the sport for the use of illegal engine turbocharger modifications –

Martin Whitaker, who had earlier been running Ford's motorsport publicity and marketing in the 1990s, became Ford's director of European motorsport in mid-1996. It was under his tutelage that the Escort WRC was developed and, more significantly, the big decision to develop the Focus WRC in 1997/1998 was made.

MARTIN WHITAKER

Following Stuart Turner's unexpected retirement from the position of Director of European Motorsports in 1990, the company's WRC strategy and programme experienced a turbulent period, where the top job changed four times over the next decade. It was not until 1996 that Martin Whitaker took over, and anything like stability was restored.

Peter Ashcroft, Turner's immediate successor and long-time deputy, had retired at the end of 1991 for health reasons. His replacement, Colin Dobinson, was more of a marketing man than a motorsport enthusiast, leading to Peter Gillitzer (ex-Ford Australia) taking over from 1994. He, in turn, did not seem to be very interested in rallying (he was much more invested in circuit racing), so there was something of a collective sigh of relief when Martin Whitaker finally succeeded him.

Whitaker, who had started his career as a junior reporter on *Motoring News* magazine, had already progressed smoothly through a series of public relations posts. These included a position with Britain's RAC MSA, the Formula 1 FISA concern in Paris, a short stay with FOCA in London, a session with McLaren, a return to FISA, and becoming motor sport communications at Ford of Europe under Peter Gillitzer, in 1994.

Gillitzer was diplomatically eased out of his post after a two-year assignment, and Whitaker's promotion was both popular and successful. He remained in the post until 2003. It was under him that the decision was taken to move the works WRC programme from its long-established base at Boreham, and awarded it to M-Sport in Cumbria. All responsibility for the WRC engine development was also moved from Mountune to Cosworth.

After his lengthy tenure at Ford of Europe, he left the company abruptly in May 2003 due to a disagreement over policy. He went on to become a very successful marketing and organisational personality in the Middle East, before returning to the UK to become CEO of the new and (at the time of writing) yet-to-be-built Circuit of Wales. His successor at Ford was Jost Capito.

that left Carlos Sainz without a drive – and I remember myself and John Taylor sitting down and saying that this sounded like too good a situation to be missed. He and I then got a flight to Madrid, met Carlos there. Carlos led us to meet the head of Ford Spain, and we also went to see the head of the Repsol oil company (Carlos was sponsored by Repsol). Literally, within the course of that day, we were able to put together a deal, whereby Carlos would join Ford. Repsol would join Ford as well, all of which effectively rescued the WRC programme for Ford. This was pretty good news for the FIA too, because at the time it was worried by

*Carlos Sainz rejoined the Ford factory team in 1996, and drove the Escort WRC,
complete with (Spanish) Repsol oil company colours in 1997.*

Toyota's absence, and might be faced with running events with less than four manufacturers."

In the meantime, Ford had made its first approaches to Malcolm Wilson of M-Sport. Whitaker, Richard Parry-Jones, and PR-supremo John Southgate, first started to talking to him in early 1996, originally on the basis of Wilson moving down to Boreham to run the existing team.

"That was in May 1996," Wilson recalls, "and initially I agreed terms to go and do it. Then, one Sunday evening, I was at home in Cumbria and decided that I could not leave M-Sport to itself. I told Ford, but thought that was it, dead and buried; I was never going to be asked again."

By mid-1996, the team's fortunes had changed considerably. Carlos (already much-loved at Boreham from his previous sojourn with Sierra RS Cosworths) had brought some real professionalism to the team, an outright victory was gained by the works team in the Rally of Indonesia, and podium position results were being returned, as expected.

When Peter Gillitzer's appointment at Boreham was terminated in mid-1996, Martin Whitaker was an obvious contender to take his place. He was duly crowned, in what appears to have been a very popular move. His first major decision was to authorise Philip Dunabin's Boreham team to produce the Escort WRC of 1997 (a very rapid cheap-and-cheerful process that has already been described in the first chapter). He also, however, began to think deeply about Ford's long-term future in rallying.

Whitaker commented: "It wasn't so much that Boreham was not delivering for Ford in a variety of aspects – there were junior formulas as well that it was involved in – but I think it was generally felt that the Escort had not delivered the potential that it should have reached, and there was considerable opinion that the programme should therefore move to Malcolm [Wilson]."

Wilson recalls that he then took two M-Sport Escorts to the Neste Rally Finland in 1996, where they beat the official works team cars. It was after this remarkable performance that Ford approached him yet again.

This time, however, the offer was different. Whitaker had made it clear to his immediate superiors, Jac Nasser and Nick Scheele, that Wilson's determination to run the team from Cumbria could not be challenged. As a result, they were more amenable to doing a deal.

"At the time," Whitaker says, "there were alternatives, which I don't now recall in detail, but I don't think they were as attractive as the programme – and the package – that Malcolm put forward. What Malcolm was able to display was his key intent to make a success of it … at the time he was running M-Sport from relatively small premises, which were actually in the stables of his house! But he had that vibrancy, the determination to succeed. To be frank, that was what Boreham seemed to be lacking at the time.

"It was a big decision to be made, because at the end of the day Boreham had huge historical significance within Ford, while Ford itself had a massive history as far as the sport was concerned. So it was always going to be difficult to move away from Boreham, but the more we all talked about it, it was clear that new impetus was needed. [The programme] needed new blood, it needed new drive, and it needed more passion and enthusiasm."

The new deal was agreed just before the Wales Rally GB started from Chester, which gave M-Sport's 18-strong staff just eight weeks to get a grip of the WRC programme, build new Escort WRC cars, and turn up at the start of the 1997 Rallye Automobile Monte Carlo:

"I was in London, and had to keep it all confidential at first," Malcolm Wilson told me, "… my wife Elaine got all the staff into my conservatory at home, at which point they didn't know what was happening. That was on 18 November 1996 …"

The rush then started; not only did M-Sport need to develop the existing and agreed programme, but the design of a new car had to be started, and more spacious premises in which to evolve new-generation cars had to be found.

"Before getting the Ford contract," recalls Malcolm, "I had already started to look for some other premises. We could just – only just – get seven cars into the existing workshops at home, and that was really full. Not only did we need to build up our engineering resource, but the idea of Boreham designing and developing a new rally car didn't sit too well with me.

Neil Ressler, Ford USA's top technical man of the period, became Cosworth's chairman when Ford took over the business in 1998. He therefore became the guiding hand for further development of the Focus' Zetec engine in 2000 and beyond.

I wanted, basically, to do it ourselves. I put some of our ideas to Richard Parry-Jones and his colleague Al Kammerer (who was running the still-secret Focus development programme). They liked our concepts, what we were thinking of doing – longitudinal transmission and all that – and fortunately we were then awarded the contract to design and develop the new cars."

This, alongside the search for a more spacious long-term home for the fast-expanding M-Sport business, occupied much of the second half of 1997. It had already been decided, in principle, that a new rally car needed to be developed around the bare bones of the Focus family, which was not due

Guenther Steiner was project boss for the design of the original Focus WRC, based at Millbrook. He would later move to the USA, and become involved in F1.

for, transformation of, and eventual occupation of the new M-Sport headquarters at Dovenby Hall in Cumbria.

Malcolm Wilson already knew that he wanted to create a new WRC around the bodyshell of the still-developing Focus, but he also knew that not a single scheme, computer test, or calculation had taken place. Yet, well before the end of 1997, he was under pressure to get a car ready to show to the world at the Paris Motor Show in September 1998, where the Focus road car would make its debut. That, to those not at the sharp end of Ford's publicity machine, was an unbreakable requirement. Wilson, however, had an equally vital commitment to meet: achieving FIA sporting homologation by the end of 1998, and having two cars on the starting line of the Rallye Automobile Monte Carlo in January 1999.

M-Sport began planning for the engineering of the new Focus WRC before the end of 1997, but could not actually begin work until the first weeks of 1998. Right from the start, Malcolm had made it clear to his main Ford contacts – Richard Parry-Jones and Martin Whitaker – that he wanted to tackle the whole thing in-house, and only involve Ford in providing technical information, drawings, and related information.

Central to this process was the appointment of Guenther Steiner as Project Leader, a well-respected engineer whom Malcolm had first got to know at the Jolly Club, when the Italian organisation was running M-Sport-engineered Escort RS Cosworths. Malcolm had helped to steer him into a post with Prodrive: "I told [chairman of Prodrive] David Richards that if I ever had a job [for Steiner], I would employ him. I told David that if ever I had a job for him in the future, I would try to get [Steiner] back …"

Which he duly did, but this was only the beginning. Although M-Sport was a permanent fixture in Cumbria, Malcolm saw that he should get the car engineered, and the first prototype constructed, much further south. He didn't want to have to make a big or long-term investment, so leasing premises was a certainty. In those days, email was only just becoming widely available, and it was desirable that the team should be closer to Ford's HQ at Warley, near Brentwood in Essex. But where? Boreham was ruled out, but otherwise the choice was endless. Each time, however, there always seemed to be a snag.

"I think it was Guenther who suggested Millbrook," Malcolm records, referring to the massive proving ground

to be officially launched until September 1998. This meant that M-Sport had just a year to turn a great idea into a real rally car. Not only that, but there were scores of FIA World Rally Car regulations to be met along the way. Oh, and by the way, M-Sport had to carry on running the existing works programme with Escort WRC cars, and also satisfy a healthy demand for new Escort WRCs to be built for private customers! Just to emphasise the time that this was going to take, in 1997 there were 14 WRC events, and in 1998 there would be 13 more. How much time was involved in all this? Well, the well-known phrase goes, 'you do the maths …'

In terms of what follows, there are two fascinating stories about this project that need to be told. One is the saga of the creation of the Focus WRC itself, and the other is the search

MILLBROOK PROVING GROUND

Way back in the 1960s, while Vauxhall (of the UK) and Opel (of Germany) were both subsidiaries of the American giant General Motors, they still pursued their own separate design, developing, testing, and manufacturing programmes. At that time Vauxhall's 'proving ground' was a modest and cramped little facility in Luton, and the company set out to build a brand-new, spacious, and very well-equipped complex. The new site was to be based north of London, close to the M1 motorway (Junction 13 served it), and squeezed between the villages of Lidlington and Millbrook.

Opened in 1969 and completed in 1970, this 600 acre facility included a banked and truly circular two-mile high-speed track, a one-mile straightaway, a tarmac hill route, a rough-surfaced cross-country route, and many other facilities. Vauxhall (and Bedford, the truck spin-off of this operation) used the test tracks extensively until the 1980s, after which Vauxhall and Opel were integrated (with all new-model activities confined to Opel in Germany).

The entire site, complete with its extensive workshops and facilities, was then hived off, and made available to all, from manufacturers and suppliers to outlets for film and other media. It provided a very secure establishment in which photography was strictly controlled.

It was there – in 1998 and 1999 – that the Focus WRC was originally designed, took shape, and first driven and tested under Guenther Steiner's control. That operation was later moved north to Dovenby Hall, as that ultra-modern HQ was being developed.

GUENTHER STEINER

When M-Sport set up its compact little design team at Millbrook to engineer the all-new Focus WRC, the project leader was Guenther Steiner. He was well known to Malcolm Wilson due to his previous connection with M-Sport as the technical director of the Italian Jolly Club, which was running Martini-sponsored Escort RS Cosworths from 1994. Steiner settled in at once, and ran the technical side until 2001, when he was head-hunted for the Jaguar F1 operation by the then team boss Niki Lauda.

Born in Merano, Italy, in 1965, Steiner started his working life as a mechanic with the works Mazda rally team – when it was running Group A 323 four-wheel drive models – and eventually moved on to the Jolly Club team, where from 1994 he was its technical director. From 1994 to 1998, the Jolly Club ran Martini-sponsored Escorts (RS Cosworths, followed by World Rally Cars), and later took a job at Prodrive. When the time came for M-Sport to start work on its new Focus at the very beginning of 1998, Steiner was an obvious candidate for the job of Project Leader at Millbrook.

At Millbrook, Steiner guided Ray Stokoe, Christian Beyer, and Hamish Robson to engineer the all-new Focus, while also liaising closely with associate suppliers such as Mountune (engines), Xtrac (transmissions), and Michelin (tyres). With the first car completed, and testing under way, he then moved his tiny operation to Cumbria, and was M-Sport's Technical Director until 2001.

At that point, Guenther relinquished the Focus programme after being lured to the Jaguar F1 programme. He then moved briefly to Opel in 2003, before returning to the newly-established Red Bull (ex-Jaguar) F1 team in 2005. After further career developments he moved to the USA, and once again became well-known in Europe (and F1) by being appointed team principal of the newly-formed Haas F1 team in 2014.

complex, close to the M1 and Milton Keynes, "… basically that would be a turnkey operation. The offices were there, so were workshops, the desks were there, and security was assured. It was a perfect location, especially as there was a big test track alongside it."

With the lease acquired, and a moving date of February 1998 assured, Steiner could immediately hire himself a tiny design team. Steiner himself was not so much a designer as a manager, and he would effectively be a ringmaster over just

three people: Ray Stokoe, Christian Beyer and Hamish Robson, all of whom had engineering backgrounds.

Stokoe himself was to be the lead designer; not only had he been working on major transmission projects at Xtrac in

RAY STOKOE

Although much of the limelight surrounding the design of the Focus WRC focused on Guenther Steiner, he was the – very capable – co-ordinator/manager of the project, rather than the person who did much of the actual design. That honour should go to Ray Stokoe, the rather restlessly independent engineer for whom this was a real voyage of discovery.

Educated at Slough Grammar School, Stokoe started work in the motor racing industry immediately after graduating, working for the engine tuner Bill Lacey, and learning all about Coventry Climax race engines along the way. Eventually he became linked to Martin Slater on chassis design, whose F3 and Formula Atlantic cars were not only competitive, but race winners.

Moves then followed thick and fast, including spells with McLaren, JW Automotive, Frank Williams, VW, and a Lyncar-designed Hesketh sports car. After this, he spent time designing much of the rear structure of the turbocharged Benetton B186, and enjoyed two spells working on March Indycars, sandwiching some serious work on the Leyton House F1 cars of 1988-1990. Eventually, he joined the transmission specialists Xtrac, taking charge of several two-wheel drive and four-wheel drive projects.

Accordingly, it was at this point that he was head-hunted by Guenther Steiner to take charge of the engineering for the still-secret Ford Focus WRC, working from premises at the Millbrook proving ground. Once his task with the new Ford completed, he was offered the chance to relocate to Cumbria, working at the newly-opening Dovenby Hall, He ultimately turned this down, and went off again to complete a freelancing career.

This was the detail of the Focus WRC front suspension strut, as designed in 1998. Note the remote fluid reservoirs, and huge Brembo disc brakes.

recent years, but he had also carried out significant chassis and suspension work on modern F1 cars from Benetton and Leyton House. Beyer came across from the Toyota WRC team in Germany, while Robson was a bright young engineer who had already been involved in Ford chassis design at Dunton for some time.

Not that this was a long-planned move for Stokoe, who later commented:

"I had worked on an Opel 4x4 DTM transmission at Xtrac for three years, until Opel won the DTM Championship. Then, I got a phone call from someone I had worked with at Leyton House, asking if I was interested in rally car design. Then I got a call from Guenther Steiner – told him that I had never before done a rally car – and after I agreed to work with M-Sport at Millbrook, found that when we arrived it was just an empty room.

"We needed a flatbed so that we could layout and build the first car on it; we needed drawing boards (we weren't on computer designing at that stage); and I said that we needed constant and immediate information from Ford about what would be the new Focus."

This was where Hamish Robson's Ford engineering expertise was invaluable. Along with Malcolm Wilson, Robson was able to set up a direct electronic ISDN link to Ford's highly confidential IT/CAD network. Ray Stokoe had always been expecting drawings, on paper, but instead found that the entire engineering layout was available, component by component, by electronic transfer.

"Even so, there were just three of us in a small room. Through a door next to it was Guenther's office, with a secretary, and the build workshop was just along the corridor."

So it all began, geographically remote from M-Sport's Cumbrian HQ, Ford UK's technical HQ at Dunton, *and* the corporate HQ at Warley. Malcolm Wilson remembers how often he had to visit Millbrook, happily being able to use a leased helicopter to make an arduous journey almost routine.

The ISDN line immediately proved invaluable, with floods of bodyshell drawings beginning to wing their way, electronically, down the line. Before long, Stokoe's tiny team had a good idea of what it would like to retain, what it would like to modify, and what could be – would be, even – discarded altogether.

Right from the start, it seems, the team was uneasy about the aerodynamic performance of the new car, as there was potentially too much lift at the rear. Ford knew, of course, what an influence (visually and functionally) rear spoilers had exerted on the Sierra RS Cosworths, Escort RS Cosworths and the Escort WRC. Similarly, M-Sport knew that it could add a rear spoiler to the shell, and so too did Dunton Design (what the layman knows as the styling department). Initially, however, there were big differences between its proposals.

The problem stemmed from the fact that the new FIA World Rally Car regulations placed limits on the dimensions of add-on spoilers, whereas Design wanted to use spoilers that were quite considerably over-size. Both Stokoe and Robson remember having to attend a top level meeting at Dunton to thrash this out, and recalling that Design was not at all happy at being outranked by the FIA!

With that said, it is surprising to note that the design of the original Focus WRC was completed in just seven months,

thus achieving the target set by Malcolm Wilson during the winter, and that defined this project. Starting from the bare room at the Millbrook Proving Ground in February/March 1998, the first prototype/test car was completed in October 1998, and was preceded by the announcement of Colin McRae's signing. Incidentally, the blue show car, first seen in September 1998, was just that: a 'show' machine, with no running gear installed, that had never even been close to completion at Millbrook!

After the basic design and concept had been agreed, the important junctures were achieved along this timeline:

- **January 1998**
  - Premises at Millbrook secured.
- **February 1998**
  - Design work at Millbrook began.
- **May 1998**
  - Roll cage design settled.
- **June 1998**
  - Suspension design finalised.
- **August 1998**
  - First prototype bodyshell completed.
  - Colin McRae first visited Dunton before agreeing to sign a deal for the first two years.
- **September 1998**
  - The first engine was delivered from Mountune.
- **October 1998**
  - The first gearbox was delivered from XTrac.
  - 21 October: The engine was fired up for the first time in the car.
  - 22 October: Car was first tested at Millbrook, with Malcolm Wilson driving. He demanded anti-roll bars (that were still not ready).
- **November 1998**
  - 15 November: Ford presented homologation paperwork to the FIA.
- **December 1998**
  - Public launch to the specialist media, at Dunton, with Malcolm Wilson driving S16 FMC.
  - Initial snow testing in Norway, in the white-painted S16 FMC.
- **December 1998**
  - 18 December: FIA objected to the remote water pump position.

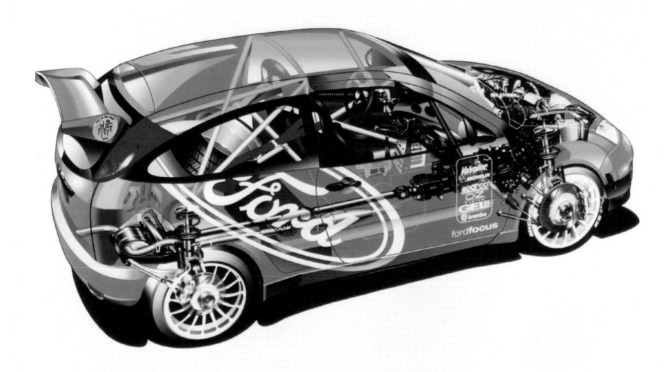

This was the anatomy of the new Focus WRC, as revealed in 1998, showing off the new four-wheel drive transmission system.

January 1999

Martini livery showed for the first time at the
Autosport International Show at the NEC.
17 January: Two Focus WRCs (S7 FMC and S8 FMC)
started the Rallye Automobile Monte Carlo.

Although concept work began on every aspect of the new car in the winter of 1997/1998, it was the evolution of the engine, and the complex four-wheel drive transmission, which had to be pushed ahead first and most rapidly to keep the timing of the project on track. By February/March 1998, both Mountune (engines) and Xtrac (transmission systems) were already well advanced and producing hardware.

David Mountain, the founder of Mountune, had been Boreham's favoured engine supplier since the late 1980s, and it was his company that had wrung the last out of the venerable YB power units fitted to the 1997/1998 Escort WRCs. When concept work on a new Focus WRC was started, it was natural – assumed, even – that Mountune would develop and manufacture the engines.

Until spare wheels and other on-board material was added, this was the equipped 'boot' area of the original-type Focus WRC. Among the kit already installed was the jack, the wheel-nut gun, and the electronic pack connected with the on-board cameras.

The cockpit layout of the original Focus WRC bore little relationship to the Focus road cars, which were already selling in big numbers!

At the time, and even before the Focus production car was ready to be launched, it was clear that the most powerful road car variant would be the normally-aspirated, fuel-injected 1988cc version in the 16-valve Zetec-M range, that output 128bhp. The WRC regulations limited engine capacity to two litres, but otherwise allowed the complete freedom of turbocharging, lubrication, and other details. The exception being that the turbocharger would have to be equipped with a 34mm diameter restrictor upstream of the turbo intake. The rules allowed the transversely positioned engine to be lowered a little, and to be leaned back in the engine bay by up to 25 degrees. However, and this became critical in the December 1998/January 1999 event, no freedoms were allowed for the location and dimensions of the engine cooling water pump.

Even before the Focus programme was agreed upon, Mountune began investigating a transformation of its engine, with a target of producing more than 300bhp. As David Mountain recounts:

"The phone call came from Philip Dunabin at Boreham, along the lines of, 'Here's a £25000 purchase order, for you to look at everything in the Zetec engine, to do some work, and to run a test engine.' We were employing a very good Japanese designer call Hiroshi; he later became Toyota's top race engine man. We knew a bit about Zetecs already, because we had built a few normally-aspirated engines, but the deal with Boreham was always that a new World Rally Car was going to use a version of the 2-litre Zetec engine.

"Shortly after that, however, it all got cancelled. I think we ran one prototype engine on our dyno [dynamometer], and

MOUNTUNE

David Mountain started work building engines for Swiftune before setting up his own small workshop operation in Maldon, Essex (just five miles from Ford's motorsport HQ at Boreham) in the early 1980s. Mountune, his staff and technicians soon proved that they could produce high-performance Ford-based race and rally engines that were at least the equal of those built by rival concerns such as Terry Hoyle, Brian Hart and – amazingly – Cosworth itself.

The company's first high-profile successes came when it began preparing ultra-fast Sierra RS500 Cosworths for touring car racing, which often bested factory-supported cars that ran with rival engines. Mountune provided the engines for the works Sierra RS Cosworths while they were at its competitive best, from 1988 to 1992. So, for the Escort RS Cosworth came along in 1993 and the Escort World Rally Car that followed in 1997, it was Mountune, not Boreham, that did most of the development work. Boreham no longer had (or needed) a test-bed of its own.

When Ford and M-Sport set out on the design and development of the original Focus WRC, it was Mountune that was originally tasked with the work on the 2-litre Zetec-M-based power unit, which was a conspicuous success. Colin McRae's first-generation Focus WRCs, that won the East African Safari and Rally of Portugal events in 1999, all used Mountune-built engines.

Because Ford had taken over Cosworth towards the end of 1998, it seemed logical that work on this engine should moved to the new acquisition, this transfer of responsibilities being carried out at the end of 1999.

Although Mountune no longer had links with the works Focus WRC, the company was still well-regarded by Ford and its engineers. The feeling was such that when Mountune eventually came to forge links with Roush of the USA in 2003 – moving to a more spacious factory at Hutton (near Brentwood) – it soon began developing a whole series of factory-approved tune-up kits for cars like the already-high-performance Fiesta and Focus RS road cars.

Mountune developed the original Focus WRC engine, arranging for it to be leaned back in the engine bay, and to have the turbocharger placed at the front of the power unit where it would stay as cool as possible.

The 16-valve Zetec engine was originally used in early-1990 Escort road cars, then in the vast majority of Mondeos, and was a mature design, especially in 2-litre form, when Focus WRC design began in 1998.

The original 1998 Focus WRC engine bay was stuffed full of kit, including a massive turbo intercooler.
The engine itself, transverse-mounted, was laid back towards the bulkhead.

did some basic work again when Boreham thought it had secured the programme. Then, suddenly, it was all announced that the works contract was going to M-Sport. That was a blow, as we had already talked to Philip, who was visually seeing the format of the new car as he would design it.

"But, it wasn't all bad news for my 15-strong workforce. Soon after Malcolm started work on the Escort WRC, we started doing all the Escort WRC engine work."

Once the Focus WRC project was officially approved, Mountune thrashed out a deal with Malcolm and his associate Marc Amblard, who came to work with Mountune during the year. At the time of writing, nearly 20 years on, it can now be disclosed that the original deal was for £500,000. This was to cover design, development, payment for tooling, and the production of the first three engines, one for the dyno, and two for test cars. It was written into the contract that each engine had to be able to perform for a minimum of 800km before a rebuild was necessary.

At first Mountune had just six people working on the design, led by Mr Hiroshi Yajima, and it was committed to delivering

engines by October 1998. Camshaft profiles were finalised by a consultant called Peter Lings. As is now well known, the firm convincingly beat that deadline. The workforce rapidly grew, nearing 30, and there were engines at Millbrook ready to fire up before the first car was completed.

In many ways the layout and operation of the engine was familiar to modern WRC rallying pundits, except that the turbocharger and related exhaust system sat up proudly, facing the front of the engine bay. The original power unit proved to be very powerful; indeed, it was totally competitive, just as Mountune had forecast. The FIA was looking for engines that would produce around 300bhp, but Mountune was instead aiming for something between 320 and 325bhp. According to Mountune's records, the first cars produced between 310 and 312bhp, and by the Portugal event in 1999 they were running at about 320bhp.

Other than what the more sensationalist publications called 'the water pump crisis' (to be detailed later), there was one further irritating design problem, which was eliminated before the power units were ever run in cars. No one can better summarise the situation than David Mountain himself:

"Marc [Amblard] wanted the engine to run without the clutch being attached to the flywheel. The idea was that, effectively, we wanted to reduce the inertia of the drivetrain as much as we could, and – by the way – Marc was very much involved in the concept of the gearbox layout too. The idea was that the clutch should not be positioned on the flywheel, but there was to be a shaft that would go all the way through the middle of the transmission, with the clutch on the outside of the main casing.

"That was fine, in concept, but when we started to run the engine with the gearbox attached on the dyno, all the spline couplings had a bit of lash in them, so what happened was that we had very high torsionals on the crankshaft; we discovered all this on the test-bed, well before we put it in a car. We couldn't keep a cambelt on it in that form … every time we ran the engine the cambelt flew off, which meant that valves hit pistons and the engine was destroyed.

"In the end I said that we were running out of time, that we had got to get a flywheel on the crankshaft. The problem, then, was that the crankshaft had never been designed for that to happen …"

In the end, the problem was solved by going back to what might be considered a 'conventional' layout. M-Sport extended its contract with Mountune to ten engines, with an agreement to build, service, and supply them all. By the end of 1999, Mountune had produced around 20 such engines.

Then there was the saga of the water pump location, an issue that didn't come to a head until the Focus WRC's first official outing in the 1999 Rallye Automobile Monte Carlo. The outcome, as is covered in greater detail in Chapter 3, was that the Focus was disqualified from the event results on the grounds that the pump, its location, and its performance, were counter to the ever-developing WRC regulations.

It was while Mountune was running the first turbocharged engine on its own test-bed in Maldon that it discovered that the original – standard – water pump, which was positioned at the end of the cylinder block, did not have a high-enough flow rate. Clearly it was adequate for the standard road car engine, but not for an engine tuned to produce between 320 and 325bhp.

Because the latest WRC regulations allowed free oil pumps and related plumbing, Marc Amblard was sure that there had

XTRAC

Mike Endean was working for the motorsport-orientated Hewland transmission company in the 1980s. Deciding to set up his own business, he founded Xtrac in 1984 with the goal of making 4WD transmission systems. Xtrac's first job was commissioned by the successful Norwegian rallycross star Martin Schanche, for a system to fit in a much-modified Zakspeed-engined Ford Escort MkIII.

As business built up, Xtrac moved from its original premises in Wokingham, Berkshire, to the nearby Finchampstead. A bigger move followed in 2000, when Xtrac relocated to a brand-new, purpose-designed, factory in Thatcham, to the east of Newbury. The move was representative of the fact that Xtrac had already become the UK's largest and best-regarded maker of motor racing and rallying transmission items. The company's first links with M-Sport came in 1997, when M-Sport was running the Escort WRC, and continued very successfully with the original generation of Focus WRCs that followed.

been an omission, and – being a fluent French speaker – was sent to discuss the matter with the FIA. According to Marc, he was given the verbal go-ahead by the FIA to move the water pump and its plumbing. Crucially, however, this was never put into writing.

In the meantime, Mountune made up a bespoke water pump installation, which provided twice as much water flow as the standard pump, and placed it down towards the end of the sump – outside the cylinder block – with a drive coming through the sump. This installation was obvious to an inspector, and passed through the original homologation procedure, only to be held up by the attitude of rival teams, to whom the original homologation papers were naturally made available.

Before the 1999 Rallye Automobile Monte Carlo, when the first (and, at the time, only) two completed Focus WRC cars arrived for scrutineering, the rival teams rejected the proposal of a regulation change allowing greater freedom on water pump design. They did, however, apparently proffer a compromise. The rival teams were prepared to allow the Focus to compete in the first three events with the non-standard water pump, on the understanding that Ford would not be able to score championship points …

This was a nightmare scenario, and one that resulted in Colin McRae and Simon Jean-Joseph being disqualified from the event. This is considered, in much greater detail, in Chapter 3, but this is surely the place to spell out what happened next. M-Sport was stung by what it considered was a betrayal at the hands of the FIA. Team boss Martin Whitaker later stated that "We felt that we had a cast iron case, and I still have a feeling – to this day – that the whole proceedings were a bit of a charade … we had been led up the garden path, then hung out to dry." Nevertheless, Mountune and M-Sport set about producing a 'Mark 2' system that would be acceptable to the FIA.

Now it can be told that the revised system was completed in a mere three weeks; conceived, engineered, and manufactured for use in the same two ex-Rallye Automobile Monte Carlo cars, ready to compete in Sweden. This time frame included bringing the cars back to the UK, preparing them, and transporting them to the start of the 1999 International Swedish Rally in Karlstad …

The result – perhaps not strictly 'sporting legal' but quite invisible to a casual observer, or an event scrutineer – was totally effective. Returned to a supposedly standard position in the block, Mountune produced a new pump impeller, bored out the housing as far as it could (or dared), and arranged to drive it at a different speed from before. Although it was very much a crossed-fingers job at first, this proved to be completely successful; so successful, in fact, that the revised engine was able to withstand the heat and dust of events like the Safari Rally, which followed only weeks later!

In comparison with all this drama, the layout, proving, and performance of the all-new six-speed four-wheel drive transmission was relatively free of crisis. Since M-Sport had already established a good relationship with Xtrac in 1997, there was much mutual trust already; in a matter of months, Xtrac had produced a six-speed sequential-change main gearbox for the Escort WRC, to replace the old-style MS90 (FFD-Ricardo) transmission on the Escort RS Cosworth. No sooner had concept work started on the Focus WRC than Ray Stokoe, as an ex-Xtrac employee himself, laid out his requirements.

Xtrac itself was ahead of the game at this point, having already started to design what it called a generic 4WD transmission, featuring a transversely-positioned engine and a longitudinal main gearbox (Type 157 in its coding). This soon morphed into the Type 240 for the Ford project. The original layout is credited to Xtrac's founder Mike Endean, but much of the project work on the Focus transmission was headed up by Paul Eastman. Paul, incidentally, would go on to join M-Sport in 1999, where he further developed many of the transmission components for future versions of the Focus WRC.

As an aside, it is no secret that at this point in its history, Xtrac also had two other customers who might be interested in using such a generic layout, and both eventually did just that: in 1999 both the Hyundai Accent and the Peugeot 206 had transmissions that were generally similar in layout and operation to the Focus.

With the first of the Focus Xtrac transmissions, the reason for the remote clutch mounting became clear. The clutch was positioned on the extremity of the shaft, and thus was able to be easily removed at a hurried service point: something that was never going to be easy with it buried in the mass of the transmission itself. Even more, such a change was essential to deal with all the torsionals that have already been detailed regarding the engine layout.

Although Xtrac had already done as much as it thought feasible to cut down on clearances, tolerances, and what it called 'lash' (technology and machining capabilities have moved on to such an extent that it would be able to produce a much more sophisticated transmission today), there was general astonishment the first time the new transmission was run on the test bed. As David Mountain himself recalls:

"We simply couldn't believe the noise that was coming out of it. We switched it off instantly, because we thought there must have been some nuts and bolts lying around in it … there were lots of drop gear sets in there – the gearbox was quite complex, and of course the gears were straight cut – and with the casing expanding quite a lot with the heat, it sounded just like a shotgun going off …"

Much detail development, and attention to tolerances, was needed, and it eventually paid off (though one would never have described this as an acceptably refined road car transmission). The gear change linkage, incidentally, started life relying on rods, but a cable linkage was adopted at a later date.

Xtrac used every ounce of its formidable experience in designing transmissions to produce the new Focus WRC system.

The rest of the structural design was relatively straightforward. The tightly-knit team of Stokoe, Beyer and Robson knew their stuff, as well as knowing what their rivals could, and might, do. Armed with this knowledge, they forged ahead to meet the October 1998 deadline.

Developing the roll cage structure – this, of course, being securely welded into the shell – was made easier by Stokoe and Beyer's previous experience on other race and rally cars. There was, however, one moment of hilarity (and this story, I am assured, is true in every detail), when a team from Ford Design made a visit to Millbrook. The group had arrived to see what changes were being made to the shell, including the positioning and shape of the rear spoiler, and to the nose of the car, where sizeable air intakes had to be fashioned to help keep the engine bay cool.

At one point the question was raised as to how the interior of the car could be 'dressed' to make it appear less stark (suggesting trim panels, arm rests, and the like). Discussion was cut short when the design team was informed that the objective was to take as much out of the car as possible: to save weight, and at the same time reduce the fire risks. That

wasn't all; although the Ford Design team understood the function of a roll cage, one individual objected to the use of the tubes that crossed the door apertures (compulsory by FIA regulations, incidentally), and suggested that they be removed. Restraining his temper with great effort, Ray Stokoe had to explain that the tubes were part of the overall structure. "If these are removed," he enquired, "how many drivers would you like to kill?" All in all, it was not a successful visit.

Design finally accepted that the dimensions and location of a rear spoiler on this new car would need to be constrained by WRC regulations. For 1999 at least, a free-standing aerofoil was mounted on struts behind and above the hatchback window glass. Testing in Ford's own wind tunnel (located in Cologne) originally revealed that there was substantial rear-end lift at higher speeds, and Stokoe's biggest problem was how and where to mount the supporting struts without having to carve into the glass itself.

To make things even more frenetic for the small team at Millbrook, during the summer it was asked to build a convincing mock-up of how a Focus WRC might look. This

Here's a study for the model makers: a test car, correctly liveried in every detail.

would allow it to be exhibited at the same time as the new Focus road cars, when they made their debut at the Paris Motor Show in September 1998 (although the WRC 'car' would originally be on show in a room at a nearby hotel). This car, as all experienced observers knew, was no more than a visual suggestion of what might follow; the show model had no free-standing rear spoiler/aerofoil, and there was a totally standard front-wheel drive 2-litre Focus chassis under the skin. The colour scheme was based around an anonymous dark blue, and the windows were blacked out so that the interior could not be inspected.

The mock-up car would appear several times in the next few weeks, notably at the October 1998 British International Motor Show at the NEC in Birmingham. As it was always seen in the same glossy blue – albeit made more striking by the presence of a massive Ford oval logo along the flanks – the media found it difficult to get excited about the team's prospects, especially as no major sponsor was yet evident. This is particularly worth noting when we remember that for their

last season the outgoing Escort WRCs had also run without major sponsorship of any type.

The sensations, when they did occur, all happened behind the scenes. Because the massive Ford oval spread down each of the flanks, whenever a passenger door was opened the oval would be broken. According to Ford USA traditions (and, let us not forget, Ford UK was a subsidiary of that parent company), to break the oval was sacrilege. Martin Whitaker now takes up the story:

"John Southgate and I did a 'reveal' for David Scott – who was the current head of Ford public relations, worldwide – in a room in our hotel. David, frankly, was horrified, and burst out: 'You have broken the oval!' He didn't think the corporate boss in attendance, Jac Nasser, was going to be happy. Well, we went through the ceremony of doing another 'reveal' for Jac when he turned up, and – guess what – he also said 'Who broke the oval?' But that was almost the beginning and the end of it, because he otherwise loved the style, and just so long as we didn't open the doors in public he was content."

Even with the understated colour scheme, the showing at the two motor shows had ignited continuing media interest, especially since Ford had already let it be known that it had signed Colin McRae to join the team for the 1999 season.

To the great relief of everyone involved in the engineering of the new car, the very first machine was near-complete at Millbrook by October 1998, and was fired up for the first time on the same day as the British International Motor Show opened its doors. Malcolm Wilson somehow found time to visit the show, answering mountains of queries about the progress of the new project, before travelling to Millbrook to carry out the first test drives around Millbrook's famous Hill Circuit. Generally satisfied with the machine (Ray Stokoe considered it "still rough, needing a lot of refining"), Malcolm commented that the car was too soft-sprung, needing stiffer front and rear anti-roll bars. His suggestions were met with the information that such anti-roll bars would indeed be fitted: they had even been designed, but had not yet been delivered.

The wait was almost over, so it was altogether fitting that Ford arranged to let many of world rallying's insiders get a better view of the mock-up, while also celebrating the imminent retirement of the existing Escort WRC from works rallying. To do this, it hosted a truly glittering 'end-of-an-era' dinner party, commemorating the most important juncture in Ford's rallying history since the arrival of the Escort Twin-Cam of 30 years earlier.

The party was to take place on the eve of the Wales Rally GB, which was due to start from Cheltenham in November 1998. Taking place at Sudeley Castle, just a few miles from the start of the next day's rally, the event was incredibly well attended. Not only was it hosted by Walter Hayes, who had masterminded the setting up of Boreham, the Escort rally programme, the Escort RS Cosworth, and so much more, but almost everyone with past and current Ford motorsport connections had been persuaded to attend.

A group photograph was taken of the 'Great and the Good,' all standing around the mock-up Focus WRC, and it was one of this author's duties to circulate the tables with a massive print of that image, so that the many stellar characters in attendance could sign it. These, incidentally, included no fewer that six World Rally Champions – Björn Waldegård, Ari Vatanen, Hannu Mikkola, Juha Kankkunen, Carlos Sainz and Tommi Mäkinen – along with such other luminaries as Malcolm Wilson, Timo Mäkinen, Ove Andersson, David Richards, Andrew Cowan, Stuart Turner, Martin Whitaker, Bill Barnett, Gunnar Palm, and Tony Mason. Naturally, Walter Hayes performed a speech, making a few kind and appropriate comments, and everything seemed to go well. All in all, it was an unforgettable evening.

Now, however, it was time for ceremony to be put to one side, and for the long-secret Focus machinery to move into the limelight. Just days later, the first (and only) Millbrook-built Focus WRC came to the fore. Testing began, Colin McRae became available as a driver as his Subaru contract ended amicably, and the team's new sponsor could be announced.

In Monte Carlo, on 17 January 1999, the Focus WRC would finally get down to business. Game on!

CHAPTER THREE

1999 – The first eventful season

Looking back after the end of the 1999 rally season, many pundits concluded that the works Focus WRC programme had been lucky to survive a year in which it had experienced more than its share of colossal highs and lows. By any standards, it had been a turbulent, eventful, controversial, and sometimes frustrating season. Even so, M-Sport could at least point to two outright World Rally Championship victories, and a great deal of evidence that – when reliability was finally achieved – the car, and the team behind it, would be competitive in all events.

The miracle – and in some respects it certainly had been miraculous – was not that there had been victories, but rather that the cars appeared at all, in time to take part in their first event; the Rallye Automobile Monte Carlo in January. Engineering of the new car had not begun until February/March 1998, and the first (and only) prototype – S16 FMC – only ran for the first time in October 1998. Yet, somehow, two immaculate new machines – registered S7 FMC and S8 FMC

appeared on the start line in Monaco on 17 January 1999, resplendent in Martini colours.

During this time the new-generation Focus WRC had been launched, with real flourish, in a banqueting suite at Ford's technical centre at Dunton, Essex. A white car – S16 FMC, still the only car that had been completed – was shown on a display plinth throughout the morning, taken down during lunchtime, and allowed out to show its paces (with Malcolm Wilson at the wheel) on the Dunton test track in the afternoon.

With Focus project director Al Kammerer presiding, and with Malcolm Wilson, Martin Whitaker, Richard Parry-Jones, and the new team drivers all present, the new project was flamboyantly displayed. This show included a separate example of the complex new Xtrac transmission, but there remained no mention of a sponsor; negotiations with Martini were still highly secret, and not close to complete.

In the afternoon session, Wilson put the test car through a whole series of passes, spins, and pirouettes for the photographers without drama or any technical hitches. It was

Colin McRae, co-driver Nicky Grist, and the newly launched Focus WRC, as seen in December 1998.

The new car was officially shown to the world's press in December 1998. One car – registered S16 FMC – was on show, and later demonstrated on the test track at Ford's technical centre at Dunton in Essex, with team boss Malcolm Wilson at the wheel. Martini sponsorship had not been obtained at that point, so the test car was in an anonymous livery. S16 FMC eventually appeared on the Safari Rally in 1999, where Petter Solberg took fifth place; but was it the same car?

a performance that was greeted with some amusement: a number of those in attendance had just returned from a similar occasion in France, organised by Peugeot, where the new 206 WRC had been shown off to them, and had promptly broken down! [It is worth recording that although the Peugeot design had been started well before that of the Focus WRC, the 206 did not appear in competition until May 1999, did not finish an event until August, and did not record a victory until the following year …]

Although cold-weather testing would begin in Norway just days after the display – and all of the team's recently-announced driving roster would take part in that exercise – the team's biggest concern was receiving approval for homologation of the new car, which used many features not previously incorporated in other WRCs by rival teams.

Every detail of the proposed new Focus WRC had been presented to the FIA authorities in Paris on 15 November (the press launch taking place just ten days later). Unhappy about many about many aspects of the proposal, the FIA team, led by scrutineer Jacques Berger, asked to see a complete car laid out for inspection at Millbrook. A number of the more 'sensational' motorsport press corps wasted no time in reporting that homologation had been refused, and that there were no fewer than 39 points of conflict between Ford and the FIA. Malcolm Wilson, for his part, rebutted these rumours as "pure speculation," especially as his associate, Marc Amblard, had enjoyed a very business-like discussion with the FIA before the car's provisional specification had been settled.

The visit was not a success. In short, Berger did not like what he saw on display. The language barrier did not help

Four happy individuals at the start of an exciting time for the evolution of the Ford works rally team in 1998/1999. From left to right: Malcolm Wilson, Colin McRae, Nicky Grist, and Ford's European Director of Motorsport Martin Whitaker.

At the launch in December 1998, Ford showed off S16 FMC, the first and only car yet to be completed. Here it is surrounded by Martin Whitaker, Malcolm Wilson, Guenther Steiner, and Al Kammerer, who was project director for the Focus road car programme at the time.

matters (Amblard was not present for the inspection), and it was decided that the rival teams – particularly Toyota, Mitsubishi, Peugeot, and Subaru – should have a chance to comment on the situation. Apparently all of those asked turned down the proposed water pump layout. It would seem that jealousy and professional pique were more of

This is how Ford publicised the format and equipment of the Focus WRC, when it was new in the spring of 1999.

From family car to World R

① GENERATING DOWNFORCE

A rally car must remain stable at very high speeds, so a rear wing is mounted on the hatchback. Like an aircraft wing - only mounted upside down - it generates 'downforce' instead of lift. Downforce from a wing increases dramatically with speed and pushes the car onto the road for better grip

② MISSION CONTROL

Co-driver is both 'car manager' and computer operator. Using a purpose-built dash-top laptop, he monitors distance, time and speed through three hectic days of rallying on every championship event

③ SAFETY CAGE

More than 40 metres of steel tubing is welded in to a safety cage inside the bodyshell to create a survival cell

Graphic by G2K/March 1999

belt h
extinguisher
have radio intercom

Championship challenger

Seven steps that transformed the Ford Focus award winning road car into a rally winner...

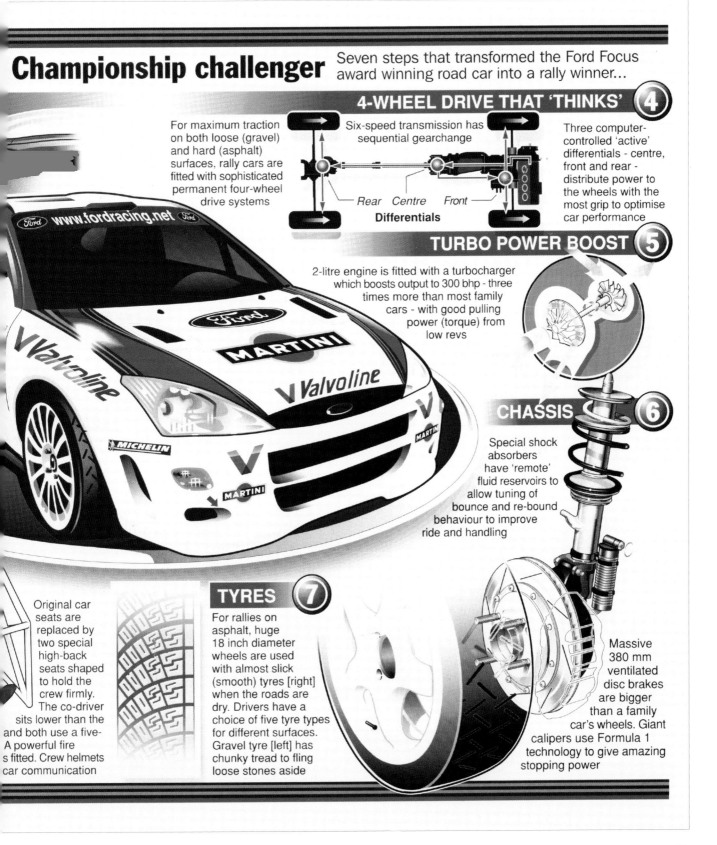

4-WHEEL DRIVE THAT 'THINKS' ④

For maximum traction on both loose (gravel) and hard (asphalt) surfaces, rally cars are fitted with sophisticated permanent four-wheel drive systems

Six-speed transmission has sequential gearchange

Rear   Centre   Front
Differentials

Three computer-controlled 'active' differentials - centre, front and rear - distribute power to the wheels with the most grip to optimise car performance

TURBO POWER BOOST ⑤

2-litre engine is fitted with a turbocharger which boosts output to 300 bhp - three times more than most family cars - with good pulling power (torque) from low revs

CHASSIS ⑥

Special shock absorbers have 'remote' fluid reservoirs to allow tuning of bounce and re-bound behaviour to improve ride and handling

Original car seats are replaced by two special high-back seats shaped to hold the crew firmly. The co-driver sits lower than the and both use a five- A powerful fire s fitted. Crew helmets car communication

TYRES ⑦

For rallies on asphalt, huge 18 inch diameter wheels are used with almost slick (smooth) tyres [right] when the roads are dry. Drivers have a choice of five tyre types for different surfaces. Gravel tyre [left] has chunky tread to fling loose stones aside

Massive 380 mm ventilated disc brakes are bigger than a family car's wheels. Giant calipers use Formula 1 technology to give amazing stopping power

the deciding factors here than any serious consideration of Ford's so-called 'mistake.'

Clearly, this stand-off could result in homologation being refused, and therefore in M-Sport not being allowed to compete in the Rallye Automobile Monte Carlo. Undaunted, the two immaculate new Focus WRCs – which had done no more than the very minimum of shakedown testing – were presented at pre-event scrutineering in Monte Carlo, only to be banned from starting the event.

Then, a last minute compromise was offered, partly influenced, to be sure, by worries over how the media would treat an event where such anticipated machines did not appear. With one hour's notice, the cars – running close to the front of the field at numbers seven and eight – were allowed to compete 'under appeal.' As is now well known, Colin McRae's car would finish third 'on the road,' but subsequently be disqualified. There followed a turgid process of protest, explanation, and appeal to the FIA International Court of Appeal. The FIA's negative decision took a few days to materialise, but with less than two weeks left before the start of the International Swedish Rally, M-Sport already knew that it would have to re-engineer the water cooling system. How this was achieved has already been detailed in the second chapter.

Motorsport Director Martin Whitaker had hired the noted barrister and legal expert, Chris Hardman, to argue his case to the very end. Though the appeal finally ended in failure (the FIA chose not to impose any further penalties, however) it resulted in Hardman accompanying the team on all its events for the remainder of the season!

At this point it should be emphasised that in January 1999, the world of rallying still didn't quite know what to make of the Focus project. It came from M-Sport – an endeavour that was still aspiring to be a top-level works team – with a brand-new driver line-up, on top of being the only all-new machine to enter at the start of the season. Its specification, and M-Sport's interpretation of the WRC regulations, was also seen as controversial, even contentious.

Major competition would come from Mitsubishi (having won the 1998 World Rally Championship, and boasting three-times Driver's Champion Tommi Mäkinen among its roster), the formidable Toyota line-up (Toyota's lead driver, Carlos Sainz, was not only charismatic but remarkably successful), and Subaru, with ageing – but still very effective – Prodrive-built machines.

Facing up to this, not only was M-Sport still quite a small team (although Dovenby Hall was already being transformed, the original team effort was still based in small premises at Malcolm Wilson's home just a few miles away), with a new major sponsor that was expecting results almost immediately. Finally, it only had one front-line driver, Colin McRae, who was still thought to be 'on the rebound' from Subaru, having driven for it since 1991.

To fill out the story of this first season, however, we must first of all see how the driving strength was assembled; how a major new sponsor – Martini – joined the team; and how the fast-expanding M-Sport company found, bought, and transformed the Dovenby Hall site to become its new HQ.

Right from the start, Director Martin Whitaker and M-Sport team boss Malcolm Wilson were determined to get the best possible drivers on board. On too many occasions in the past, securing truly stellar works drivers had been foiled by budget shortcomings, as both Boreham and – in recent years – M-Sport had suffered from having only limited financial resources. For Ford, the problem was that it had been in world-level rallying for a long time, and was slow to catch up with the colossal fees drivers now commanded in the sport. Ford had been operating along the same lines throughout the 1970s – when there might have been serious inflation, but drivers' fees were still manageable – and even the 1980s, long after other companies like Mercedes-Benz, Audi, Lancia, and Toyota had all opened up its over-flowing bank balance to drivers. In the 1990s Ford had sometimes benefited from the support of generous sponsors – from Q8 fuels, Mobil, and later from Repsol – but in 1998 the two-car team looked to be only able to operate with limited support from Valvoline.

Martin Whitaker, having taken over from Peter Gillitzer, was determined to put a stop to this. Thanks to this, along with Malcolm Wilson and some carefully-nurtured 'sponsorship finders,' the new Focus WRC was able set out on its quest to become 'number one' with massive financial support from Martini (the Italian drinks giant) and Valvoline oils, as well as substantial technical back-up from Michelin tyres.

The Martini connection came from two sources – one of them sporting, the other a simple sponsorship-seeking operation. Martini had been close to motorsport – both rallying and racing – for some years, and its strongest rallying link had developed with Lancia. Until 1992, Martini livery appeared on Lancia's Rally 037s, Delta S4s and works Delta Integrales.

Details of the Martini sponsorship colour scheme changed greatly over the four year period. In the first year, 1999, the cars featured mainly red flanks, with two-tone striping from front wheels to rear spoiler …

… while in 2000, the arrival of Carlos Sainz with (Spanish) Telefónica Movistar sponsorship, saw the flanks become blue, with red-and-blue diagonal side sweep colours …

… in 2001 there was considerably more red/two-tone blue Martini colouring on the bonnet and the roof. Then came another change …

… for 2002, when the roof and bonnet became white again, and there was a delicate pattern of Martini red/blue/blue 'teeth' on the doors.

M-Sport then began the engineering and development of Ford Escort RS Cosworths, used by the Italian Jolly Club from 1994, and knew all about Ford's capabilities thereafter.

In 1998, while the Focus WRC was still being designed at Millbrook, Martin Whitaker – aided (and introduced to Martini) by 'sponsorship finder' Jonathan Bancroft – approached the Italian giant. He proposed that it took up headline WRC sponsorship of the brand-new (and, at that time, still secret) Ford motor car. This, it was suggested, would then make it possible to sign the 'people's favourite,' Colin McRae, as the team's number one driver; a potential match that was surely made in heaven?

Whitaker was delighted to learn that Martini considered that this was a very promising link-up, and was also amazed to learn that Martini would also be happy to be joined on the car by other sponsors. As it happened, this would not occur

MARTINI IN RALLYING

The Italian drinks giant Martini had already enjoyed a long and distinguished record of sponsorship in motorsport before it joined hands with the Focus WRC programme in 1999. Particularly linked to Porsche and Lancia, the first overt Martini sponsorship showed up on racing Porsches from 1968, and the brand became successful and prominent in many motor racing events, all the way up to F1 involvement.

Strong Martini sponsorship in rallying began in the 1970s, and began to make spectacular headlines during the 1980s and 1990s when it was adopted as title sponsors by Lancia, on cars such as the Rally 037, Delta S4, and Delta Integrale.

Martini's links with Lancia ended after the 1992 season, but its interest was revived in 1994 when a new team titled Team Ford-Martini Racing-Jolly Club was founded, using distinctively-liveried Ford Escort RS Cosworths and, later, Escort WRCs. That team's principal driver was Gianfranco Cunico (who had driven for the Ford works team in the recent past), and the cars were engineered by Malcolm Wilson's young and ambitious team.

It was this successful sporting and commercial enterprise (covering 1994-1998), and the several outright victories at European Rally Championship level, that were important factors in persuading Martini to return to the World Rally Championship scene. Its return was with the M-Sport Focus WRC operation in 1999: a collaboration that coincided with the team's links to Colin McRae, as both of them would leave the team at the end of 2002.

shade to a brighter, more fluorescent hue. The sparkling red was agreed upon, and dominated an artfully-arranged livery (in layouts that would then be changed, in detail, every year for the next four seasons). The new deal, alongside the sparkling new Focus livery, was unveiled during the Autosport International Show at Birmingham's NEC in January 1999.

The race to find a new driving team had already occupied Whitaker and Wilson for several anxious months in 1998. They had realised that they would have to release Juha Kankkunen and Bruno Thiry at the end of the year (both would join Subaru for the 1999 season). To fill this gap, they had great – and well-funded – ambitions to attract both Colin McRae and three-times World Rally Champion Tommi Mäkinen to the team.

During 1998, approaches to Mäkinen were made in total secrecy (Stokoe and Hamish Robson recall being banished "to the pub" one lunchtime, so that a "famous driver" could privately visit the Millbrook workshops and look at the new car). These talks ultimately came to nothing, as Mäkinen elected to stay with Mitsubishi, and went on to become World Rally Champion again in 1999.

Attracting Colin McRae was a long, and somewhat complex business. Ford and M-Sport had originally made him an offer for 1997 and beyond (which would therefore have seen him driving Escort WRCs). He did make visits to Cumbria in order to test the cars at M-Sport's local forestry-stage location, but as it was thought that his contract with Subaru was both long-term and set in stone, it was decided that he should not be approached again until mid-1998.

When that time came, McRae visited Millbrook (where there was still no car ready to be driven), and once again tested an Escort WRC. He was clearly impressed by the potential of the new project, and negotiations turned to concentrate more on finance and personal commercial deals. The deal was agreed in August 1998, and finally went public in September, where Ford's PR statement quoted Malcolm Wilson as saying: "With the recent signing of Colin McRae, we think we have the world's fastest rally driver. We are determined to put him in the world's fastest rally car …"

With the negotiations centred more on money than on the car itself, and as Martin Whitaker confirmed, the final agreement between McRae and Ford broke all previous records; McRae was signed for the largest amount of money in his career to date. Final approval had to come down from Richard Parry-Jones, because the sometimes byzantine Ford

in 1999, but would become central to the livery of the 2000 car, when Carlos Sainz rejoined the team, bringing Telefónica/Movistar from Spain with him.

So the deal was done, with Martini even agreeing to a modification to its colour scheme for use on the new Focus. Everyone, including Ford Design, apparently recognised that the two blues of Martini's corporate colours were beautiful, but that its rather dominant red would be more striking if brightened up; from what was described as a rather dull

COLIN MCRAE

Colin McRae had no time to do anything slowly. Everything in his life seemed to be enjoyed at top speed, the toys had to be big, complicated, and fast, and his career reflected all of that. His top-line rally career may have already been over in 2007, but there was surely still much high-profile motorsport to be enjoyed from him. Alas, McRae was tragically killed, along with his son Johnny and two family friends, in a helicopter crash near his home in Scotland in 2007, while he was flying the craft.

Colin was the eldest son of five-times British Rally Championship winner Jimmy McRae. Before he took up rallying, McRae had indulged in motorcycle trials and scrambles, but it was after watching his famous father win so well – and so stylishly – in rally cars that he took up that sport. His rallying life was never dull, and his sport was never tackled cautiously. Along the way he notched up an impressive total of bills for crashed cars, and seemed not to care how much this was sometimes costing his employers: an attitude which eventually weighed against him.

On Colin McRae's first British rally, he could be seen picking tree branches out of the bodywork of his battered Vauxhall Nova. The second time, he was doing the same to a Sierra RS Cosworth, and the third … well, suffice to say his long-standing nickname was 'McCrash.' David Sutton once described Ari Vatanen's progress as "Crash, win, crash, win …" Colin was like that too. In fact, that sequence was rarely broken.

It was in 1986 – while his father Jimmy's career was at its peak, driving works-blessed Ford Sierra RS Cosworths – that Colin started out in the Scottish Rally Championship in a Talbot Sunbeam, soon turning to a Vauxhall Nova (with help from DTV). He was aged only 18.

Ford, who had Jimmy McRae on long-term contract, decided to encourage Colin, too, providing a Group N Sierra RS Cosworth for the British Rally Championship. The car struggled in the championship, and often crashed, but his most astonishing performance was to take fifth overall in New Zealand driving D933 UOO, an ex-works Group A Sierra (on an event where four-wheel drive cars were already considered essential).

Ford still indulged him, giving him full backing in 1990, where he started the year in a rear-wheel drive Group A Sapphire Cosworth, and ended it in a Sierra Cosworth 4x4. Although he took second place overall in the British Rally Championship that year (a seven-event series in which he had one victory, placed second twice, and third twice), his first stint with Ford works cars came to an end immediately after he badly damaged yet another works Sierra Cosworth 4x4 in the Wales Rally GB. In a way, Boreham seemed relaxed when it became known that McRae had turned to Subaru (and Prodrive), where he would stay until 1998

It was at Subaru that he firmly cemented his relationship with the British rallying public. Not only did he win the British Rally Championship twice in four-wheel drive Legacies, but he began winning at the World Rally Championship level, using steadily-improving Imprezas.

Despite becoming World Rally Champion in 1995, his demeanour, and his treatment of his cars, remained unchanged in this period. He finished second in the WRC in both 1996 and 1997, but was often at odds with his team management, and with his so-called team-mates (in particular with Carlos Sainz). Even inside the car, he dumped co-driver Derek Ringer in favour of Nicky Grist in 1997.

His demands on the team and his financial demands on Prodrive eventually led to his being released at the end of 1998. By that time he had already agreed to a mega-contract with M-Sport and Ford, where he was made team leader for a reputed (and colossal for the time) fee of £3 million a year. You may be sure that Martini, the headline sponsor of these cars, had to spend much of its budget on him!

The financial outlay was seen to be worth it, as, grappling with the all-new Focus WRC, he startled everyone by winning the 1999 Safari Rally and Rallye de Portugal events in his first few months. These were only the third and fourth events ever tackled by the complex new four-wheel drive car.

Colin continued to be hard on his cars, expecting them to put up with his methods, and the team to put up with his sometimes sullen temperament. When things were going well he could be the best of hosts, but when the gloom descended (which it sometimes did), he was better avoided. Malcolm Wilson's M-Sport organisation, rose above this as the car kept on improving. The company loved him because of his unstoppable ambition to win, and ability to keep a battered car going. Colin was always 'on the pace' unless – or until – the Focus WRC let him down. It often did in 1999, with eleven retirements in that first year, three of them due to crashes. Whenever and wherever he appeared in the Focus, though, he continued to set standards and – usually – fastest times.

His second season with the M-Sport Focus (2000) was typical of his flamboyant career at Ford. Having started all 14 World Rally Championship rounds, he won twice (in Spain and in Greece), and took second on three occasions. His cars suffered four engine failures (Cosworth was not best pleased), and had two big accidents. He was apparently so unhappy about this that he threatened to leave at the end of the year.

However, things improved greatly in 2001, when he won three WRC events, all three consecutively: Rally Argentina, Cyprus Rally, and Acropolis Rally. Amazingly there was only one accident this season, in front of his adoring fans in the Rally of Great Britain at the end of the season.

Colin always gave everything to his sport, and his employers. In fact, he came close to death for Ford when a high-speed crash in Corsica, in 2002, left the car upside down in the trees and below the level of the road, with him trapped inside and fuel dripping on to his overalls. It was a miracle that co-driver Nicky Grist was able to get out of the wreck and summon help.

To the very end of his Ford career, he was the darling of the national and motorsport press (much like Nigel Mansell, it didn't necessarily like him as a man, but he certainly provided many good headlines). The coverage was, particularly, a great thing for his personal publicity, especially as the media encouraged the myth of his rivalry with Richard Burns (the two were friends, and found the idea of a 'feud' quite laughable). With a total of 25 WRC event victories and many other podium placings to his credit, one can see why.

Bargaining on his worth to the sport, Colin soon became rallying's richest driver. When more than ten million copies of the *Colin McRae Rally* video games were sold, he took the decision to become a tax exile in Monaco for some years, with the trappings of a helicopter and other toys to be enjoyed.

It was these financial demands (he reputedly demanded £5 million for the following year) that eventually forced M-Sport to release him at the end of 2002. At this point he moved to Citroën, but he was never happy, nor successful, under this new deal. Just one season later, there were no other substantial offers on the table, and he found it impossible to gain any further regular works drives.

Apart from dabbling with the design of a new 'clubmans' rally car – the McRae R4 – which he personally demonstrated at the Goodwood Festival of Speed in 2006, a one-off drive in the Le Mans 24 Hour race, and the commissioning of an ultimate Escort MkII 'just for fun,' his motorsport career was effectively over.

budgeting system meant that it was the Product Development department that would provide the funds. Neither party would ever admit to exact figures, but it seems understood that McRae stood to gain at least ten million US dollars in the first two years.

Even today it is not known whether, in an ideal world, the arrival of a new Focus WRC, and the signing of Colin McRae, could have led to an immediate relaunch of Ford's famous 'RS' brand. Unhappily, Ford's well-known tardiness in taking advantage of motorsport successes meant that this did not happen at the time. As Martin Whitaker commented, many years later:

"Malcolm, Richard, and I all thought that some sort of performance road car should come out of this effort. John Southgate was very much behind that sort of project, and I am still sure that it would have been fantastic if we really could have gone that step further; to a four-wheel drive Focus RS, which could have come with all the 'Colin' branding. As it was, when it came in 2002, Colin was supportive of the two-wheel drive RS, but clearly for him it didn't quite cut the mustard. To this day, I think that Ford missed a massive opportunity …"

Because of the astronomical fee allocated to Colin McRae, M-Sport's options for back-up drivers were limited. Tommi

It wasn't all dust and drama! Colin McRae, watched by his more cautious teammates, getting acquainted with a friendly leopard in Kenya on the 1999 Safari rally.

The Swedish driver Thomas Rådström joined Ford for only one season in 1999. His opening performance (third on the Swedish Rally in February) was also his best for the team. He broke his leg at a pre-Safari function, returned to take sixth in Argentina, seventh in Australia, and sixth in the Rally of Great Britain, remaining always out-shone by Colin McRae.

Mäkinen had already refused, Kankkunen had turned down a modest offer in favour of joining Subaru instead, while Carlos Sainz – flattered to be approached yet again – preferred to stay with Toyota.

So, Malcolm Wilson turned to less renowned drivers. Thomas Rådström, an up-and-coming 32-year-old Swedish hero, joined the team after having driven Toyota Celica GT-Four and Corolla WRCs in previous years. Petter Solberg (Norwegian-born, and only in his third year of rallying) was another relatively well-known driver Ford recruited. It was the last signing of all – Simon Jean-Joseph, from the French-controlled Caribbean island of Martinique – that was the wild card. Already known for his rallying exploits in that part of the

world, he was thought to be a great prospect for the tarmac events in the World Rally Championship. The experienced Fred Gallagher was drafted into the team to act as Jean-Joseph's co-driver and, in many ways, his mentor.

It was perhaps Britain's *Autocar* magazine that best summed up the scenario facing the new Focus WRC at the start of what was to be a tumultuous first season:

"Martini money and McRae magic – the perfect cocktail or a concoction likely to be shaken and stirred? Ford has signed the world's fastest rally driver to drive the world's most radical rally car. Only time will tell if the money has been well spent …"

Setting the water pump controversy aside for a moment, it is fascinating to see that the new Focus was instantly

Simon Jean-Joseph, a French driver thought to have youthful potential, signed up for M-Sport in 1999. However, he would drive the Focus WRC only four times, finishing seventh in Sanremo, but retiring on the other events. He was not re-signed for the following season.

Colin McRae (right), Nicky Grist, and their brand-new Focus WRC at the start of the 1999 Monte. They finished third, but were then disqualified because of homologation problems with the engine installation.

competitive in the Rallye Automobile Monte Carlo, though it tells us much that Britain's *Autosport* magazine devoted two entire pages – and a large action shot of the Focus – to covering the pre-event drama, compared with a total of six pages of the rally report. The magazine was clearly sympathetic the team's dilemma, and made reference to McRae's pace:

"You could hear the whoops of delight over the radio as team co-ordinator John Millington acknowledged co-driver Nicky Grist's message. Colin McRae had just recorded the fastest stage times on the last two stages of the Rallye Automobile Monte Carlo's opening leg. They were the first such successes for the Ford Focus …"

McRae might have easily 'won' the event outright if his engine had not suffered a misfire on an early stage, and transmission trouble at a later juncture. Nevertheless, the team was very happy with the car's performance in its very first event.

As detailed in the previous chapter, M-Sport developed a 'legal' way of engineering the Focus engine's cooling system, which was done in a matter of days. As a result, the ex-Monte Carlo cars – after being suitably refreshed back at M-Sport's HQ – made it to the next start-line in Cumbria. Thomas Rådström made his debut in S8 FMC, and achieved a fastest stage time, while McRae's car was forced out of competition with an engine problem.

Action at last! Colin McRae's Focus WRC in the snows of Monte Carlo, January 1999.

Then came the Safari, where two Focus WRCs took the start. The first was the brand new S9 FMC, while the hard-working original test car, S16 FMC, was the other (having been carefully rebuilt, and with a new livery). Before the event, no-one expected too much from this outing; the severe and unique conditions of this event lent it a certain reputation. It used to be said that to even *finish* one's first Safari was an achievement, and it was certainly not feasible to expect a victory until the third, or even fourth, visit. Ford's most recent Safari victory had come 22 years earlier, in 1977 …

There was more. Before the event, on a practice trip in Kenya, Thomas Rådström had fallen down the stairs of his hotel, suffering a broken leg. Unable to drive, Rådström had to be replaced in the event by Petter Solberg, who had never before competed in the Safari.

This classic event provided more than 600 miles of competitive motoring, spread over four days on the 1999 Easter weekend. As ever, it was a rough, fast, dusty, and

gruelling challenge, but both the Focus WRCs proved their durability. McRae had won the event as recently as 1997 in a Subaru Impreza WRC. True to form, he took the lead after seven competitive sections, from which point he was never headed again. This was in spite of spirited opposition from Tommi Mäkinen's Mitsubishi Lancer and the two works Toyota Corollas driven by Carlos Sainz and Didier Auriol. Petter Solberg had to undergo intense on-event tuition from co-driver Fred Gallagher, but remarkably still managed a sturdy sixth.

Everyone – Ford, M-Sport, Colin McRae and almost every British enthusiast – was overjoyed by the result; when the season had started, optimistic predictions had placed the Focus on its first podium sometime during the 1999 season, and allowed that victories might follow in 2000.

To this day Martin Whitaker retains vivid memories of what immediately followed:

"I remember getting the news from Kenya on the Sunday afternoon, and immediately calling Jac Nasser in the USA –

A famous victory, for the Focus WRC, Colin McRae and Nicky Grist, when they won the Safari Rally in 1999. It was the first outright win for the Focus.

The young Norwegian, Petter Solberg, was a 'rookie' driver for M-Sport in 1999 and 2000 (his best placing was fourth in New Zealand in mid-2000). Later in his career, with Subaru, he became World Rally Champion in 2003.

very excitedly – to tell him that we had won. It was very early in the day for him, but he didn't mind that. I also remember breaking down after making that call; it was just a colossal release of pressure, knowing that we had finally won a WRC rally, and the Safari of all events …"

Colin McRae was interviewed immediately after his ground-breaking Safari success, where he was asked for a tip as to his next win. "Portugal!" He replied with a big grin, apparently not clear as to whether he was joking, or deadly serious. What's more, Portugal wasn't the only event he had in his sights:

"We can certainly win more events this year. Having won the Safari, I'd have to say I'm pretty confident about the Acropolis because essentially we'll be using the same car."

Although the team now felt that it was on top of the original water pump problem – much testing had confirmed this, and victory on the Safari confirmed the findings – it was still agreed that the Focus WRC needed to go on a diet. As soon as there was sufficient time to make some adjustments, it was hoped the car could slim down by 155lb/70kg, dropping it down to the lower weight limit allowed by WRC regulations.

For the Portugal event, M-Sport turned up in Matoshinos (close to Porto on the Atlantic coast) with the same two cars that had already tackled Monte Carlo and Sweden, this time with Petter Solberg at the wheel of S8 FMC. Monte Carlo had featured some snow and ice, and Sweden even more, but Portugal was an all-gravel rally. The event was to take place in

The winning Focus WRC leaping into the record books on the 1999 Safari Rally: first outing in Africa, first victory …

You don't usually get to see pristine rear views of works rally cars. This was the original 1999-spec Focus WRC in Portugal.

Ford's second victory of the 1999 season came in March 1999, when Colin McRae (driving S7 FMC) won in Portugal.

dry and relatively warm conditions, yet another combination of challenges for the still-new car.

Right from the start, Colin McRae proved that he could make the new Focus work in all conditions; he won the first two special stages on gravel, and pulled away from the two works Toyotas of Carlos Sainz and Didier Auriol. At the end of day one, he found himself running first on the road. Over the course of the 19-stage, four-day, event his lead gradually – but manageably – eroded from 50 seconds to just 12 seconds.

Was it easy? McRae certainly made it look so, but there was much more of this 14-event Championship left to play out. Martin Whitaker, for his part, was sanguine about it all:

"So, we came back home from the Safari, then went out and won in Portugal too, so it was suddenly beginning to look easy. Then, of course, we came down to earth with a bang! However, I certainly believed that we thought we were on to

something special, but I'm also sure that we never thought it was going to be easy.

"More than anything, I think I was relieved with what I found with Colin. I think he 'broke the mould' when he came out. There was something unique about this man; he was totally fearless. He had the most extraordinary driving ability, which was legendary, wasn't it?"

So, after four events, the Focus WRC had already recorded third (but disqualified), third, victory, and a second victory. This was, however, to be the height of its fortunes for a time. After Portugal – and let us never forget that this was still only nine weeks into the rallying programme for a brand-new project – the team's fortunes took a real slump. In the next ten events, from Spain's Rallye Catalunya in April to the Rally of Great Britain in November, it would score only minor points on three occasions. At the other rallies, it scored nothing at all. M-Sport (and Colin McRae in particular, having scored only once in all that time) was deeply depressed about this outcome, and could do nothing but look forward to the 2000 season with high hopes.

This turn of events would have been difficult to foresee. Take Rallye Catalunya, for example. Based in Lloret de Mar, the event had a total of 18 stages, all of them on tarmac. This should surely have suited the Focus, but ultimately neither team car made it to the finish. Jean-Joseph, driving S7 FMC (which was tackling its fourth WRC event in three months), was still struggling to make his mark at this level of the sport. In the end he was forced to retire before the end of the second day, when the car developed an electrical problem. Colin McRae was as fast and fiery as expected; driving the brand-new S10 FMC, he set two fastest and two second-fastest stage times early on in the event. However, he also lost time when his engine's anti-lag mechanism broke and crippled the power unit. M-Sport decided to withdrew the car before it could tackle the final day; the company was fully aware that at this stage it was still short of newly-developed Mountune engines, and didn't want to risk 'grenading' this one!

Corsica's all-tarmac Tour de Corse event, which followed, was dominated by two front-wheel drive Citroëns, and McRae did well even to take fourth place after his Focus developed problems with the gearshift. He recorded only a single fastest stage time in the event. Rally Argentina was next, far away from – and relatively unfamiliar to – M-Sport. The event was another disaster for the team. McRae, reunited with the Focus he had

Colin McRae wasted no time in aiming for victory in Portugal in 1999, managing to shot-blast some of the livery around the rear quarters of his car. S7 FMC had already tackled the Monte Carlo and Swedish rallies, and was on its third outing in two months.

driven in Monte Carlo, set fastest stage time on the second stage, before crashing comprehensively on the very next section. Having, as he put it, "clouted a rock the size of a house," the Focus ended up on its side, with the front end very severely damaged. It was quite clear that it could go no further.

Two weeks later, M-Sport turned up in Athens for the Acropolis Rally of Greece, with two freshly prepared cars (the cars were by no means new, of course; McRae's had appeared in Corsica, while Rådström's had been driven in Monte Carlo). The team had high hopes, not only because it was confident about the abilities of the Focus on rough stages, but because Colin had previously won the event twice, driving Subarus. Its hopes were somewhat dented after Rådström's engine blew on the first day. McRae, meanwhile, battled for the lead until the end of the second day, at which point his gearbox failed and immobilised him.

M-Sport now had a break of six weeks, allowing it to have fresh cars ready and air-freighted out to Auckland in time for Rally New Zealand. Even with this, though, it was difficult to see how the team's spirits could be raised. Unhappily, it was to be a wasted journey for the team, as neither car made it to the finish. Colin McRae led the rally after eight stages, but before the end of the ninth his car expired with an electrical

malfunction. Thomas Rådström fared no better, with an event that started badly, and ended up worse. After just three stages, he rolled the Focus, when (as he commented at the time), "the car slid wide, the rear wheel clipped a bank, flipping the car on to its side, and then the roof …"

Even with almost everything on the car seemingly twisted or battered, the wreck was somehow made moveable again. The Norwegian continued for two more days, setting three fastest times in the process, before crashing yet again and having to retire. Those two cars – one of them having to be extensively rebuilt – would then stay Down Under for months, as they were already allocated to Rally Australia, scheduled for November.

It wasn't going to get any easier in the rest of the season, and there must have been times when Ford and Martini both worried about their investment. The team's speculative investment in Simon Jean-Joseph also seemed to have stalled, and he would not be retained after the end of the season.

Neste Rally Finland (some historians with long memories still preferred to call it the 1000 Lakes) was another complete disaster for M-Sport, as was the China Rally that followed three weeks later. Three Focus WRCs started in Finland, but only one finished; Rådström retired after suffering an accident, and McRae – who was set to finish fourth after setting three

No luck for Ford or for McRae in Spain, in 1999. His Focus developed engine problems and had to be withdrawn: but not before he had set two fastest stage times …

fastest stage times – was stopped when a piston let go in his engine. Petter Solberg struggled on alone against world-class opposition in this high-speed event, and ended up placing 12th.

In China it was not the cars that failed, but the drivers. Both Colin McRae and Thomas Rådström crashed their cars just one mile into the very first special stage; both colliding with the same rock, with the same front wheel, and both with the same suspension-wrecking results. McRae, clocking up his fifth straight retirement in a Focus (and with memories of his double victory, Safari and Portugal, fading fast), was honest enough to have this to say afterwards:

"It must be my shortest rally ever. I saw the rock, but other cars had been over it. It must have gotten dislodged, and damaged the suspension too badly to go on …"

Rådström no doubt agreed with this sentiment, as his car ended up parked at the side of the track, just yards away from the other Martini-liveried machine.

M-Sport then 'enjoyed' (if that is a word that can ever be applied to the relentless lifestyle of works technicians and engineers) a full four-week break before three different cars arrived in Italy for the start of the all-tarmac Rallye Sanremo. In

the downtime, a weight-saving exercise had been carried out, with two of the cars now approaching the minimum weight limit. Following Ford's instructions, plans had been laid to use Cosworth-built engines (instead of Mountune units), but following a spate of pre-event cylinder head gasket failures these were not used on the rally cars themselves.

None of this helped much, as Jean-Joseph struggled to take seventh place (also failing to set any fast stage times). Solberg dropped to 27th after a major accident that damaged the rear suspension. S8 FMC – the car in question – was on its seventh event of the year and, if cars had souls, likely wished for a more restful weekend. Colin McRae was always up among the leaders, until his engine suffered a water leak that was soon stemmed. Punctures followed, and he finally had to retire after crashing his car and rolling it down a bank.

Could the team's fortunes get worse? With only two events remaining to complete a very eventful first season, one would think not. Amazingly, it could. At the end of October, M-Sport flew halfway round the world to Perth, Australia, where its advance team of technicians had already repaired/restored the two cars that had last competed in New Zealand. Colin McRae, who had won both the 1994 and 1997 Rally Australia events in Subarus, was looking forward to it. His team-mate Thomas Rådström was, he said, just there to learn. The Cosworth-built engines were used for the first time during this event.

McRae led the event outright in the early hours – setting two fastest and six second-fastest stage times along the way. However, early in the morning on day two McRae's Focus flew off the road after a big jump, coming to a very abrupt halt among the trees. The very high speed crash totally wrecked the Focus (S11 FMC); the entire right-side front suspension, and much of the front end of the car, was ripped off in the impact. McRae and co-driver Nicky Grist were lucky to emerge unscathed. According to M-Sport, the data logging shows that the car went from 100mph to zero in just 1.3 seconds!

Ford bought Cosworth Racing, in Northampton, in September 1998. Although Mountune had originally designed and developed the Zetec engines used in the Focus WRC, at the end of 1999 Ford transferred the build/maintenance/ development contract to Cosworth. Ford and Cosworth made much of the handover: Ford's Martin Whitaker is on the left of this study, shaking hands with Cosworth's then managing director, Dick Scammell. Cosworth would retain the work on this engine, which it coded YC, until 2004.

"We landed heavily," Colin later admitted, "and the steering wheel flew out of my hand. Nicky and I were passengers from that moment. That was one of the biggest and most frightening accidents I've ever had …"

The final event of the season approached, with the Network Q Rally of Great Britain, starting and finishing in Cheltenham. This time M-Sport provided three cars for the event – the drivers being McRae, Rådström and Solberg – but the results were distressingly familiar. Once again McRae crashed out of the competition, making it his eighth consecutive retirement of 1999, while the other two were not on the pace. In comparison with what had just taken place in Australia, this was quite a mild affair. Colin bent the Focus' passenger door against a straw bale at Cheltenham race course, and didn't seem to be enjoying the second day in mid-Wales, when he went off the track in Myherin forest in very foggy conditions. To add insult to injury, he collided with a private owner's rally car. The car had already crashed on an earlier run in precisely the same place, and the collision managed to wipe both ride-side wheels of the Focus chassis.

With a high-profile season ending in such a manner, big changes – and a big improvement – would be needed in 2000. Even in the depths of the gloom covering M-Sport after the end of the season, Malcolm Wilson was able to take heart from one important development: Carlos was coming!

TECHNICAL DEVELOPMENTS MADE IN 1999

During this frantically busy first season, M-Sport had several aims. It wanted to achieve mechanical reliability, continue building up its stock of cars and engines, and also come to terms with the long-planned – but nevertheless major – change over of engine supply from Mountune to Cosworth (which began in the autumn). Over the course of 1999 the team used nine different cars in events, their numbers spanning S6 FMC to S16 FMC, almost all visually identical to each other in their startling Martini livery.

Apart from the panicked engineering of the engine's new water pump layout, which followed the Rallye Automobile Monte Carlo in January/February, much of the in-season innovation was concentrated on the transmission layout and detailing (a cable gear change was adopted from October, and the Sanremo event), and the evolution of the four-wheel drive differential settings and function. Before the end of the year, Cosworth (see below) had taken over from Mountune as the builder, developer and supplier of engines for the cars.

Some weight was trimmed from the cars that were thought ideal for tarmac usage (S12 FMC and S14 FMC). This was part of an ongoing campaign that Steiner's team would continue to pursue in the seasons that followed.

WORKS CARS USED

To satisfy the WRC regulations and homologation rules, the FIA required the building of 20 cars or complete kits of parts, which M-Sport duly achieved. Some machines were used only for testing, the first customer examples were also delivered, and the records show that all told just nine cars were used in WRC events. As there was now to be no possibility of reshelling a car after an accident and retaining the same registration plate, it's a simple matter to determine which car worked hardest.

S8 FMC – one of the two original cars that had taken part in the Rallye Automobile Monte Carlo – topped the list, having started in no fewer than eight rounds of the World Rally Championship. S7 FMC and S10 FMC both started six times each.

DOVENBY HALL OPENS

Further important developments would follow in 2000, but the end of this tumultuous first season marked the beginning of the progressive occupation of M-Sport's new permanent HQ, Dovenby Hall, just a few miles north west of Cockermouth. Up to this point (the first workers moved in after Christmas in 1999), M-Sport had operated from cramped workshops close to Malcolm Wilson's house at Threlkeld Leys. Malcolm had always harboured big ambitions for this business, and even as early as 1997 a search for new premises had been under way. In a single stroke, M-Sport left behind workshops that had struggled to fit more than six Focus-sized cars, and began work in a space that would be able to accommodate well over 20.

The conditions of the space were something new, too. Malcolm's aim was always to produce a facility that would not only be a match for any of its rivals, but also be unique for Cumbria (where nothing remotely as modern had been attempted for many years). Jumping through all the usual hoops for local authority planning took time, and even before that he had to work through no fewer than 39 different potential sites. Some were new, some old, some empty and pristine, some well-equipped but positively decrepit; all

DOVENBY HALL

The history of Dovenby Hall's development as a motorsport centre is told in detail in the text on this page. For the record, though, the original Dovenby Hall estate, north west of Cockermouth, dates from 1154, when it was the principal residence of Dovenby village. It extends to 115 acres, and the house that still stands as the centre-piece of the site was developed in three phases.

Among the names of the owners of the estate are the Lamplugh family (who first came to Dovenby Hall in 1400), and the Dykes family (who took over in 1791). The Dykes family retained ownership until 1930. During the 19th and early 20th century, the hall's prosperity was assured by the development of a coal pit at the bottom of the village, as the hall received a royalty for every ton of coal extracted.

In 1930 Colonel Ballantine Dyke moved to another resistance, at Broughton in Furness (close to Barrow-in-Furness, the modern home of British submarine building). The Dovenby Hall estate was sold to a local authority: the Joint Committee for Carlisle, Cumberland and Westmorland. After the sale, it was turned into a mental institution, and over the years the hospital was gradually extended until at its peak it provided accommodation for 400 patients. The hospital was closed in 1997, and the entire site – buildings and grounds – was then sold to M-Sport in January 1998 (a figure of £761,000 was quoted at the time, and never denied). The site was not only restored under M-Sport's ownership, but extensively redeveloped and expanded.

of them had to be filtered down into a list of winners and losers. Malcolm also had some tempting development grant offers from the North East (County Durham in particular), from various sites in the Home Counties, and of course from Millbrook itself, but he was determined to stay near home:

"I was lucky, in the end, with the Allerdale planning office," Malcolm recalled, "where there was one planning guy who probably shared my vision, and was very understanding of what the Ford contract meant to the area. It was he who mentioned that the place called Dovenby Hall was coming on the market.

M-Sport purchased Dovenby Hall, near Cockermouth, in the winter of 1997/1998, when it was little more than a closed-down mental health institution. M-Sport then completely modernised and expanded the site, so that by 1999/2000 (as seen in these two images), it not only had a magnificent new workshop suite, but also ample space for further expansion, which took place as the years passed by. Each and every Focus WRC started life here.

"Initially I had no ideas at all about the place, and I had never been there. You could – still can, of course – drive past the driveway and have no idea of what's going on behind the trees. The original entrance was down in the village, not off the main road … I was persuaded to go look at it, and as soon as I drove in through the entrance, and saw that there was not only this historic house, but lots of space and 115 acres of land, I knew would have to have it …"

As is made clear in the panel on page 57, the estate was centuries old. The house itself was a gracious Georgian mansion, which originally tapped the village for many of its staff. In the 20th Century, however, it had been sold off to the local authorities and – with several hideous new buildings added – had been used as a mental institution up until its final closure in 1997.

The decision to buy the property and build new workshops was one thing, but the practicalities took more time:

"There were queries about the 'change of use' aspect. We had a fair number of battles, but the Allerdale planning authority was always very helpful and receptive. The biggest problem I had was when buying the place, because it was then owned by the North Yorkshire Health Authority. Basically, it took me about eight months before I actually owned the place and could start making the changes."

20 years on, the changes made quite outstrip what was retained, though the beautifully restored (yet very functional) house itself is still the part that looks after central administrative work. A massive building was erected on what had been the kitchen garden, becoming the main workshops. This had plenty of space for all the competition activities, which included the ever-increasing demand for 'customer' Focus WRC machines. The first of these was delivered to Mohammed bin Sulayem in the Middle East (it won for the first time in July). The second went to the Jolly Club in Italy, for what was agreed to be the going rate: around £350,000. Other buildings and departments were soon added to the workshops, including bodyshell manufacture, engine machining, testing and assembly areas, and every other aspect required for a modern motorsport business to operate.

The team would complete its initial occupation of the site in May 2000 (the 2000 Acropolis Rally cars were the first to be prepared in their entirety at the new location), with Ford's global boss, Jac Nasser, officially declaring it open at the very end of June 2000. On one wall of the immaculately restored

COSWORTH AND THE FOCUS CONNECTION

As described in the main text, from 2000 Cosworth was closely involved in the manufacture, development, proving, and persistent improvement of the original Focus WRC engine. It was already working on the engine's replacement (the light-alloy blocked Duratec-R) when M-Sport's policy change resulted in it taking engine assembly in-house, with further development being granted to the French company, Pipo Moteurs.

Cosworth was founded by Keith Duckworth and Mike Costin in 1958, and the link between it and the Ford Focus was a logical one, reconfirming the close relationship that the two companies had forged over the previous forty years. The first Ford-related project was a series of Formula Junior/Formula Three power units, based on the then-new Anglia 105E/109 power unit. Overhead-camshaft conversions then followed, the Lotus-Ford twin-cam engine was finalised and made road-reliable, and in 1967 the now-legendary DFV 3-litre F1 engine followed suit.

Once the DFV had made Cosworth famous for all time, the company turned to the design of the 16-valve twin-cam BDA power unit. This was the engine used in many race and rally teams (including Ford-backed operations), and that powered such world-winning machines as the Escort RS1600, the Escort RS1800, and (in turbocharged form) the Group B RS200.

Cosworth followed this up by designing, developing, and manufacturing the YB series of engine. These were used in turbocharged form in the Sierra RS Cosworth and Escort RS Cosworth families during the '80s and '90s.

Cosworth, originally an independent concern but eventually a subsidiary of Vickers, was finally absorbed by Ford in 1998. As a result, it was totally logical that the original Focus WRC engine development programme should be allocated to it within a year.

and presented complex was a modest plaque stating, 'Ford: Home of the World Rally Championship Team.'

Additions to the site would be phased in over the years that followed. More recently, in fact, a test track has been constructed within the grounds, and the state-of-the-art operation now seems to be bursting at the seams.

As far as the team was concerned, the only downside to this major development was its geographical location; it seemed somewhat remote from what we might call 'motorsport valley' (roughly the broad swathe of land stretching from London and the Home Counties to the Northampton area, taking the M1 motorway as its axis). Although Guenther Steiner moved willingly to become M-Sport's de facto technical director, Ray Stokoe decided not to follow. Christian Beyer and Hamish Robson also took up residence, though only for a limited period.

Malcolm Wilson was undaunted, carefully picking and choosing from the mass of accomplished technicians and designers who were willing to join him in Cumbria. The workforce expanded rapidly.

COSWORTH INSTEAD OF MOUNTUNE

One of this project's most controversial moves was, before the end of 1999, to see Focus WRC engine building, testing and development moved increasingly from Mountune to Cosworth. Naturally, Mountune was unhappy about this, feeling that the move reflected on its image in the industry. Commercially, though, it made a lot of sense: Cosworth had recently become a subsidiary of Ford.

What's more, Mountune's problem was not merely that it was a contractor and supplier, now competing for Ford's business against one of its own subsidiaries; the 325bhp engines it was building were still not reliable enough.

Throughout 1999, and until Cosworth supplies began arriving in October, M-Sport had suffered engine failures in Sweden, Spain, Corsica, Greece, and Finland: all on Mountune-built engines. This was not considered satisfactory, but in other circumstances the problems might yet have been settled amicably. However, as Malcolm Wilson recalled:

"I was quite happy with Mountune, to be honest, but Ford then purchased Cosworth [towards the end of 1998] and purchased PI Electronics too. Obviously David Mountain was pretty cut-up about it at the time, but as Ford had just spent lord-knows-how-many millions on buying Cosworth, it made sense for it to promote Cosworth in the World Rally Championship.

"Carlos Sainz had a lot of influence then … he could see that work needed to be done on the engine, and it was he who got Alex Hitzinger to join Cosworth from Toyota at the same time. After that, Ford made big investments in the engine – upping the ante – and we then had a fantastic engine, but a very expensive engine …"

David Mountain tells a very similar story:

"We learned about this very early on in the programme, and I think it was Martin who first raised the subject. We were testing somewhere – probably Portugal early in 1999 – so, in fairness, we had getting on for a year's notice of a change. It certainly didn't happen overnight, and Ford was very good about it. It gave us a lot of notice.

"Martin pulled me to one side on this test and told me that he was sorry, but it was only right to give me a lot of warning that Ford had a plan – having bought Cosworth – for it to do the rally car engines as well as all the F1 work for which it was famous.

"It wasn't a big shock to me. It actually paid us quite a lot of money to help hand over the project. In fact we made more money out of that project in 2000, after we handed it over, than when we were making doing the engines. The reason was that in 2000 we had to continue supplying all the parts to Cosworth, and we just couldn't believe how much Cosworth kept on ordering. In 1999 our running budget had been about £1 million for the year, but when it went to Cosworth the rumour was that its budget was about £5 million. We'd be getting orders for 20 crankshafts and so on … we made more money in supplying the parts than we would have done by doing the job like the previous year.

"But was a very clear-cut move. Cosworth supplied one or two engines towards the end of 1999, but for 2000 all the engines would be fully Cosworth-built and Cosworth-supported. Our job then was to supply whatever parts Cosworth needed. We had done everything in 1999, and Cosworth was not supplying anything to us in that year."

Well in advance of a complete changeover, Cosworth elected to prepare engines for use in the October 1999 Rallye Sanremo, but pre-event testing showed that the engines had not been satisfactorily tuned, for the engines suffered cylinder head gasket failures. As a result, Mountune engines were substituted in for the cars that reached the start line. Even so, Cosworth became the team's regular supplier before the end of the year, and was fully ready for a team assault when 2000 began.

CHAPTER **FOUR**

2000-2002 – The McRae and Sainz years

After all the traumas, sensations, and controversies of 1999, everyone connected with the Focus WRC programme was hoping for a more ordered, successful, and memorable future for the cars and the team. They got their wish; in 2000, not only did Carlos Sainz rejoin the Ford ranks, but he immediately became competitive, and was soon clearly at home in the car.

For Ford, M-Sport, and rallying in general, the return of Carlos Sainz to the 'Blue Oval' was the biggest possible news. Finally, the team had all the signs of a potential winner in every event: an already-competitive car (it had already won two WRC event victories in 1999, don't forget), and two front-line drivers who had already won the World Rally Championship for Drivers three times, and achieved 40 individual WRC rally victories between them.

Although Sainz had enjoyed his two years with the Escorts (the RS Cosworth, then WRC, over 1996 and 1997), he had been happy to return to Toyota and get his hands on the new Corolla WRC for 1998 and 1999. It was in those cars that he recorded two victories, and no fewer than nine second places.

Carlos Sainz was delighted to rejoin Ford for the 2000 and subsequent seasons. Here he is talking tactics to team boss Malcolm Wilson.

Despite this, something – some spark or other – was missing this time around. This feeling was compounded after Sainz lost the World Rally Championship crown in 1998, when his Corolla blew its engine on the last stage on the Wales Rally GB, literally within sight of the finish line.

In 1999, Toyota intensified its racing sports car activities, announcing its intention to move up to F1 racing, and forecasting an end to WRC competition at the end of 2000. At first, this appeared to be a protracted but business-like withdrawal, so – as early as August 1999 – Ford started up

CARLOS SAINZ

Is there anyone else in rallying who is so admired, respected, and even hero-worshipped as the charismatic Spaniard, Carlo Sainz? He did not quite win as many events outright as, say, Colin McRae, or make as many 'loveable' headlines as Markku Alén. Nevertheless, he was the sort of rallying character of whom almost everyone would speak positively. Not only that, but as an elder statesman, he is also known as the father of Carlos Sainz Junior, who burst onto the Formula One scene in 2016.

Between 1987 and 2005, Carlos started 196 World Rally Championship events, and won 26 of them. He finished in podium positions countless other times, and drove for no fewer than five fully-fledged factory teams along the way. He had a long and incredibly successful WRC career, driving continuously and fully competitively to the very end, and then topping it all off by graduating to long-distance rally raid events, winning several major rallies and championships for VW.

It was a measure of Carlos' reputation, his dedication, and the way that he was so endearing to his employers, that he enjoyed not just one, but three separate series of contracts with Ford: originally driving Sierra RS Cosworths (1987-1988), then Escort RS Cosworths/WRCs (1996 and 1997), and finally in M-Sport Focus WRCs (2000-2002).

Carlos a supremely talented rally driver, who was dedicated to his craft, rarely crashed, and tried to do his best at all times. Not only that, but he was the sort of handsome, debonair, friendly, and totally promotable individual that made him ideal for his multi-faceted career. Born in Madrid in 1962, these qualities became clear even at an early stage in his life. As a teenager, he had trials with the legendary Real Madrid football club, became Spanish squash champion at the age of 16, and started out in motorsport rallying in a Renault 5TS, having already sampled motor racing in Formula Ford single-seaters.

Sainz had been noticed even before he joined the Ford works team, when driving a mid-engined Renault 5 Maxi Turbo in Spain, then continuing on to drive works-blessed Sierra RS Cosworths to victory in the 1987 and 1988 Spanish Rally Championships. Although he did not win any WRC events in the Sierra, he was soon head-hunted by rival teams and, in search of a competitive four-wheel drive mount, he moved to Toyota (whose team was based in Cologne, Germany) for 1989-1992. It was there that he became World Rally Champion in 1990 and 1992.

After moving to Lancia in 1993, and on to the British-based Subaru team for 1994 and 1995, he was then attracted back to Boreham-based Ford to drive Escort RS Cosworths in 1996, where he achieved one victory and five other podium placings. He decided to stay with M-Sport for 1997, when he started 14 WRC events, winning twice, and notching up four second places.

Toyota then lured him back to its team for 1998 and 1999, before Malcolm Wilson's M-Sport organisation persuaded him to return to drive the Focus WRC for three happy years, 2000-2002 inclusive. Later, and as a last hurrah, Citroën tempted him to move to its Paris-based team for 2003 and 2004, and it was there that he announced his retirement from full-time WRC rallying at the end of that season, at the age of 42. Rallying guru Martin Holmes later summed up his glittering career:

"The end of Carlos Sainz's career was met with genuine emotion from his countless friends and admirers. He was undoubtedly the greatest world championship driver in history …"

He was, in truth, the most popular, if not the most explosively fast, driver ever to join a Ford works team. It is no exaggeration to make the point that anyone in the M-Sport team would do anything for him, not only to help the cars be improved, but to keep its most revered driver content.

yet another conversation with Carlos. His was not the only expensive scalp that M-Sport considered at this time, as it also approached the existing World Rally Champion, Tommi Mäkinen, at the same time. It was soon discovered, though, that Mäkinen's financial demands would be even more eye-watering than McRae's had been!

Then, in October 1999, Toyota astonished the rallying world. It announced the sudden and imminent closure of its rally programme, putting both Carlos Sainz and Didier Auriol on the market in time for the 2000 season.

Within hours of this news, it seemed, Malcolm Wilson was on the case. As Martin Whitaker confirms:

"Malcolm was very much at the forefront of this move, this time. Malcolm doesn't sleep many hours at night, and he had done a lot of thinking. He thought that for sure it would be a risk in putting Colin and Carlos back together again – because obviously they hadn't much enjoyed the healthiest of relationships at Subaru – but although it might have been one of the worst things that we could ever do, on the other hand Malcolm and I had always believed in healthy internal competition inside a team.

"Carlos was very expensive, of course. Not as expensive as Colin, though. It wasn't as bad as all that, as on this occasion we got some very positive financial support from Telefónica of Spain, with its brand Movistar. We loved him then, and to this day we still do. It was a real coup to get him back, and on this occasion we had a lot of help from James Gilbey, doing a lot of work on sponsorship for the team.

"The great thing about getting Carlos again was that it opened up a lot of opportunities for us in Spain. Not least with Ford, and of course with Movistar. It was, and still is, a very large telecommunications company. As a result, too, we also re-energised our relationship with companies like Pepe Jeans."

Immediately after Sainz's contract with Toyota was terminated, in December 1999, both he and Colin McRae began testing and development on new-for-2000 Focus WRCs. Carlos in particular was meticulous in his assessment of every aspect of the latest machines.

2000

The immediate result of signing Sainz was obvious. In 2000 alone, M-Sport cars won three events outright, scored points on all but two of the 14 World Rally Championship rounds, and finished second only to the Peugeot factory team,

whose 206 WRCs were top-class competitors throughout. Sainz and McRae finished third and fourth in the World Rally Championship for Drivers respectively, notching up three victories and five second places between them. There were crashes and disappointments, of course, but what team is ever likely to be totally committed – and totally competitive – without those? The cars themselves usually looked immaculate (until one or other of the drivers suffered what we might call an 'indiscretion') and were likely to win if they remained healthy throughout an event. In all, this was a different, more successful, and progressively more accomplished team than it had been in 1999.

The season got off to a good start in January's Rallye Automobile Monte Carlo. Two Focus WRC cars – S6 FMC and V2 FMC – started the winter classic, facing up against the massed works ranks of Mitsubishi, Peugeot, SEAT, Škoda, and Subaru (though, of course, there were no factory Toyota vehicles for the first time in many years). This was the usual ultimate ice- and snow-driving challenge, and if Tommi Mäkinen had not been at his usual superlative best, in the latest Mitsubishi, then the Sainz's Focus would surely have won. The winning margin was just 86 seconds. Where Sainz's run was encouraging, however, McRae's was frustrating. His 1999 car – totally refreshed for 2000, of course – suffered from steering, transmission, and finally engine problems. Even so, the Scot generally kept pace with Sainz, but ultimately had to give in when the engine expired on the very last special stage. This made nine consecutive retirements for McRae; what would this do for his morale?

The team's performance on the International Swedish Rally, which followed, was coloured by controversy over engine reliability. It was perhaps at this time that the first mutterings against Cosworth began to be heard; various minor problems were encountered before the event started, and even before the cars (V2 FMC and V3 FMC) had left Cumbria for Sweden, some engine swapping had needed to take place.

The outcome of the event itself, however, was mildly encouraging, even though there was still no outright victory to shout about. Although the engine oil pump failed on Sainz's car after ten stages, he had at least only been in sixth place at the time. Meanwhile, McRae fought tooth-and-nail against Grönholm (Peugeot) and Mäkinen (Mitsubishi) for a podium position. McRae set four fastest stages times, as well as placing second and third four times apiece. He eventually lost out by a mere 14 seconds, to claim third overall: his first finish for nearly a year!

The Safari Rally was held unusually early in the 2000 season. No-one could remember the event ever starting at the end of February, and traditionally it had been an Easter occasion. As a result, M-Sport had a real scramble to get three cars on the start line (driven by McRae, Sainz and, on this occasion, Petter Solberg). Because the Safari Rally was well-known as a rough event, it was decided to send S10 FMC, S12 FMC, and S14 FMC: three proven cars that had already been seen in 1999.

This was undermined somewhat when the cars utilising Michelin tyres (which, of course, included Ford) suffered a spate of punctures in the early hours of the event. Everything had seemed to start well for the M-Sport team, but before the end of the first leg McRae's car suffered a failed front suspension strut, which punched its way up through the front wing of the Focus. *Autosport*'s reporter, John McIlroy, described it as looking "… gruesome to the eye, and the car almost failed to make the tight turn at the service in-control, but once the Martini mechanics got their hands on it, the damage was fixed without further penalties."

Then came misfortune, pure and simple. With McRae up in third place, and fighting to go even higher, he elected to run his Focus – S14 FMC – without the snorkel that many Safari competitors fitted to their cars, allowing them to forge deep streams. To quote Martin Whitaker:

"I think he thought he could do without it, because it was causing quite a lot of aerodynamic drag, and this was a 'dry' event this year. The last thing anyone expected was for a dry river bed suddenly to become a raging torrent, but it did fill up. When the gravel crews had gone through in the morning, it was dry, but then the locals had dammed it up – to make the crossing more interesting – so that the water level rose a lot, and came in over the Focus' bonnet level …"

The engine was drowned out, and subsequently ruined. Sainz and Solberg, however, had both elected to run with the snorkels in place, forded the torrent successfully, and ended the event in fourth and fifth places. It may be no coincidence that two of the cars – S12 FMC and S14 FMC – were never driven by the team again.

Portugal had been the scene of a great Ford triumph in 1999, and M-Sport was surely hoping it would deliver a better result than the Safari Rally. Once again, however, the McRae jinx struck. Despite setting two fastest stage times, and leading the rally in the early stages, his power steering pump drive failed. The transmission progressively began to lose gears, and on the ninth stage his engine oil pump failed and a connecting rod came out through the side of the block. Sainz kept going well in V4 FMC, though with at least one major power steering failure. Over the course of the event, he set three fastest times and 13 other second- or third-fastest times. Nevertheless, this could only deliver him into third place overall.

McRae had now suffered 12 retirements in the last 13 events; would this sequence never end? Rumours began to spread that McRae was looking to leave Ford, and M-Sport, as soon as his contract would allow. His father, Jimmy, (who was also managing his affairs) admitted that there had already been approaches from both Peugeot and Subaru. Then came Spain, just two weeks later. Amazingly, it was here – the very next event – that McRae would break his streak of bad luck.

Rallye Catalunya was a mind-bogglingly competitive all-tarmac event. A victory by Carlos Sainz was heavily favoured among those watching, but there was intense yard-by-yard rivalry with McRae (both of them in new cars, V5 FMC and V6 FMC), Richard Burns (Subaru) and Tommi Mäkinen (Mitsubishi). Fastest stage times were shared almost equally between these four, but – tellingly – it was Colin McRae who took the lead before the event's midpoint, and held it until the very end. He beat Richard Burns by just 5.9 seconds, with Carlos Sainz another 5.8 seconds behind that.

Even so, it was not quite the turn of the tide. Six weeks later, in Argentina, both McRae (engine failure) and Sainz (an accident while leading) failed to make it to the finish. The team's 'apprentice,' Petter Solberg, made it to the end in sixth place, however. Carlos admitted that his crash was self-inflicted, while McRae's engine failure was later identified as being due to the totally unexpected entry of a piece of gravel through the air intake and into the engine itself, with predictable results.

Then came Greece's Acropolis Rally. Hot, rough, and dusty, the event was one in which Ford, M-Sport, and its star drivers had traditionally excelled in the past. M-Sport therefore entered three strong and reliable cars (Solberg's machine – the third in the line-up – not carrying Martini livery, of course), and dominated the event from the very start. Setting no fewer than 14 fastest times out of the 19 stages, one or other of the Focus WRCs looked certain to win. The only question that remained was, which one?

Having survived a traumatic 1999, Colin McRae rebounded in 2000, in this case winning in Spain in fine style.

A huge amount of controversy to was follow the event results. Petter Solberg having crashed on one early stage (and finding that spectators were unwilling to help him retrieve the car for seven minutes), astonished everyone when he overtook his team-mates on the FTDs (Fastest Time of the Day). In all, he topped the charts six times, with five other podium placings. Unhappily, his transmission failed on the 20th stage, and his dream ended there.

McRae took the lead overall on Stage 3, and Carlos Sainz followed up close behind. Sainz then overtook McRae on the final morning, only to be ordered to ease off by Malcolm Wilson in order to let McRae take the victory. Carlos was furious (similar situations had arisen when they were both driving for Subaru in the 1990s), and until the very last minute it looked as if Carlos

On loose surfaces there was rarely anything separating Colin McRae's and Carlos Sainz's pace.
This was Carlos, fighting his way through the dust in the Acropolis Rally of 2000, on his way to second place.

Carlos Sainz thoroughly enjoyed his return to Ford in 2000. His luck deserted him, however, on the Neste Rally Finland when his engine encountered electronic problems, there was a fire in the transmission tunnel, and he suffered a roll on the second day.

In his last outing for M-Sport, on the 2002 Wales Rally GB, Carlos Sainz took a fighting third place.

would defy his team orders. Then, according to *Autosport's* John McIlroy, "Sainz had actually been some 20 seconds up on his team-mate at the mid-stage split, but he stopped just 100 yards from the finish, and posted a time more than two minutes slower. Orders had been obeyed – just." TV news cameras had witnessed, and recorded, the whole sordid scenario.

Four weeks later, as the entire team flew over to New Zealand, the cracks in the relationship seemed to have healed. This was an event that seemed to suit the Ford cars, and there were hopes of another great result. In the end, it was only the brilliance of Marcus Grönholm (and his Peugeot 206 WRC) that got in the way of a perfect result for the M-Sport team. McRae, Sainz, and Solberg finished second, third, and fourth, with Colin just 15 seconds behind the flying Peugeot at the end of the event.

Back in Europe, in the Neste Rally Finland, it was almost the same story; Grönholm again leading McRae to the finish, this time by more than a minute. It wasn't all good news, however, as Petter Solberg (who was beginning to keep pace, second for second, with his 'seniors') crashed out on an early stage. His car, V2 FMC, ended up so far into the forest that trees had to be felled in order to get it out afterwards. An engine control unit (ECU) failure mid-stage ruined Carlos Sainz's chances, and he had to settle for a 'honourable finish' in 14th place.

In September, M-Sport's cup overflowed again. This time it was the Cyprus Rally, which was almost a clone of the Acropolis Rally, in terms of temperature and conditions to be experienced, albeit with more twisty stages. The team ended with another victory and second place finish, but this time with Carlos Sainz edging out Colin McRae, and leading the event from start to finish. It was Sainz's first WRC victory since joining M-Sport, and it was smiles all around on the result. With eight fastest stage times against one by McRae, Carlos won by 37 seconds.

Petter Solberg, meanwhile, did not figure in Cyprus. Rather, he was publicly playing M-Sport off against Subaru for his services in 2001, despite having what was thought to be a rock-solid five-year contract with M-Sport. Solberg's advisors thought otherwise, and the upshot was that he would never again drive a Focus, joining Subaru for the remainder of the 2000 season. Lawyers were involved, and the atmosphere between the two companies was distinctly frosty for some time.

M-Sport's fortunes then took a further tumble, in more ways than one, in September's Tour de Corse. Sainz fought valiantly to finish third behind two Peugeot 206 WRCs, but Colin McRae and Nicky Grist were fortunate to survive a massive crash on the ninth stage. McRae was never at his best on such narrow and twisty tarmac stages, but was fighting hard. In an incident caught by the in-car TV camera footage, the car clipped a rock face on the inside of a corner, spinning off to the unprotected right of the tarmac road, before plunging into the undergrowth of a ravine. The car came to a rest there, upside down.

Team boss Market Whitaker recalls that for a time there was a real fear for Colin's life; the mangled car had stopped in an manner that allowed co-driver Nicky Grist to scramble out, but Colin had remained trapped.

"He was upside down, and couldn't get out of the car. Nicky couldn't do anything for him, but climbed back up the hill to get help. I'm not sure he had a fire extinguisher, but he didn't want to jolt the car in case he caused any sparks, and started a fire."

Autosport's report noted that Colin's crash helmet was wedged into the twisted roll cage, until the rescue crew could cut him free. He had a fractured cheekbone and bruised lung, and was hospitalised for a day or so before being flown back to Scotland in a private air ambulance. Amazingly, he recovered remarkably quickly, and was back in action for the Rallye Sanremo in October. The wrecked Focus, on the other hand, was just that: wrecked. It was never repaired.

After such a traumatic weekend, the M-Sport team's attack on WRC event honours seemed to sag a little. This coincided with the inexorable rise of Grönholm and his Peugeot 206 WRC. Even in November's Network Q Rally of Great Britain, where a fully-recovered McRae might have been expected to shine, M-Sport was met with no luck. McRae did, though, set four fastest stage times before he suffered another big accident on the 11th stage.

M-Sport had entered three cars for this final event of the season. The third car was running without Martini livery, and had Tapio Laukkanen at the wheel (he had finished sixth in Rally Australia, driving a sister car). Although the British event had never truly been Carlos Sainz's favourite (a ban on high-speed reconnaissance motoring was one factor), he tried as hard as he could. Even though he damaged his car, Sainz managed to take fourth place overall, without setting a single fastest time. Colin McRae, on the other hand, set four fastest times, and achieved the second-fastest time and third-fastest time twice apiece. All of this was within the first ten stages, as he rolled his car on special stage 12. The crash damaged the car's radiator and McRae, seeing all the cooling water disappear, had to retire with a crumpled machine.

Quite suddenly, and in a very downbeat way, the season ended. M-Sport finished a rather disappointing (to it) second in the World Rally Championship for Manufacturers. Up until the Cyprus Rally it had been leading, and been bullish about the outcome, but Peugeot (led by Marcus Grönholm) soon pulled in front after Colin McRae's Corsica accident. Sainz and McRae finished third and fourth in the prestigious World Rally Championship for Drivers.

2001

Colin McRae still thought that he could win the Drivers' Championship in the ever-improving Focus WRC, and Carlos Sainz seemed to be gradually restoring his mojo in the same car. Nevertheless, Malcolm Wilson was looking for significant improvements all round. Wilson had, it's said, become convinced that Michelin would favour Peugeot over Ford in 2001 and beyond, and that Michelin's return to F1 tyre supply was also bound to affect its attention to rally teams. Regardless, the change from Michelin to Pirelli had been flagged up well in advance. Within days of the end of the 2000 British rally, a Focus WRC was sent out to Spain for three days of Pirelli tarmac testing – with Sainz at the wheel – followed by more work in France.

More important, however, was the unexpected news of Phil Short's arrival at M-Sport, effectively becoming Wilson's right-hand man. Short was originally a successful co-driver coordinator at the WRC level in the 1980s. Since then, he had become Ove Andersson's team manager at Toyota, and moved on to become a major influence on the Mitsubishi team, of which Andrew Cowan was team principal. Short had signalled his resignation from Mitsubishi well before the end of 2000, and it was a pleasant surprise to every observer of the sport to see him suddenly appear in M-Sport colours.

As Short later told the author:

"I joined M-Sport in February 2001, after six successful years as Team Manager at Mitsubishi Ralliart. My title was 'Sporting Adviser' and, yes, I suppose right-hand man to Malcolm is a fair description. My brief was to look after the sporting side of things – regulations, dealing with organisers, stewards, protests, appeals, etc – as well as the tactical aspects of the events themselves. I also introduced the Ford mid-stage signalling, which at first was done manually by myself with a 'pit-board,' but I'm quite proud that I initiated the later electronic in-car info systems that allowed crews to monitor their progress at various split times along each stage, and us to warn them of incidents and problems ahead. This was later copied by all factory teams …

"I was also handed responsibility for the weather forecasting, on the basis that I used to be a private pilot and, supposedly, understood such things! With the increasingly

Having done much to make the Sierra Cosworth 4WD and Escort RS Cosworth models competitive in the 1990s, François Delecour rejoined M-Sport in 2001, running cars that did not carry Martini sponsorship.

Phil Short had previously been a high-ranking manager at word-class rally teams such as Toyota and Mitsubishi. He joined M-Sport in 2001 as what was colloquially called an 'eyes and ears' expert. As Malcolm Wilson's close confidant, he had much to do with seeing the Focus WRC programme mature in the early 2000s.

specific nature of the tyre choices, this aspect became even more critical than earlier …"

Phil was, and is, modest about his achievements and importance within the team, but it is worth recording that he stayed at M-Sport until the end of 2008, when M-Sport's budgets had to be cut considerably.

The other major news was that M-Sport had juggled and, it seems, enhanced its operating budget for 2001. This resulted in the great news – for it, and for his many fans – that François Delecour, the fiery Frenchman, would be returning to Ford. He would be driving on a one-year contract, piloting Focus WRC types throughout the season. Delecour, of course, had leapt to fame with Ford in the 1990s, when the works team operated

from Boreham. He had begun by taming Sierra Cosworth 4x4s, before giving the Escort RS Cosworth a startlingly successful beginning to its career (which, for him, meant victory in the 1994 Rallye Automobile Monte Carlo).

After a serious road car crash in mid-1994 (when driving a friend's Ferrari F40), he took time to recover and eventually moved away from Ford. He then rebuilt his reputation by driving works Peugeot cars, most recently the very fast 206 WRC. He left the team in 2000, after a tempestuous series of clashes with team-mates and management, and was speedily snapped up by M-Sport. The combination of McRae, Sainz and Delecour must surely have been the most promising works line-up ever seen.

Design students, and those fascinated by the minutiae of modern rallying, immediately realised that Delecour would not be a 'Martini' driver. The drinks company's sponsorship still appeared on the cars of Colin McRae and Carlos Sainz, whereas the Delecour cars were simply liveried in white, with very strong 'RS' decals on each flank. Technically, however, the two sub-types were identical.

With the line-up arranged, M-Sport approached the opening of the season with real relish. Monte Carlo, three

Just for kicks, in 2001 the M-Sport mechanics produced this one-off 'World Rally Transit.' It was great fun, both to look at and to drive, and could also be very useful as a high-profile service/support vehicle for M-Sport.

The interior of the 2001 World Rally Transit looked like a kitted-out rally car. The Sparco seats and the roll cage were very real, but it still had a standard 2.4-litre diesel engine.

world-class drivers, not much snow in the Alps at the turn of the year, and a great deal of confidence in the latest Focus WRC? What more (except complete, boring, dominance), could a works team require? Even so, with six full works teams now in the lists – of which Peugeot, Subaru and Mitsubishi were the major rivals – this promised to be a stimulating 12 months.

The snow duly arrived just before the start of the event. All three works Peugeot vehicles expired before three stages had been completed (engine failure, accident, and accident, respectively), while the Subaru Impreza driven by Richard Burns was also forced to retire with an ailing engine. Perhaps

M-Sport's occasional exasperation with Cosworth was not as unusual among WRC teams as might be thought. At the end of the first leg, with six stages completed, Colin McRae led the field, Carlos Sainz was third, and newcomer Delecour was sixth. A good start, then.

Colin McRae and Mitsubishi's Tommi Mäkinen then battled – head to head – until the final morning, at which point just 2.5 seconds separated them. Then, on the 13th stage, a small electric motor in the drive-by-wire system of the Focus throttle failed, immobilising McRae. In the end, therefore, Sainz took second overall behind the Mitsubishi, only 62 seconds adrift, with a delighted Delecour up to third place.

It was a similar performance, with slightly different results, in Sweden just three weeks later, where M-Sport sent three entirely different cars. Although it was the Finnish Peugeot driver Harri Rovanperä who won the event outright, he was only 37 seconds ahead of Carlos Sainz, who took a storming third place overall. Delecour took fifth, meanwhile, and Colin McRae finished ninth.

This result partially hid the fact that McRae set seven fastest times (out of 17 special stages). He blotted his copybook, as it were, on only the third stage when he used what he thought was a friendly snow bank to help him get around a corner, only to find that the bank was softer than expected. The bank swallowed the car, and it took eight minutes (and a lot of spectator power) to get him back in business. At the end of the day, he was just four minutes off the pace …

By this time, team-mate Carlos Sainz was becoming quite desperate to add to his record of WRC victories. After winning the Cyprus Rally in 2000, he had been sure that he would be able to repeat the trick several times. Ultimately, though, it wasn't to happen in 2001, though he would have another second, and two third places before the end of the year.

His second place came in Portugal in March, where he battled head-to-head with Tommi Mäkinen, and his Mitsubishi Lancer Evolution, throughout. The weather was awful (cold, wet, foggy, and muddy throughout), and spectator control seemed to be non-existent. The Focus/Mitsubishi battle was ferocious; so much so that, after Colin McRae's engine failed, Cosworth received an aggrieved phone call the following day. François Delecour settled for a finish without heroics, ending ten minutes off the pace, in fifth place. Carlos, on the other hand, had a marginal lead going into the last stage, but ended up just 8.6 seconds – 8.6 – behind Mäkinen.

François Delecour rejoined the works team for 2001, running without Martini sponsorship but always having a completely up-to-date car. Using V3 FMC, he took fifth place on the Swedish rally.

Spain's Rallye Catalunya was just two weeks later, and one border away. Could M-Sport do even better there? Everyone, especially Carlos, probably the most famous sports star in Spain at this time, hoped so. M-Sport provided three freshly-prepared (ex-Rallye Automobile Monte Carlo) cars, specifically set up for tarmac rallying, to harden resolve. Even so, M-Sport realised that Peugeot and Citroën, each having a mountain of tarmac experience in this part of the world, would make it very difficult for the team to achieve a victory.

Unhappily, its fears were well-founded, and the Focus failed to be competitive in the event. All three cars suffered engine problems, with a rather mysterious malady in fuel pump operation (McRae retired because of this, with the other cars struggling on to the finish). On top of this, there was a suspicion that – on tarmac events – Pirelli (the suppliers for M-Sport and Subaru), was not as technologically adept as Michelin (the continued supplier for the rest of the works field). Whatever the root cause, M-Sport suffered humiliation; Sainz only finished fifth, and Delecour came in behind him at sixth.

Brr ... service in the open air in a wintry Sweden for the Focus WRC team. The white Focus is François Delecours' car, and number three is that of Carlos Sainz, who finished third.

Everyone in the team, particularly the disgruntled technicians, was delighted to have nearly six weeks before the next event in Argentina. The time was used to complete the building, testing, and transport of three 'gravel' cars to

*Carlos Sainz jumping, all askew, on his way to taking third place in 2001's Rally Argentina,
an event that Colin McRae's Focus WRC won outright.*

Rally Argentina, an event that Ford and M-Sport had never yet managed to win. Colin McRae had the pleasure of driving a brand-new car (X5 FMC), but the other drivers were assigned vehicles that already performed in European events.

Suddenly – quite suddenly – it all came right for the hard-pressed team. Colin McRae not only had a trouble-free run, but his car was sturdy, reliable, and fast; he won the event outright. What's more, in a head-to-head battle with Richard Burns in his Subaru (both cars running on Pirelli tyres that, for once, appeared to have an edge over Michelin on these loose surfaces), McRae set ten fastest times on the 21 specials. Indeed, he led throughout, and never looked like losing. The fact that Sainz took third place overall, and Delecour seventh (even after rolling his car on the very first stage), was a real bonus.

The relief in the team was palpable. McRae had finally finished a rally in 2001 – five months after the season had begun – and all the cars had proven themselves on what was

a rough and demanding event. This was Colin's 21st victory in a WRC event, and – some suggested – the sweetest so far.

Then it all happened again. Just four weeks later, when the entire WRC circus left South America and moved to Cyprus (where Carlos Sainz had won in 2000). Based in Limassol, and held in scorchingly hot and dry conditions throughout, the event boasted 22 special stages and rough, dusty conditions. The event also played host to a titanic battle between McRae's Focus (X7 FMC, out on its very first event), Richard Burns' Subaru, and Marcus Grönholm's Peugeot 206.

There was little between the cars for days; McRae was 'only' fourth at the end of day one (by 14 seconds), second to Burns by the end of day two (by three seconds), before claiming victory by a mere 16.4 seconds. Along the way, Sainz set seven fastest times, McRae five, and Delecour two. The hapless Frenchman was forced out after 11 stages (at which point he was in a sturdy third place), after the engine blew. To add insult to injury, various regulations had obliged Carlos to

*Driving X7 FMC, Colin McRae won the Cyprus Rally of 2001 in fine style.
The same car would also win, in the Acropolis, a year later.*

act as 'sweeper' ahead of the field during one phase, in order to clear the road of any 'marbles.' Had he been spared this, he must surely have taken second place from Richard Burns.

Surely, such a result couldn't happen again. Yet just two weeks later – and a short trip across the Mediterranean – Colin McRae made it three in a row at the Acropolis Rally in Greece. These were the same sort of hot, dusty, and rough conditions, but McRae was at the wheel of yet another brand new Focus WRC (Y4 FMC). Such results led to some pundits suggesting that the Focus would always win in such conditions, especially with such a formidable driver line-up. With this latest victory, McRae brought his career total up to 23 WRC event victories, putting him equal with Carlos Sainz. The Spaniard, however, was less than happy with his results at this self-same event. Despite matching McRae's times stage after stage (he set five fastest times, compared to Delecour's four and McRae's two), he was brought to a halt when a piston in his Cosworth-prepared engine expired on the very last special stage. He had been only five seconds behind McRae

at the start of it. Delecour, for his part, had injured a wrist after falling off a mountain bike the day before the event, and then suffered a power-steering failure on one stage during the event. Somehow, it seemed it wasn't to be his season …

At this point in the year, Ford had notched up its 40th WRC event victory (only Lancia and Toyota could match that, and not for long), and it led the World Rally Championship for Manufacturers, ahead of Mitsubishi, with Peugeot looking unlikely to catch up. Would the team be able to hold on for the remainder of this 14-event season? It had six weeks to prepare for the next event, which was to be the Safari Rally. Unfortunately, it was here where the team's luck suddenly disintegrated, leaving neither Martini-liveried car in the running, and François Delecour struggling to keep up with the revivified Mitsubishi and Peugeot vehicles.

While the team was preparing for the Safari, Delecour had been sent off to compete in a non-WRC event in Germany, where he used his refreshed ex-Argentina car to take third place. This was not only a good result, and came with great publicity for the Focus, but it also gave M-Sport good experience for an event that looked sure to join the WRC series in future. As expected, it did, in 2002.

Sainz had, need one say, performed as consistently well as ever in the Safari Rally. Unfortunately, the engine on his Focus expired before the end of the first leg, by which time Colin McRae's hope of making it four in a row had already vanished; a steering joint had broken on one of the roughest sections, and he burnt out the clutch in trying to retrieve the car from the bush without help from onlookers. François Delecour, meanwhile, was tackling his very first Safari, and was in fifth place after the first and second days (having suffered punctures and transmission problems). He finally took home a fine fourth place

Then came another four-week break, which – by the frenetic standards of modern rallying – felt almost like a holiday to some of the hard-pressed technicians, managers, and drivers. Neste Rally Finland (now affectionately nicknamed the 'Finnish Forest Grand Prix'), was due to start from Jyväskylä in August. M-Sport had hopes for the event, though it had been a decade since a non-Scandinavian had won the rally. It posed a daunting combination of gravel stages, high jumps at speed, and an average speed throughout of more than 75mph. M-Sport entered its usual three world-class crews, while the Finnish legend Markku Alén entered a privately-owned and financed Focus WRC (which, ultimately, took only 16th place after struggling with a recalcitrant transmission towards the end).

The Peugeot 206s set the pace, and for once – this had, so far, been a disappointing season for Peugeot – dominated proceedings; not even a rampant Colin McRae could match up to Marcus Grönholm's pace. In the end, after 21 warm, dry, and dusty stages, McRae took third place, just 32 seconds behind the winning Peugeot. Sainz arrived sixth, while the luckless Delecour had to retire with fuel pressure supply problems.

In the next three months, every active WRC team – obviously including M-Sport – had to complete five major events, spending much of their downtime jetting from one continent to another. To start, they had to set off half-way round the world to New Zealand, then back to Sanremo in Italy, a trip across the sea to Corsica, then a return to Australia (where, hopefully the ex-New Zealand cars would have been prepared again), before a final return to Britain for the last

rally of the season. There would then be a chance to sit back, albeit only for a matter of days, before it would be time to start building cars for Monte Carlo in January 2002.

The New Zealand event rapidly became a strategist's game of chess, with most teams trying every method of moving cars back from head of the queue. This was done so that some other unfortunate driver would be obliged to sweep all the loose gravel from the route, leaving a more grippy road behind! Richard Burns, in his Subaru, proved to be just 44 seconds quicker over the 24 gravel stages than Colin McRae. McRae nevertheless held on to a joint lead in the World Rally Championship for Drivers, and M-Sport consolidated its place at the front of the Manufacturers counterpart. Carlos Sainz placed fourth, a mere 7.6 seconds behind McRae, while Delecour took 12th after rolling his car on the first stage of the second morning. Without this incident he would likely have achieved seventh or eighth place, and was not best pleased.

Two weeks later the teams took to the serpentine tarmac roads of Rallye Sanremo. M-Sport did not expect to beat Peugeot at the event – and, indeed, did not – but Carlos Sainz took a very gritty fourth place, with Delecour placing sixth and Colin McRae eighth. For McRae, it was probably a weekend he would rather have forgotten. His Focus (Y5 FMC, brand new for the event) suffered a lot of transmission trouble, more a problem with the electronics in the control systems than in the mechanical 'mangle gears' themselves. He later described the event as a "s**t weekend" …

Two more weeks, and a brisk hop over the sea from northern Italy to Corsica, the three-car M-Sport team was hoping for a more relaxing time in the Tour de Corse. However, on tarmac roads even narrower and less suited to the Focus WRC chassis, this was a delusion. Ominously, pre-event it also became clear that M-Sport's Pirelli tyres were no match for the Michelin ones chosen by most other teams. Suffice to say that François Delecour's tenth place was the highest that the team could achieve, and even his car had brake problems. Both his team-mates struck rocks (one of which was in the road itself, and was, funnily, never hit by any of the top French cars in the event). The result was that Sainz's engine and oil system was terminally damaged, and McRae's car suffered a power-steering pump failure that cost him three minutes on the final stage of the first day.

Was it even worth trekking back around the world to Perth, Australia, for the penultimate event of the year? So far

High jumping in Australia came naturally to Colin McRae, though in later years he had a big accident to throw that into question. This was 2001, when he finished fifth.

as the championship was considered it certainly was, but for the entire rallying 'circus', it was exhausting. For M-Sport, the trip to Australia must have felt like an expensive waste of time and money. Of the three cars that started the event, one was crashed seriously, injuring the co-driver. A second also crashed, putting its driver out of the running for the top spot. The third, meanwhile, was not quite able to deal with the combination of the Australian road surfaces and the high jumps on the stages. The fact that Colin McRae and Carlos Sainz did not let this discourage them was a real tribute to their courage and professionalism; they achieved three and four fastest times, respectively.

Sainz was the first to suffer, when his car clipped a tree stump on the sixth stage. The impact tore off a rear wheel, and started a fire. Although the team repaired the damage, the incident had dropped him from fourth to 11th place, and he eventually clawed his way back up to eighth. The unfortunate Delecour almost replicated this series of disasters, hitting a

tree in a very large accident on the 14th special stage. Co-driver Daniel Grataloup was badly hurt, with a broken shoulder blade, collar bone, and multiple broken ribs, and had to be hospitalised for several days. Amid all this, McRae somehow (for he had stopped at the scene of the Delecour crash) held on to fifth place. He would go into the final event of the season – the Network Q Rally of Great Britain – immediately ahead of his rivals in the World Rally Championship for Drivers.

Colin McRae versus Richard Burns. Ford versus Peugeot. Hyped up beyond all measure by the British mass media, this was a dramatic end to the season for M-Sport, for which it produced three fully-backed Focus WRCs. With François Delecour released from his contract prematurely (in any case, his regular co-driver would not have been fit enough yet to accompany him), his place was taken by Mark Higgins. Higgins was allocated Delecour's ex-Germany/ex-Argentina car (X3 FMC), repainted in a rather sombre, dark, Ford Performance Blue with no Martini exposure.

There is no delicate way to describe this final event; the team's outing was disastrous. Almost everything went wrong. Initially living up to the pre-rally hype, Colin McRae went out and set two fastest and a fourth fastest time on the first three stages, but then on the very next stage crashed at very high speed. The car rolled several times, reducing it to – effectively – an expensive ball of junk. It was a write-off, and would never again feature in the M-Sport line-up. Richard Burns went on to finish third, usurping McRae at the top of the World Rally Championship for Drivers, and taking the title.

Carlos Sainz was very well placed until stage 11 – the Brechfa stage – where he went off, unfortunately colliding with a radio car, and a group of spectators who were standing nearby. Immediately after alerting the rescue crews (13 spectators were injured, but fortunately all recovered remarkably well after medical treatment), M-Sport advised him to drive to the end of the stage, where he was immediately withdrawn. Mark Higgins, who had been up to fifth place by this time, was also instructed to withdraw. This was how Ford's M-Sport operation ended its season. It ceded the World Rally Championship for Manufacturers to Peugeot, as it was Marcus Grönholm – driving for Peugeot – who won the event, and clinched the crown.

2002

As far as the fans were concerned, the big news was that – even before the end of 2001 – both Colin McRae and Carlos Sainz extended their contracts with M-Sport for the next season. The third man, François Delecour, who had been so unlucky in the 2001 season in so many ways, had not been retained.

In Delecour's place, M-Sport signed up Markko Märtin, the 26-year-old Estonian driver who had already made a name for himself driving Subaru vehicles. For Markko, this was to be just the start of a three-year contract. In a 'wild card' deal, revealed at the same time, Malcolm Wilson signed 21-year-old François Duval of Belgium. Duval seemed to have taken well to racing Ford Pumas in the slightly lower-level Super 1600 rallying formula, and was engaged to drive a mixture of Pumas and Focus WRCs throughout the season.

In the winter of 2001/2002, Malcolm Wilson made one of the most important (and, it later transpired, successful) job appointments of his life when he hired Christian Loriaux to become M-Sport's technical director. As is made clear in the panel on page 75, Loriaux had already made a distinguished

Markko Märtin of Estonia took his first M-Sport works drive in 2002, but would become a very successful team leader soon thereafter.

To show off the latest Focus WRC livery for 1992, and Boreham's latest thinking on a 'junior' 1.6-litre Racing Puma, Ford showed this car at the beginning of the year.

CHRISTIAN LORIAUX

Born in Charleroi, Belgium, Christian Loriaux has spent his entire working life in the engineering side of the motorsport industry, beginning as an unpaid 'intern' with RAS Sport, and becoming the technical director of M-Sport in the winter of 2001/2002.

After working at RAS Sport, Loriaux then moved to the UK to study automotive engineering at Cranfield University. From there, aged only 22, he moved to the Prodrive organisation in Banbury, where he was involved in the engineering of race and rally cars from 1991 to 2002.

Having become chief rally engineer in 1998 (his immediate superior was Technical Director David Lapworth), he was responsible for the fourth-generation Subaru Impreza WRC, which won three events outright in 2000, and which helped Richard Burns to become World Rally Champion in 2001.

Unhappy at Subaru, however, Loriaux moved to M-Sport in Cumbria in the winter of 2001/2002, as technical director – a post that he held throughout the Focus WRC programme, and that of the Fiesta WRC (rally) and Bentley (racing) programmes that followed thereafter.

himself at Prodrive as its chief rally engineer, responsible for the design of the Subaru Impreza that had helped Richard Burns to become the World Rally Champion in 2001.

When interviewed in later years, Loriaux admitted that while he had loved working in the Prodrive team, towards the end of his stay there he had begun to feel under-appreciated:

"For a time I actually considered moving into F1; spoke to various people, particularly at Benetton, where someone closely connected with Ford heard my name mentioned. I now know that Guenther Steiner was leaving M-Sport, and they obviously heard about my search for a move.

"Malcolm gave me a call … I'd thought that I might move anywhere in the UK, but not to M-Sport because it was too far up north. But, Malcolm asked me to go up for a chat, telling me it was only a two-hour drive (but it took me four hours), and while I was there he mentioned that Colin McRae had mentioned me to him already."

What followed next was important. At the same time Loriaux was considering a move from Prodrive to M-Sport,

M-Sport was finalising a deal to continue using Pirelli tyres for 2002. As Loriaux then told Malcolm Wilson:

"We would have won many more titles at Subaru if we had been running on Michelin [tyres]. I told Malcolm that of course I wanted to win, but that 'if you want to win, you'll have to switch back to Michelin …' which we did, but not until 2003."

Loriaux, a straight speaker with ready opinions on many subjects, agreed to join M-Sport in November 2001. He then summarised what impressions he had gained about the current ready-for-2002 Focus WRC. Beforehand, he had assumed that claims of the car having a low centre of gravity and amazing aerodynamic figures were all true, but soon realised that this was not the case.

Rather, he concluded that the centre of gravity was higher than he would wish, the weight distribution needed to be improved, but that the engine was very strong … and the car had Colin McRae and Carlos Sainz driving, which helped enormously! All of his conclusions would affect the layout of the 'Mark 1½' Focus WRC, or the Focus WRC 2003, as he called it. He worked diligently on the machine until it was launched in mid-2003.

Although it was already too late to affect the layout of the car that started M-Sport's 2002 season, there was scope for detail improvement throughout the season. Loriaux made the point that, when he arrived at Dovenby Hall, Christian Beyer was his immediate subordinate, with seven other designers working for him. Work began at once on Loriaux's 'Focus WRC 2003'. Initial priorities were to deal with an ongoing power-steering issue, to raise the sump guard by 40mm/1.6 inches (improving the ground clearance on rough events like the Acropolis and Cyprus), and to persuade Cosworth to make changes to the sump of the engine to make the raising possible.

"We also needed to take 100kg/220lb off the weight of the car, but that was going to take some time …"

Loriaux's biggest worry – that of the performance of the Pirelli tyres (in comparison with the Michelin tyres used by other teams) – was echoed by Colin McRae in a pre-season interview, in which he stated: "We've got a big step to make on sealed surfaces. I'm not overly confident that I'm going to be able to compete for wins on asphalt … The Pirelli [tyres] work very well in the wet. In Corsica and Sanremo we were right up there when it was raining, but we have to marry the car to the dry tyre properly."

Markko Märtin joined the Focus WRC team for 2002, starting with a steady 12th place in Monte Carlo.
Later in the year he would take a remarkable second place in the Rally of Great Britain.

Even so, the team started the year in Monte Carlo, in January, with very high hopes. It was immediately obvious that there had been significant visual changes to the combined Martini/Movistar colour scheme, and that all three cars would start in that guise. Later in the year matters were confused somewhat, as Markko Märtin's cars would sometimes sport Martini/Movistar livery, but at other times they would appear in Ford Performance Blue.

All in all, the Rallye Automobile Monte Carlo was a good, if not sensational, start to the season. Almost a new beginning, if the talk of restructuring the management team at M-Sport, and the reliable behaviour of three cars in the event, bore out. Carlos Sainz was just as consistent as expected, and a power-steering failure meant that his third place, only 76 seconds behind Mäkinen's Subaru Impreza, was a real achievement. Colin McRae took fourth, and new-recruit Markko Märtin was 12th. "Still learning all about the car," as he said afterwards.

In February, M-Sport brought three new cars to tackle the snowy International Swedish Rally (for McRae and Sainz, these were the first for some years not to carry familiar FMC registrations). If the truth be told, no-one really expected the Focus to win this event, especially as the M-Sport team was up against Scandinavian drivers in well-developed Peugeot 206s. So it transpired, with Sainz (third place), and McRae (sixth), not even backed up by Markko Märtin. Märtin had crashed his car on the 'shakedown' test, held just hours before the start of the event proper, and didn't have enough time for it to be repaired to compete. There was less publicity for young François Duval, driving an all-blue Focus WRC (X8 FMC), and finishing tenth.

By this time, and after persistent nagging from new Technical Chief Christian Loriaux (as well as Subaru, also a Pirelli user), Pirelli had embarked on a big programme of change to its tyres; it was hoped that it could make up an acknowledged performance gap on Michelin. During February, M-Sport spent nearly two weeks of tarmac testing in Spain (all three of the main contracted drivers were involved), and the team was hoping that this would do the trick.

In the event, M-Sport's visit to Corsica for the third round of the 2002 series was an unmitigated disaster. Although four team cars started – with high hopes – two of them crashed out, while the other pair struggled to keep up with the flying Peugeot 206 WRCs. The results – sixth for Sainz, and eighth for Märtin – were disappointing enough, but the accidents of François Duval and Colin McRae were even worse.

By the start of the last day, McRae had driven his heart out to hold on to fourth place. Yet, only two stages from the end, he found his Focus caught out on a mud-strewn S-bend in the mountains. Slewing sideways, his car then hit a tree – writing itself off – with the hapless driver suffering a badly broken little finger on his left hand. Although McRae was brave enough to suggest that the digit could be amputated, if that would help

seed his recovery, it would eventually heal. The car – Y5 FMC – was never driven again.

M-Sport was now in one of those 'down' periods from which it would take time to recover – it would take until Argentina in May, in fact – but still it struggled valiantly on. The Focus was no more successful in Spain, two weeks after the Tour de Corse. Before the Rallye Catalunya even began, Carlos Sainz crashed a car during tyre testing, resulting in his long-time co-driver Luis Moya suffering a broken rib, and Sainz himself a performing a serious piece of soul searching. Colin McRae, for his part, was determined to get back into action, so M-Sport's mechanics modified a brand-new car (EK51 HXZ, one of the first Focus WRCs not to carry the charismatic FMC identity), to have an altered gear-change installation that McRae could operate with either hand. In the circumstances, his performance in Spain – sixth place,

The Focus WRC was so spectacular – as was its leading driver Colin McRae – that it led to great adulation from the fans. Here, X7 FMC was on its way to winning the Acropolis Rally in 2002.

though never at blistering speeds – was a remarkable comeback.

M-Sport was now faced with a tightly-grouped series of rough-road events – Cyprus Rally, Rally Argentina, Acropolis Rally and Safari Rally – that was something to which the entire team looked forward. After a disappointing foray to Cyprus, a remarkable sequence of three victories followed, two by McRae (who seemed to have recovered all his strength and stamina), and one by Sainz.

It could even have been four victories; in Cyprus, Colin McRae was leading up to the final five stages, but then rolled his Focus into an expensive ball. The result was a complete write-off, but nevertheless McRae struggled to finish sixth overall with the car whose cabin was comprehensively crushed. The Argentinian event, which followed in May, was extraordinary in many ways. Not only were leading Peugeot cars disqualified due to servicing infringements, but also the Fords were suddenly competitive once again. Peugeot's last-minute exclusions led to Carlos Sainz being elevated to outright victory (his 24th in a stellar career), while Colin McRae finished third, and Markko Märtin a very welcome fourth.

Could M-Sport repeat this in Greece, which followed three weeks later? It could, for not only did McRae take his third consecutive Acropolis victory, but Sainz and Märtin also placed third and sixth. What's more, Märtin led the event for the first eight stages, while McRae stroked his way to victory without setting a single fastest stage time. This must have been a disappointment for Märtin, as without incurring a puncture that cost him more than three minutes in stage time penalties, he would have set six fastest stage times and won the event himself. And as for Carlos? As consistent as ever, he did not set a single fastest time, but still took third place …

From M-Sport's point of view, this was much more like it. Then, a month later, things went even one step further. Colin McRae proved that he was back to his fighting best, not only in body and stamina, but in attitude and commitment too. He not only won a gruelling Safari Rally, but also marked his 25th WRC event victory. To give an idea of how different the Safari was (and would remain) compared to other rallies of the day, Technical Chief Christian Loriaux revealed that the three cars weighed up to 60kg/132lb heavier than usual. He also noted that they ran with bull bars, a snorkel (for the engine, to deal with flash floods), a heavier sump guard, two spare wheels, reinforced Pirelli tyres, an enlarged fuel tank, and a different set of gear ratios.

Carlos Sainz in Y6 FMC, on his way to third place in the 2002 Acropolis.

Colin McRae and Nicky Grist used X7 FMC to win their third consecutive Acropolis Rally in 2002, with (to their left) team-mates Carlos Sainz and Luis Moya in third place. To their right are Peugeot drivers Marcus Grönholm (who would soon join M-Sport in the mid-2000s) and his co-driver Timo Rautiainen: all grouped at the finish in Itea.

Markko Märtin – in Y3 FMC – was a real star on the 2002 Acropolis rally, regularly outpacing the entire field (including Colin McRae and Carlos Sainz) in this plain blue-liveried car. One tyre failure caused him to lose the lead, but he finished a stirring sixth overall, which looked promising for his future.

With McRae and Sainz (himself on 24 victories) in the team, M-Sport knew that it was still employing the best of the best. It was for this reason that it redoubled its efforts to make the still-secret 2003 car even better. Unhappily, this was to be M-Sport's final victory of 2002 and – if only we had known it at the time – brought the triumphant Focus WRC/McRae/Sainz era to a rather downbeat close. M-Sport's biggest rivals, Peugeot, finally achieved a peak of reliability with the 206 WRC and, along with its lead driver Marcus Grönholm, won five of the last six events in the season.

In comparison, the Focus team's best showing was second/third/fifth/sixth in the Network Q Rally of Great Britain, and fourth overall on four other occasions. There were, of course, the usual dramas; such as McRae's machine catching fire during Neste Rally Finland, when his car's rear differential was cracked open by a big rock, the leaking oil ignited, and the resulting fire could not be extinguished. A final shot of drama was found when – in spite of still being what can be described as 'the apprentice' in the M-Sport team – Markko Märtin set two fastest stage times, and was second fastest six times, on the Rally of Great Britain. He not only beat all his team-mates, but led the rally until the final morning, eventually finishing a storming second to Petter Solberg's Subaru Impreza, only 24 seconds off the pace.

The fact that Ford took second in the World Rally Championship for Manufacturers, and that Sainz and McRae came third and fourth in the Driver counterpart, was very creditable. Nevertheless, by M-Sport's increasingly high standards it almost counted as a failure. At the end of a tumultuous season, Malcolm Wilson must have sat down in his office at Dovenby Hall, and forced himself to acknowledge that his colourful organisation empire would need a major rebuild for 2003. Although this had been brewing for some months – Malcolm had not missed any of the signs – he had to face up to the imminent end to the Martini sponsorship deal, and to losing the high-profile services of both Colin McRae and Carlos Sainz. Long courted by Citroën, McRae had announced his defection as early as September, while Carlos Sainz had carried out a lengthy courtship with Motor Sports Development's Hyundai team before finally accepting a much-reduced offer from Citroën, delaying that announcement until December.

Not only that, but Ford's continuous struggle to turn the Jaguar F1 team into a credible organisation meant that M-Sport would have to face up to a serious belt-tightening process; its budgets were certainly going to be drastically cut for 2003. The only good news, it seemed, was that Christian Loriaux's efforts to rejig the Focus WRC were about to bear fruit.

TECHNICAL DEVELOPMENTS MADE IN 2000, 2001 AND 2002

Although the cars were officially known as Ford Racing Focus WRC models in 2000, this was no more than a courtesy title given to the rehomologated cars. Visually, the changes were restricted to a slightly different nose, with extra cooling slots on the extremities, channelling more cool air to the front brakes, and a larger main inlet for radiator/engine bay cooling. At the rear, the original free-standing spoiler had been discarded in favour of a smaller and much more discreet spoiler atop the hatchback. Amazingly, although this style did not look as aggressively 'aero' as before, the figures recorded in Ford's wind tunnel told another story.

All this, of course, was quite overshadowed by the new presence of Carlos Sainz's major sponsor, Telefónica Movistar, which resulted in the rear quarters of the cars now being mostly blue (instead of the bright red of the 1999 models).

Mechanically, Cosworth had already phased in several changes to the engines, which were now all being built at its Northampton base, at least for the works machines. Some Mountune units were still supplied to the 'customer' clients, as well as the fitment of smaller, more specialised, turbochargers. Co-operation with Xtrac (suppliers of the complex Focus transmission) meant that changes were able to be made to the layout, and positioning, of the clutch. There was much detail work with regard to differential controls.

Although M-Sport was quite reticent about this at the time, it eventually became clear that Sainz had been less than impressed with the Focus engine, which he did not consider to be as 'torque-y' as the Toyota to which he was accustomed. Cosworth, stung by this, carried on a steady programme of incremental improvements ("expensive" was one quote from Malcolm Wilson), which included new camshaft profiles and work on the electronic engine management systems.

For 2001, the 'Ford Racing Focus WRC' name of 2000 was dropped, the cars returning to their basic (and still correct) 'Ford Focus WRC' title instead.

A major technical change was the move from Michelin to Pirelli tyres (this had been confirmed as early as September

2000, and was supposedly for a three-year deal). The decision proved to be somewhat controversial; indeed, only one other team – Subaru – opted to use Pirelli in 2001. The move was so contentious that when Christian Loriaux was interviewed for the technical director role at the end of the season, he insisted that he would only move to M-Sport if the team would return to Michelin as soon as possible!

Aerodynamically, more wind-tunnel work had encouraged the change to the rear spoiler (abandoning the Gurney Flap), and the elimination of the brake cooling slots at the extremities of the front bumper moulding. Progressive developments on the Cosworth engine included the fitment of drive-by-wire throttle facilities, a ceramic turbocharger, changes to the engine/transmission traction control installation, and continuing work on the brakes. The January 2001 statement that this latest Focus WRC had 'new' Cosworth-built engines was more hype than fact, as the same basic iron block was retained. Cosworth had done a great deal of work, though, not only to improve the breathing and the high-revving output, but to make the power unit more responsive from low- and medium-rate revs too.

For 2002 (and increasingly under the influence of the new technical director, Christian Loriaux) there were many evolutionary changes. When it was realised that more improvements could be made than the WRC regulations would allow, car was rehomologated. Cosworth had continued to make improvements to the Zetec-M engine, which – it claimed – was three per cent lighter than before (a saving of about three or four pounds). Further changes had been made to the reprofiling and 'porting' of the cylinder heads, and improvements had been made to the crankshaft, connecting rods, and flywheel, all allied to a different Garrett turbocharger and its fittings. Pi Research (a Cosworth subsidiary) had worked yet more wonders on the electronic engine management system, while Xtrac had phased in different gearbox internals.

M-Sport still acknowledged (internally, if not always in public) that it needed to further reduce the car's weight, so that it could run at the minimum regulatory weight on tarmac (and even, sometimes, on gravel and more demanding outings). During the year, this 'diet' led to lighter suspension mountings, a lighter front cross member, an improved aluminium sump

guard, and new gearbox mounting cross member. As new cars were built, a different roll cage layout was introduced, and through the year changes were made to almost every aspect of the running gear, notable among which was the adoption of a 'paddle' type of gear change.

Even so, there were major changes to follow in mid-1993, as the first of what we might call the 'Loriaux cars' was made ready.

WORKS CARS USED
2000

Of the 20 Ford Racing Focus WRC cars that featured at WRC level in 2000, nine carried 'V' registrations, and several were sold to private customers. M-Sport officially used only four 1999 models (S6 FMC, S10 FMC, S12 FMC and S14 FMC) in front-line action during the season. V2 FMC was hardest-worked of all, starting nine times with no fewer than four different drivers.

2001

Because M-Sport was running a three-car team throughout the series (McRae, Sainz, and Delecour, though Delecour's car never carried Martini livery), it used no fewer than 18 works cars during the year. Six of these were 'V' registered machines – encompassing V3 FMC to V10 FMC – while the other 12 were brand new, and progressively introduced during the season.

2002

Although Christian Loriaux had now joined the team as the new technical director, the team would not be ready to launch vehicles that had been much modified until early 2003 at least. In 2002, therefore, a mixture of refurbished and updated 2001 Focus WRCs were campaigned alongside newly-built examples of the current model. Because a number of the older cars had been sold off to private customers, no fewer than 25 such machines appeared in WRC events.

As to M-Sport controlled vehicles, there were no fewer than 16 in the 14 events. Y6 FMC appeared five times, with four other cars appearing four times each. In between events some of the off-duty cars were used extensively in testing, development, and on publicity occasions.

CHAPTER FIVE

2003-2005 – Markko Märtin's star shines

As far as M-Sport and its Focus WRC was concerned, almost everything about the 2003 WRC season was new, unfamiliar, and – in some ways – a shot in the dark. Not only was a radically re-engineered car due to appear early in the year, but there would soon be new headline sponsors, and a fresh driver line-up. The problems – and the opportunities – were considerable, yet the question of finance overshadowed them all.

Even as early as September 2002, Ford had made it clear that it was intending to slash its WRC budget for 2003, with some at the time claiming that the grant was to be halved (something that neither Ford nor M-Sport would ever confirm). Colin McRae's financial demands, meanwhile, were such that M-Sport never even approached a compromise with him. McRae therefore accepted an offer from Citroën for the 2003 season (which, as it happened, was a grave mistake), and before the end of the year he would be joined there by Carlos Sainz.

To recap: for 2003, M-Sport would have no Martini sponsorship, no immediate replacement for that outgoing sponsor, and no McRae or Sainz either. A much-rumoured partnership with BP/Castrol would remain as just that – a rumour – until mid-season at least. In the meantime, the cars would have to operate in rather undistinguished corporate Ford livery, although the brave showing of a very large 'RS' down the flanks of the cars was surely a teasing 'wait-and-see' …

Malcolm Wilson had been hoping to run a high-profile team for the 2003 season. Ultimately, though, he concluded that while he might still be able to run three drivers, all of them would be up-and-coming rather than current superstars. To that end, the 'apprentice' of the 2002 season, Markko Märtin, became de facto team leader. He had, after all, occasionally outpaced his 'seniors,' and completed all but one of the events that he started. Markko was accompanied by the 22-year-old François Duval, who, despite originally having been a Puma-driving star in the Junior category, was still unproven. The real surprise (but whose name would be present until the very end of Focus rally history) was Mikko

*The new sponsorship deal was finally publicised in mid-2003.
This was the Castrol type …*

… and this was the BP version.

François Duval would mature as an M-Sport driver during 2004.

*In 2003, Mikko Hirvonen's car was basically
unsponsored by M-Sport, but carried its own
support from Scandinavian sources.*

*This was the Focus WRC's latest front suspension/
braking layout for 2003: there would be more
advances later in the season.*

Mikko Hirvonen was M-Sport's third-man/'apprentice' early in 2003, but would go on to be a king-pin of the team in later years.

Hirvonen. A 22-year-old Finn, who had already won the Finnish F2 title, Hirvonen would sometimes compete with private support from Finland. He was clearly a rising star, whom Malcolm Wilson was sure to mentor. This last signing was a gamble, for sure, but in retrospect it was to be seen as a very shrewd decision.

Wilson, the seasoned team boss/publicist/commercial operator, was cautious about the team's prospects when interviewed before the start of the 2003 season. He stressed that his drivers were all young, the new version of the WRC car was not quite ready for competition, and even that the team had started looking ahead to what the next Focus WRC should look like. This would be the car based on the second-

generation Focus road car, which was due for launch in the autumn of 2004. The 2003 Focus WRC, meanwhile, would be subjected to test after test in the first months of 2003, and finally received its homologation approval on 1 April, just in time to compete in New Zealand.

After all this caution, then, Wilson must have been delighted by the performance of his 'young guns' in Monte Carlo. Their fourth and seventh places were taken in a hard-fought battle with Sébastien Loeb, driving a Citroën Xsara (this being a combination that was going to loom large in rallying over the next few years). Markko Märtin was only on his third Rallye Automobile Monte Carlo – his first in a Focus with Michelin tyres, and his first as effective team leader – yet he finished only seconds behind McRae and Sainz (in works Citroëns), which was extremely encouraging. New recruit Mikko Hirvonen, driving an all-white car, unfortunately rolled his Focus, hitting a tree and rendering the car immobile.

There was a similar scenario on the wintry International Swedish Rally that followed; Märtin once again took fourth place, only seconds behind Richard Burns in his Subaru, for a podium placing. On this occasion, it was François Duval's misfortune to crash his Focus on a narrow stage, leaving it damaged, and blocking the route for cars that followed, meaning that the stage had to be cancelled.

Yet another results reshuffle followed with the Rally of Turkey, perhaps proving that Malcolm Wilson had been very wise in choosing three such young, ambitious, and well-matched drivers to replace Colin McRae and Carlos Sainz. In this event, where there were loose and rough surfaces rather than snow and ice, it was Duval's turn to finish top of the three Fords, and third overall. Märtin finished down in sixth place (a transmission problem, requiring a transaxle change, didn't help), and Hirvonen was obliged to retire with steering problems brought about by an accident that damaged the Focus front suspension.

This early-season success had all been achieved with 2002-specification cars, meaning that there was a real buzz of excitement among the specialist media when M-Sport was finally ready to launch the 'Loriaux Focus.' When the launch came, it was in time for the vehicles to appear in the Rally of New Zealand, taking place in April. Christian Loriaux was convinced that the technical changes made to the Focus were a real step change. Details of the changes are detailed at the end of the chapter, but the initial media reaction to the new

Markko Märtin started his 2003 season in a Focus emblazoned with massive 'RS' livery. He finished fourth in Monte Carlo.

car may be summarised by this quote, from David Evans (of *Autosport*) on seeing the car for the first time:

"The 2003 version made a mockery of [the 2002 model]; made it look like a car from a bygone era. This year's machine, which makes its WRC debut in New Zealand later this month, looks mean, purposeful, and downright sexy. The Focus' boxy shape is disguised by a plethora of swooping lines, spoilers and deep scoops. It's more Super Touring than World Rally …"

The new cars had no luck on their first two events. New Zealand saw Märtin and Duval set four fastest stage times between them, before Märtin's engine threw a cambelt when he was in a strong second position. Duval's car suffered hydraulic problems connected with the gearshift, though he kept going. Then came Argentina, where Märtin's

The new-for-2003 Focus WRC made its debut in New Zealand, being sleeker, lower, and faster than ever before.

The first of the 'Loriaux-Focus' WRC types featured a horizontally-positioned engine cooling radiator, with twin cooling fans exhausting through vents in the bonnet.

Christian Loriaux was relieved to see his new-for-2003 Focus WRC finally in action, and to find that it was just as effective as hoped.

This was the latest Focus' sturdy sump shield being removed for service attention, in Greece in mid-2003.

Sheer delight at Markko Märtin's success in the Acropolis Rally of June 2003: it was the Focus' fourth successive victory in this high-profile event.

car suffered an engine failure on the final day, at a point where he was leading the event and looking for an outright victory. Malcolm Wilson is reputed to have reassured the team immediately after the event, saying: "Don't worry, the Acropolis is next …"

As predicted, M-Sport's dreams came true in Greece. Not only did Markko Märtin chalk up his first-ever outright victory at WRC level, but the 2003 Focus WRC performed fluently and successfully too. What's more, its long-awaited major sponsor – BP/Castrol – was finally in evidence. Castrol took precedence on Märtin's car, with BP more in evidence on François Duval's sister machine.

Ford and the Acropolis Rally certainly seemed to have a close relationship; this was Ford's fourth successive victory, with Colin McRae having won in the three previous years. Nor was this result by chance, as Märtin set five fastest and four second-fastest stage times, eventually beating Carlos Sainz's Citroën by 46 seconds.

In fact, when the fates did intervene, it was to throw a spanner in the works for Märtin. On the fifth stage, the bonnet on his Focus came unpinned, flying up and almost completely obscuring his view of the track ahead (and of course also exposing the intricate way in which the radiator cooling vents were arranged)! With 12 miles still to go, he somehow made it to the end of the stage – just – flirting with off-route disasters several times along the way. Amazingly, this entire ordeal took only six seconds longer than the fastest time on the same stage!

Team-mate Duval, on the other hand, was not so lucky on the same stage. While in second place, and aiming to close the gap on his team-mate, Duval came off the road and ended up in the only ditch for miles from which extraction was not possible.

Just two weeks later, once the entire WRC circus had made the relatively short voyage from Greece to the Cyprus Rally, M-Sport was hoping for a repeat performance. This event promised to be as rough, dusty and hot as the Acropolis Rally, and the Focus had won it on two previous occasions. Even so, there was no hint of complacency, and two different cars were prepared for Märtin and Duval. Unfortunately, there was no luck being dished out on this occasion; both the front-line 2003 Focus WRCs were eliminated on the fifth stage, both of them with engine failures caused by serious amounts of dust getting into their power units. There hadn't even been a chance for them to set fast times in those early hours, so it was a great relief for M-Sport to see Mikko Hirvonen (still the 'apprentice' on the team) take sixth place in his 2002-spec car.

The team then had something of a rest (relatively speaking, that is; it was only four weeks away) before Rallye Deutschland was held in Germany. This was an all-tarmac event, and one expected to favour the Citroëns and Peugeots (or the 'French go-karts,' as some rivals called them). As expected, those cars occupied the first four places, with Markko Märtin's car following closely home in fifth place, and Duval placing seventh.

M-Sport's drivers line up in mid-2003, proud to be alongside newly-sponsored cars. From left to right: Markko Märtin, Michael Park, Stéphane Prévot and François Duval.

If Märtin's car had not twice been afflicted by serious transmission problems, though, he might even have been battling for another outright victory. His Focus started well, before suffering transmission problems and dropping to tenth place at the end of the first day. One day later, he had set a whole series of fastest stage times, caught up with the leaders by nearly a full minute, and lay in third. On the final day it was only another bout of transmission bothers – and the loss of 23 precious seconds – that spoiled his weekend. Even so, ten fastest stages times out of 22 stages: how dominant was that?

Märtin was even more dominant in the Neste Rally Finland, where high speeds, high jumps and sheer naked bravery had to be added to the basic strength of the machines. Having battled with Marcus Grönholm's Peugeot from the very beginning – which led the event nearly the entire time – the Estonian ended up setting eight fastest, five second-fastest and six third-fastest stage times (out of a total of 23 stages). Once the Peugeot retired with a defective front suspension, which led to a wheel coming off the car at high speed, it was game over in favour of M-Sport. Märtin won outright, in front of famous rivals such as Petter Solberg, Richard Burns, Carlos Sainz, Sébastien Loeb and Tommi Mäkinen. This was no fluke, and it showed.

By this time in the season Märtin had realised that he could not win the World Rally Championship for Drivers (nor could Ford take the Manufacturers counterpart), and the media's attention turned to the still-erratic form of his teammate François Duval. Malcolm Wilson was quoted as saying: "Look at his record over the last 18 months; accidents in Corsica, Australia, Sweden, Greece, Finland, this year and last …" Although Märtin seemed secure in a long-term contract, this surely meant that his team principal was looking for improvement.

Märtin did not win again in 2003 (though there were more, many more, victories to come in the future), but both he and the Loriaux-adjusted Focus WRC were now clearly 'on the pace,' in all conditions. Except in Australia, that is, as now seemed to be traditional with Ford. This was an event best forgotten (though never by the historians); Märtin was never fighting for the lead, and at one point was seen to have a large rock unloaded from his car at a service point. He was subsequently disqualified for running under weight limits. M-Sport responded with the claim that the rock had been used as a get-you-home cure to a broken holding strap for the spare wheel. The car was later weighed and found to be 23kg/51lb over the limit, yet the officials would not budge.

The season ended in a real flurry for M-Sport, with tarmac events in Italy (Rallye Sanremo), Corsica (Tour de Corse), and Spain (Rallye Catalunya). These should have been good for the fast-improving Focus WRC, but there were no more late-season victories to come. In Sanremo, Märtin set the highest amount of fastest stage times, but could never quite elbow his way past Sébastien Loeb's Citroën in the overall result. Engine overheating problems – caused by a mass of autumn leaves clogging up the front air intake – did not help, and he had to settle for third place. Two weeks later, and it was François Duval's turn to take a well-deserved third place in Corsica (he led the rally at one stage). Märtin countered this good news, though, by effectively writing off his car in a very large accident. Even so, both drivers were on full form in Spain, with Märtin once again posting several fastest stage times. Despite this, they had to settle for third and fourth places overall.

The season ended distinctly downbeat with Wales Rally GB, where Märtin was forced to retire with a blown engine (following a water leak, the cylinder head gasket had failed). Duval, while demonstrably faster than he had been at the start of the season, was not comfortable with British forestry-type stages, and could only take fifth place. This final result meant that M-Sport finished fourth in the World Rally Championship for Manufacturers.

While all this late-season action had been unfolding, M-Sport was going through what had become a familiar process: trying to line up a likely reduction in available funds for 2004 with even more activity than before. There would be 16 events in the WRC calendar. To quote Malcolm: "We need to know if the proposed testing ban is coming, and we need to know if things like flexi-service are coming …" Even before Wales Rally GB took place, Malcolm had to take big decisions, which included scheduled testing before the 2004 season. Ford's confirmation of backing came at the end of November 2003. Not a moment too soon, even with yet another budget cut (there were no McRae or Sainz sales to rely on, after all). To those who wondered why so much money was needed to go towards the WRC series, Malcolm confirmed that his company currently employed 170 people …

For 2004, M-Sport started its World Rally Championship effort with a settled team and a settled programme. The company

Markko Märtin in the snow in Monte Carlo, hoping to notch up several outright wins in 2004.

made it clear that it planned to reserve both technical effort and investment capital for work on a new-generation Focus. At M-Sport this soon became known as the 'wide Focus,' and was due for launch as a mass-production road car before the end of that season. This Focus, however, was not expected to start rallying until the very end of 2005, nor to begin a concentrated motorsport programme until 2006.

For 2004, therefore, cars built for the early-season events were slightly-developed versions of the late 2003 model, still with the tasteful and distinctive BP/Castrol sponsors' livery. Both Markko Märtin and François Duval had also been re-signed for the entire season and, as in previous years, major competition was expected to come from Citroën, Subaru, and Peugeot. The FIA had also phased in a number of new WRC regulations, including the freedom to use lightweight bodyshell materials. This (as Christian Loriaux explained) allowed companies to move a car's centre of gravity even lower, and even cause the cars to need additional ballast for certain tarmac events.

An unpredictable start was mirrored in the early events; it was Citroën's Sébastien Loeb who set the pace on the Rallye Automobile Monte Carlo and International Swedish Rally. Märtin might have expected to win either of these events, especially after he had recorded more fastest stage times in 2003 than any of his rivals, but could not quite match Loeb at this stage. He took second place in Monte Carlo, but only seventh in Sweden (after leading the event, then suffering an accident that tore off a rear wheel and cost him more than five minutes).

Then, in March, Markko Märtin and François Duval were provided with the best cars in which to tackle Rally Mexico, and M-Sport won its first event of the year. New to the WRC series, this was an all-gravel event run mainly in warm weather, and at higher than usual altitudes, both of which clearly suited the Focus and its crews. Although not immediately the fastest car of the field (a Subaru, then a Citroën headed that column at first), Märtin's Focus broke through mid-event, and took the

Making a rare M-Sport appearance, Janne Tuohino took fourth place in Sweden in 2004.

*The 'big three' in 2004. From left to right: Markko Märtin, Malcolm Wilson, and
François Duval, celebrating a splendid victory in Mexico with first and second places.*

victory with team-mate Duval less than a minute behind him. First and second places in this high-profile event, and a good lead in the World Rally Championship for Manufacturers: who could ask for more?

The Focus WRC that was homologated from 1 April 2004 was a revised version, rather than being a comprehensive redesign like the mid-2003 update. Once again there were visual changes to the style, particularly in the front moulding where there were extra scoops/vents to channel more air to the engine bay and the front brakes. Several easy-to-replace exterior body panels were also in the newly-authorised 'lighter material' specifications. Cosworth had made a whole series of changes to the engine specification, with cylinder head gaskets, pistons, and connecting rods all coming in for attention. Before long, it became clear that M-Sport was planning to take over engine assembly and testing at Dovenby Hall, while Cosworth would continue to provide a multitude of components.

M-Sport therefore targeted reliability rather than outright pace for the next few events, and it duly got it; although the latest car was certainly competitive, it was not startlingly faster than before. The 2004-specification cars first appeared in Rally New Zealand, where they were rapid and reliable, but not sensational. Markko Märtin set three fastest stage times, but had to settle for third place, while François Duval was looking good until he went off the track on the final morning. The crash wiped off a front wheel, and Duval ended up way down the lists, no fewer than 24 minutes off the pace.

A month later it was the Cyprus Rally. The event was hot, very hot, causing a bit of a buzz in the press and among seasoned competitors, who hated having to rally inside ultra-hot WRC cars. Not that François Duval had much chance to over-heat, when – on the very first stage – his Focus broke several front wheel studs, lost a wheel, and could go no further. Markko Märtin, on the other hand, was as steady and resourceful as always. Although he set only one fastest stage time, he also made no mistakes and finished up taking second, only 15 seconds behind Loeb's winning Citroën. There were, incidentally, memories of the very first rally appearance the Focus made, when both the team Peugeots (which might otherwise have won the event) were disqualified for the use of illegal engine water pump!

Only two weeks later, the rallying circus moved over to Greece, to tackle the Acropolis Rally, where the Focus had a four-year winning streak to defend. No luck this time, though,

as Märtin put his Focus off the road, and down a steep bank, on only the third stage. Duval (not a rough road specialist) was left to fight for the lead. In the end he took a fine fourth place, unhappily allowing Citroën to sneak in front of M-Sport in the World Rally Championship for Manufacturers.

Time for a holiday? Only if you consider three weeks between events instead of two as 'taking it easy.' M-Sport mechanics, in fact, were immediately put to work on refurbishing Duval's ex-Cyprus car and Märtin's victorious ex-Mexico car. They needed to be ready in time to tackle the Rally of Turkey, the third in a sequence of Mediterranean loose surface/hot weather events. Not that this seemed to help, as for unknown reasons the Fords were not at all competitive. Märtin set only one fastest stage time, and at one point he even had to tackle some DIY electronic wiring repairs, after

Ford's motorsport supremo Jost Capito enjoyed his outings with M-Sport.

Markko Märtin going for the Finnish 'long jump' record in 2004 (that's what the markings at the roadside are all about)! He finished second overall.

his Focus plunged in a water crossing and the engine bay suffered.

This setback, however, was positively minor compared with what happened to Märtin in the next event. During the Rally Argentina, he not only incurred a $20,000 penalty fine for cutting across a stage (through a camp site, in fact), but also ended up sustaining a massive high-speed accident on the fifth stage. Team boss Malcolm described the car as looking worse than he had ever seen before. This, apparently, was caused by a mistake in Märtin's practice notes, and the car was not blamed for any part of it.

M-Sport, of course, was unhappy about all this – and deservedly so – as the car had been brand new for the event,

had apparently cost up to £400,000 to build, and would never again be used as a front-line car by M-Sport.

Fortunes improved substantially, though not quite dramatically, for the Neste Rally Finland. Märtin set two fastest stage times, 12 other podium times, and ended up second overall, just 34 seconds behind Marcus Grönholm's winning Peugeot. This was despite the substantially-improved M-Sport-built engines still being tested back at Dovenby Hall, not yet ready for use.

The tides of fortune had definitely changed, but outright victory eluded the team once again in Germany; this time, it was François Duval's turn to get close. Once again a Focus WRC took second place, once again losing out by a short

François Duval performing in front of a vast crowd in Rally GB in 2004.

margin, in this case 29 seconds. Controversy arose over the timing on one stage that, had it been resolved, could have made that gap even smaller …

A long and unfamiliar trip to Japan followed. The event itself was frustrating for the entire M-Sport team, not only because François Duval slid off the road towards the end of the event while disputing fourth place, but also because Markko Märtin could somehow not come to terms with his hastily compiled pace notes until later in the event.

Already, the make-up of the team for 2005 (if it was indeed to continue) was in turmoil. Malcolm Wilson had still not secured a longer-term commitment from Ford, and therefore the assurance of necessary finances was not in place. M-Sport therefore found itself forced to state that

it would release Duval from his contract. Even as the team flew off to Japan, Markko Märtin let the world know that he too was leaving the team, picking up a new contract with Peugeot for 2005.

In what was almost a defiant reaction, M-Sport then set up not two, but three, well-developed Focus WRCs to contest the Wales Rally GB. Märtin and Duval were joined in the cars by Janne Tuohino of Finland. Not that this additional support helped, in the end. 'Guest driver' Tuohino had to retire after his transmission failed, Duval's car suffered under-body/chassis damage after losing a battle with a big rock, and Märtin – as usual fighting for the lead, against Solberg (Subaru), Sainz (Citroën) and Loeb (also Citroën) – was hampered by a turbo failure at one point. For Märtin, third was the best he could

Markko Märtin's (and the Focus') second victory of 2004 came in the Tour de Corse.

hope for in the circumstances. Two weeks later, in Rally d'Italia Sardegna (which took over from Sanremo as Italy's WRC qualifier), the news was equally depressing. Märtin was well up among the leaders when, on the final morning, his engine's turbocharger blew. An oil leak led to an under-bonnet fire, damage was caused to wiring and hydraulic systems, and the car suffered instant retirement.

It wasn't all bad news, however. In the season's last three events – Tour de Corse (Corsica), Rally Catalunya (Spain), and Rally Australia – M-Sport notched up two outright victories and one third place. Both victories went to Markko Märtin, using the same car on each occasion.

Corsica was a specialist tarmac event that had not seen a Ford victory for many years, yet Märtin not only beat all the Citroëns and Peugeots (they were local favourites, of course), but was demonstrably fastest of all for the whole weekend. In Spain the competition was close and fierce, but Märtin's car was as dominant as before. The two M-Sport team drivers disputed the lead between them throughout the first two

days, but for Duval it all went wrong on the final morning when his car's engine faltered, then expired completely. Märtin continued on alone, and at the end of the day won outright, with works Focus WRCs setting fastest stage times on ten of the event's 12 special stages. If only it could have been like this earlier in the season …

Less than two weeks later, Märtin did it again, enjoying the warm dry tarmac stages of Rally Catalunya (based in Lloret de Mar, southern Spain), and using the same car as he had driven in Corsica. François Duval led in the early stages of the event (setting three fastest stage times), but suffered an incident on the fifth stage that was graphically described later by Christian Loriaux: "The impact [of hitting a large rock on a corner] exploded the suspension. It ripped the upright of the damper, but the wheel was still on. He got out of the stage and started on the road section, but the impact had also ripped a driveshaft out. When that started flailing around, it cut an oil pipe that killed the engine, and set the f*****g thing on fire. He wasn't going any further."

Against what had become a very familiar backdrop in Spain, Markko Märtin was well on his way to his third outright win of 2004, in Catalunya.

Victory at the WRC level is always sweet: especially when it comes on a tarmac rally in Spain. This was Markko Märtin and Michael 'Beef' Park celebrating their win in 2004.

Retirements aren't often more violent than that. Märtin, on the other hand, swept serenely on. He took up the lead almost immediately, and held it to the end. After 19 special stages, he had set top-three times on 16 of them, and never had a single bad result.

The 2004 season was brought to a close with Australia. After the recent results, it was something of a come-down Märtin's car blew its engine on the very first special stage, while Duval still couldn't come to terms with certain track conditions particular to Western Australia. To compound matters, in this same period he also announced that he was defecting to Citroën for 2005 (he would then discover that Citroën was proposing to withdraw completely from rallying at the end of that year).

Even before the end of the 2004 season, there had been all manner of horror stories floating around the specialist media. Not only were both Markko Märtin and François Duval about to leave the team – and a new world-class signing was financially unlikely – but Ford's interest in expensive WRC rallying was about to end completely. From August or September 2004, therefore, Malcolm Wilson must have spent as much of his time planning for an uncertain 2005 future as he did running his current business.

The major problems he faced were numerous, but inevitably centred around costs: the cost of competing in 16 WRC rallies, that of developing super-expensive cars, and also of meeting the financial demands of a handful of drivers.

Sometimes it's quicker by air: this is François Duval jumping high, and long, in the Rally Australia of 2004.

*François Duval's highest finish of 2004 came in Germany when he took second place overall,
a mere 29 seconds behind the winning Citroën.*

With Carlos Sainz publicly stating that he was about to leave the sport, and with Colin McRae's salary demands inflated to the point where they were no longer attractive to any of the top teams, the balance in the sport had been upset. François Duval had been offered a long-term commitment to stay at M-Sport, but was ultimately tempted away by a big-money one-season offer from Citroën.

With the source of his funds undetermined, Malcolm did not know how – or if – he could complete development of a new-generation Focus WRC and have it ready to compete in 2006. Then, amazingly, Ford chose early November to announce that it would continue to back M-Sport's efforts (Markko Märtin's two end-of-season victories must surely have been a factor). With that, design and development work on a second-generation Focus WRC could get underway in earnest. Christian Loriaux issued a great sigh of relief; he had been preparing to leave if there was no prospect of him having new work to inspire him, and he had already been courted by more than one rival organisation.

Late in November, M-Sport revealed that Toni Gardemeister of Finland would become its leading driver for 2005, and that both sides of the deal were amenable to converting it into a longer-term association if the partnership looked promising. Just a week later, M-Sport then signed up Roman Kresta, a Czech driver who had rallied very little during 2004. It was suggested that he had brought additional finance along with him, making the signing more attractive for all concerned.

Even before the 2005 season got underway, M-Sport had made it clear that this was to be very much of an interim period for the team. Financial budgets were stretched to the limit, with 16 events to tackle and an all-new Focus WRC to be designed, developed, and signed off. With these constraints, and with two new (to M-Sport) drivers on the roster, the team was pleased when Toni Gardemeister finished all but two of the season's events. Although he did not record any outright victories, second place was achieved in Rallye Automobile Monte Carlo, the Acropolis Rally of Greece, and in the Tour de Corse. At the end of the season, M-Sport, in what was described as a 'semi-sabbatical' year, finished third in the World Rally Championship for Manufacturers.

The season started well. In Monte Carlo, the two Focus WRCs took second and eighth (carrying their, by now, familiar individual BP and Castrol livery). This was swiftly followed by Gardemeister placing third overall in Sweden, with Henning

Roman Kresta joined the M-Sport team for 2005.

High hopes for the new season in January 2005. Toni Gardemeister taking the start in Monte Carlo.

Gardemeister's Focus WRC heading purposefully on in the chilly mountains behind Monte Carlo in 2005.

Roman Kresta in the snow of Sweden, on his way to eighth place.

Mark Higgins enjoying himself in the Stobart-supported Focus on the 2005 Acropolis before an accident ruined his chances.

Toni Gardemeister celebrates a splendid second place overall, in the 2005 Acropolis Rally.

Henning Solberg joined the M-Sport team on selected events during 2005.

Toni Gardemeister's second place in Corsica, beaten only narrowly by Sébastien Loeb's Citroën, was probably his best drive of the year.

Toni Gardemeister performing on the super special stage in the packed Olympic stadium in Athens, at the start of the 2005 Acropolis. He finished second overall.

Solberg acting as 'guest driver' for the team and taking fifth place. Rally Mexico, in March, saw a slump in the team's fortunes. Although three cars started (Daniel Solà, a protégé of Sainz, piloting one of them), two cars crashed out, while team-leader Toni Gardemeister arrived at the start suffering under a bad bout of influenza. He never really shrugged the illness off during the week, and it was a miracle that he finished sixth overall.

Things weren't about to get better for the team; the result in the next few events showed that the combination of new drivers and an ageing car wasn't quite enough to fight for the lead. After Roman Kresta set a single fastest time in Monte Carlo, in January, no Focus WRC driver would achieve another until May's Cyprus Rally. Toni Gardemeister revelled in the rough conditions at this event, achieving a fastest stage time twice. Two events later, at the Acropolis Rally of Greece in June, he added one more.

This was not, it seems, the razor-sharp team that Markko Märtin had led with such panache in 2004. The situation was not helped by the fact that Kresta rolled his car in the pre-rally shake-down in New Zealand, and was unable to start. In Cyprus, at least, the three major team cars took fourth, fifth and sixth overall (Solberg, Gardemeister and Kresta, respectively), but it would not be until June, at the Acropolis, that Gardemeister once again achieved a podium position. He finished second overall, 1min 36sec behind Loeb's flying Citroën Xsara.

Gardemeister's fifth place in Cyprus meant that M-Sport had scored championship points in every one of the previous 50 events. While M-Sport could boast of such an achievement,

Continued on page 106

In celebration of a fine performance. From left to right: Toni Gardemeister (fifth), Malcolm Wilson, and Roman Kresta (sixth), after the end of the 2005 Cyprus rally.

Left to right: Jan Možný, Malcolm Wilson, and Roman Kresta, before the start of the Cyprus Rally in 2005.

M-Sport team co-ordinator John Millington talks tactics with Toni Gardemeister on the Cyprus Rally of 2005.

Proud father Malcolm Wilson with his son Matthew, before the start of the 2005 Wales Rally GB. Matthew finished 15th overall.

Mark Higgins, in the Eddie Stobart car, finished eighth on the 2005 Wales Rally GB.

Toni Gardemeister in the dust, watched by agile spectators in the mountains of Sardinia, in 2005.

Time for a celebration in Corsica, October 2005: it was the Focus WRC's 100th appearance on a WRC rally since its debut in Monte Carlo in 1999.

Christian Loriaux was relieved and delighted to see his all-new rally car perform so well in Australia in November 2005.

A dusty baptism, in Australia in November 2005, for the all-new second-generation Focus WRC ...

The new-for-2006 Focus WRC – the first of the second-generation types – made its debut in Australia, in November 2005. Toni Gardemeister proved its promise, before a broken alternator belt killed the engine close to the end of the event.

*Mark Higgins enjoyed support from the
Eddie Stobart team during 2005.*

*Mark Higgins and Malcolm Wilson spent many hours testing
and improving the Focus WRC during the early 2000s.*

*Important talks, or just a social get-together? Left to right:
Jost Capito of Ford, Lewis Booth, and Malcolm Wilson.*

this was about the height of its fortunes until late autumn. Gardemeister took two fastest stage times in the high-speed Neste Rally Finland, where he finished sixth overall. Then came the Wales Rally GB, and the entire world of rallying was thrown into deep gloom on hearing of Markko Märtin's accident, where his popular co-driver Michael 'Beef' Park was killed.

For everyone at M-Sport – who had known, liked, and admired Märtin and Park for several years – this was devastating, and it required enormous resolve for the team to continue with its season. Weeks later, to the rather muted joy of everyone involved, Gardemeister put up his best performance of the season, taking a stirring second place overall in the all-tarmac Tour de Corse, behind Loeb's Citroën. Although the gap between the two was a mere 1min 52sec, it was the fact that Loeb set the fastest time on every single stage that made the rest of the sport sit up and take such notice. Loriaux, in an (at the time) off-the-record comment, made it clear that he just couldn't wait for the new-generation Focus to be ready …

The last two events of the season – Spain's RallyRACC Catalunya and Rally Australia – were completed in a rather sombre mood due to 'Beef' Park's tragic death. As far as M-Sport was concerned, attentions were now turned to the all-new 2006 Focus WRC. Gardemeister crashed his car in Spain, slumping to a miserable 14th place, and no Focus driver even notched up a fastest stage time. The new car (covered in detail in the next chapter) drew much attention thanks to the secrecy with which Ford surrounded it in Perth. There was hope, it seemed, for the future; both Gardemeister and Kresta took one fastest stage time each in the new model.

Immediately after the close of the season, M-Sport had to briefly sit back and assess what could be done for the near future. Because much of the 2005 season had been spent on preparing the new model for 2006, it seemed that it had been merely marking time with the existing car. An analysis of results showed that other rival manufacturers seemed to have improved their machines over the course of the season, while the 2005 Focus WRC merely stayed still, and the driving team had not quite lived up to hopes expressed early in the year.

One statistic, perhaps, makes for a telling story; in a total of 16 events, Toni Gardemeister had only set seven fastest stage times, and Roman Kresta only two. Regrettably, therefore, both were released from their contracts at the end of the year. For 2006, with Marcus Grönholm joining the team, better things were expected.

Toni Gardemeister with M-Sport's Phil Short and John Millington, in conference in Corsica in 2005.

TECHNICAL DEVELOPMENTS MADE IN 2003, 2004 AND 2005

Compared with 2002, 2003 saw many major changes to the M-Sport line-up, not just visually but also hidden from view (though equally significant). Not only had Colin McRae and Carlos Sainz both left the team at the end of 2002, but the Martini sponsorship deal had also come to an amicable close.

The team cars showed little in the way of commercial sponsorship livery at first. From mid-season, though, the long-rumoured deal with BP and Castrol (BP owning Castrol, of course) materialised, with their support visually displayed in more than one way. Not only that, but the two-year deal with Pirelli was abandoned, so from 1 January 2003 the works Focus WRC cars all ran on Michelin tyres, joining every other competing World Rally Championship team except for Subaru. That change was apparently a late decision, as testing was carried out with both brands of tyre before the early-season Monte Carlo and Sweden events.

M-Sport had hoped to start the season with its new-type Focus WRC, but ultimately development, build, and supply arrangements were not completed in time. This (as already noted earlier in this chapter) meant that the first 2003-type models did not appear until April, in the far-flung Rally of New Zealand.

Although the layout of the original Focus WRC was retained, there were many end-to-end improvements. To quote technical chief Christian Loriaux; "Really, the 2003

Focus was a complete redesign of the original in so many ways. It was very different from the original, because now we were effectively working from the American-manufactured [SVT170] type of the car ... it was longer, [so] we moved the engine, and we moved the wheelbase ..."

Visually, the new-type 2003 car featured a slightly longer nose, and a longer tail moulding (both being lifted from the USA-manufactured version of the Focus that was, after all, a 'world car'). These allowed changes to be made under and around the engine bay, and – more importantly – a big rear spoiler to be added, which Loriaux freely admits was inspired by that used on the rival Peugeot 206 WRC. In terms of changes invisible from the outside of the car, there was better cooling for the brakes, and greater airflow through into the engine bay itself.

Not only that, but the Loriaux philosophy of lowering the Focus' centre of gravity, while simultaneously getting rid of surplus metal and carbon fibre wherever possible, had been carried out with fanatical attention to detail. Some of this had already been applied to the outgoing 2002 car, but, even so, when the new version of the car was finally unveiled, Loriaux claimed that up to 80 per cent of the design was either new or substantially updated from 2002.

The use of the US-type front moulding was also a change in the car's aerodynamics, being longer than the original type. This was used along with a modified bonnet, which included extra cooling vents because the radiator and twin engine cooling fans were now mounted horizontally ahead of them (and were therefore exhausting their hot air upwards). The main frontal air intake was even larger than before, and there were extra cooling vents located at the corners of the front moulding where it met the front wheel arches.

Mechanically, Cosworth had been persuaded to pare down even more weight from the basic castings that it was obliged to use, and made the proud claim that the 2003 engine was 25 per cent lighter than it had been in 1999/2000, and eight per cent (~25bhp) more powerful. The same Xtrac transmission was retained, but Loriaux made it clear that he thought it was too heavy, and that he would love to abandon it one day. A 30mm diameter titanium propeller shaft was as state-of-the-art as could be arranged (this also saving weight), and there were changes to the rear suspension geometry that the company was not yet prepared to itemise.

Large efforts had been made to simplify the interior, the control layout, and to reduce the weight of as many components as possible, as much as possible. The co-driver's seat, for instance, was so low that Loriaux quipped that he would have liked to see it even lower, with the co-driver sitting on the floorpan!

Much was made of the fact that this latest car could now run at the minimum-allowed 1230kg/2712lb weight limit, and Malcolm Wilson was very bullish as to its potential for winning outright in the future, especially on tarmac events where the earlier Focus WRC had been deficient.

There were several important reasons why the Focus WRC enjoyed very little development attention during 2005. One, clearly, was due to the big squeeze on finance that the team was working under (for the same reason, the driving strength was somewhat limited). The most important factor, though, was that most of Christian Loriaux's concentration had to be focused on getting what was originally dubbed the 'wide Focus' ready for 2006. Because that car was to use an entirely fresh bodyshell, almost every aspect of the car needed to be redesigned.

One of the most important factors of the 2005 programme was that M-Sport took over the complete preparation/repair and assembly of the iron-block engine from Cosworth, locating it in Dovenby Hall (Cosworth continued to supply some components). It was also made clear that the new-generation car would have a new-generation engine – complete with an aluminium cylinder block – and that this was being developed by the noted French engine tuning/development business Pipo Moteurs.

Thanks to a special dispensation given to M-Sport by the governing body of the sport, the team revealed the new-generation car for competition in Australia, in November 2005, before the winter break allowed further development to proceed. Since this was effectively a 2006 model, a full technical analysis follows in the next chapter.

WORKS CARS USED
2003

Two different types of Focus WRC were used by M-Sport in 2003: the original generation (as gradually updated and refined between 1999 and 2002), and – from April 2003 – what one might call the 'Phase 1½', or 'Loriaux' type. However, there was no instant cut-off mid-season from one type to another. Examples of the 2001/2002 type were still in use until almost the end of the 2003 season.

Therefore, and to make it clear for number plate collectors, here are the identities of each type used as M-Sport works cars during the season:

2001/2002 type	2003 type
X7 FMC	EJ02 KMU
Y6 FMC	EK02 KMV
EX51 HYA	EO03YRJ
EX51 HXZ	EO03 YWC
EX02 OBB	R55 OTH
EX02 OBC	EK52 LNP
EX02 OBD	EK52 NWN
EX02 OBE	EX03 XYG

All in all, therefore, M-Sport used 16 'official' cars during the season. However, because a number of older ex-works Focus WRC types (along with a handful of newly-built cars) were sold to private customers, no fewer than 28 different machines were seen throughout the year. As it transpired, new type cars were used by Markko Märtin and François Duval from New Zealand onwards (the fourth event of the season), while original-type cars were used by Mikko Hirvonen and Jari-Matti Latvala for the entire 2003 season.

R55 OTH deserves special mention, if only for its clearly out of sequence registration number, which hints at a story

Parts laid out ready for a quick service/rebuild during the Acropolis Rally of 2005.

all of its own. The number was allocated to a new car that first competed in the Rallye Deutschland in mid-2003, and was the 50th Ford Focus WRC to be manufactured by M-Sport in the first five years of the project. By reading the digits and numbers on the number plate in a certain way, and viewing it through a bit of a romantic filter, this car could be seen as 'RS 50th!'

On its first outing, it was specially decorated with gold-painted wheels and a gold registration plate to mark the occasion. It went on to compete in five WRC events in 2003 and 2004, before becoming what M-Sport called an R&D/test car.

2004

As the Focus WRC fleet grew steadily larger, and M-Sport sold off some of the older cars, more and more of these machines appeared in World Rally Championship events. In 2004, therefore, no fewer than 20 of the currently homologated type, as well as seven older types, took to the start of one or other of the 16 events.

14 machines were entered as official M-Sport/Ford Motor Co Ltd entries. Of them, it was K52 NWN that appeared most often. It made a showing five times, driven by both Markko Märtin and François Duval, while ET53 UJP appeared just three

times, but winning outright twice and finishing fourth once on those occasions!

Seven of the 2003 cars used in the previous season were brought out again, accompanied by the following seven new-for-2004 examples:

EF04 VVB
EG53 BDU
EG53 CCN
EN02 UCT
ET53 UJP
ET53 UNY
ET53 URO

2005

As already noted, this was something of an interim/hand-over season for M-Sport, with much of the team's efforts going into finalising the design and development of the new-generation Focus WRC, in readiness for 2006. Even so, there was never a lack of entries (or work for statisticians), as four official cars were nominated for many of the events.

As far as what I might now unkindly call the 'older models,' only 11 2003-type Focus WRCs appeared as full works cars during the season, with nine of them having previous experience in the earlier seasons. The two newly-blooded cars, therefore, were:

EG53 AVD
EF04 WBW

Finally, the first two examples of the new-generation Focus WRC, were briefly seen in the last event of the season – Rally Australia – in November 2005. This was car intended for regular M-Sport use from then onwards, and based on the Focus Mk2 road car that had gone on sale in 2004/2005. They were:

EU55 BMY
EU55 BMZ

The new-type Focus first appeared, briefly and secretively, in the Rally Australia event at the end of 2005. Before we can even begin to analyse the remarkable success achieved by the car, though, a quick review of the launch of the project in November 2004 is pertinent. At the time, Ford of Europe chairman Lewis Booth commented that "We have developed a motorsport strategy that builds on our rallying heritage, and is integrated into our core business. I'm delighted to say that the headline news in this strategy is that Ford will enter into a long-term commitment to the World Rally Championship."

At the same time, the director of Ford Team RS, Jost Capito, made similar encouraging noises, confirming the fact that the sport was trying to limit costs, and adding that "The proposals to reduce costs convinced us to continue in the long-term."

For Malcolm Wilson and his senior colleagues it was clearly a great relief, and he rather unwisely suggested that he aimed "to be in a position to win the championships with the new car in 2007 and 2008." Every Ford enthusiast was delighted to

see him proved wrong when his forecast came to pass a year earlier than stated, in 2006 and 2007.

The team was confident that it would be back in a position to win events outright during 2006, especially as the new car had run for the first time at the end of September 2005, and had already competed – with honour albeit without much success – in November's Rally Australia event. It had been a good portent for the future that both Toni Gardemeister and Roman Kresta had used the new cars to set fastest individual stage times in Australia, despite it never having been a location where Ford enjoyed much success.

No one, probably not even Malcolm Wilson, originally expected the new car to be as dominant as it became. This may go some way towards explaining why M-Sport received permission to run the new car in the final event of 2005, granting vital operating experience that would be used in the build-up to 2006.

There was still, however, the question of drivers. After M-Sport's 'semi-sabbatical' from the World Rally Championship

No, not the Starship Enterprise, but the centre console of the 2006/2007 Focus WRC.

in 2005, it was considered that the team's drivers had done a good, though not outstanding, job. This was partly because M-Sport had not been able to find enough money to attract the very best two drivers in the world to join it in 2004/2005. Toni Gardemeister had competed in all 16 WRC rounds without ever quite being exceptional (but had nevertheless placed second three times), while his team-mate Roman Kresta had not shone at any point.

This time though, it would be different. Ford had publicly recommitted to the sport in the long-term, BP/Castrol had confirmed its continued support of the M-Sport team, and everything was tied together with the obvious promise of a new car for the 2006 season. To keep pace with the tidal wave of new technology that this new car represented, M-Sport emptied its coffers and went out to hire two new truly front-line drivers. In mid-2005 it had already approached Citroën's star driver (and, by the end of that season, two-time World Rally Champion) Sébastien Loeb. Citroën had, at this time, already stated that it would withdraw at the end of the 2005 season.

Loeb admitted at the time that he was talking to several teams, emphasising that he wanted a longer-term deal to make it worthwhile for him to move his allegiance from Citroën. He tested Focus WRC cars on forestry stages in Cumbria, but even at that early stage asserted that he knew Citroën would return for 2007. Citroën wanted him continue to be available

Preparation time at Dovenby Hall in 2005/2006, with two new cars for Marcus Grönholm and Mikko Hirvonen closest to the camera. By this time the Stobart team was also prominent, and other cars, for private owners, were also being worked on.

For 2007, M-Sport had a formidable driving team who won eight WRC events outright between them:
Marcus Grönholm (left) with five victories, and Mikko Hirvonen (right) with three.

from the end of 2006, and the notion of M-Sport building up a 'dream team' died soon after that.

Even before Citroën confirmed that Loeb would lead a semi-private team for 2006 and beyond, rumours had spread that he would be joined there by Marcus Grönholm (who was currently Peugeot's joint team leader, and known to be unhappy in that position). In view of this, what would shortly take place at M-Sport was quite astonishing. Within days, Malcolm Wilson startled the rallying establishment by signing Grönholm for 2006 and 2007, and before long he would also announce that Grönholm – a two-time World Rally Champion, who had already won 18 individual WRC events – would be joined by Mikko Hirvonen. Hirvonen was a rising star in 2005, who had recently been impressing everyone with a handful of fine drives in a privately-financed 2003-model Focus WRC. In his last appearance of the year – in Spain's Rallye Catalunya

in October – he finished third behind the dominant works Citroëns, a timely defeat of all three of the officially-sponsored BP Ford entries. With generous sponsorship already guaranteed from BP and Castrol, this was an extremely promising-looking line-up.

Until the last moment, incidentally, M-Sport had hoped to persuade Markko Märtin to rejoin the team. The trauma of his accident, while driving a Peugeot in the Wales Rally GB, had clearly doused the Estonian's love of the sport, and he refused the opportunity. He would finally announce his total retirement from rallying at the very beginning of the 2006 season.

All in all, M-Sport's arrangement proved to be inspired. In 2006, Grönholm won no fewer than seven of the 16 events, along with placing second three times and third twice, while the 25-year old 'apprentice' Mikko Hirvonen won once, finished second three times, and earned four third places. The

MARCUS GRÖNHOLM

Here was the classic case of a rally driver who was very well known in his sport, but little-known within Ford. He only drove for the company for two full seasons, in 2006/2007. It was almost a case of 'he came, he won, he left.' He had already been the winner of the World Rally Championship for Drivers twice, in 2000 and 2002, and yet Ford made little of his stupendous publicity potential while he was in its team for two extremely successful seasons. In a stellar front-line rallying career, he competed in 152 World Rally Championship events, and won no fewer than 30 of them.

Born in the Finnish city of Espoo, in 1968, Marcus Grönholm took up rallying in 1987, in a privately-owned Ford Escort 1300, and competed several times in the Finnish 1000 Lakes Rally. He went on to join the works Toyota team (which was based in Cologne, Germany) in the mid-1990s.

There was no good fortune before 2000 (his previous best result was second place in the 1995 1000 Lakes Rally), but he was then captured by Peugeot for a full 206 WRC programme, at which point the big headlines then began. He notched up his first outright victory in Sweden in February 2000, and won three more times in 2000 to become World Rally Champion. Thereafter, he was always competitive, winning three more times in 2001, and a further five times in 2002, when he became World Rally Champion once again.

More Peugeot victories followed in 2003, 2004, and 2005, but he wasn't as happy with the 307 WRC he drove in that final year as he had been with the lighter 206. Perhaps it was the tragic death of his friend and colleague Michael Park (Markko Märtin's co-driver) in an accident during the 2005 Wales Rally GB which left him deeply unhappy. Originally it seemed as if he would transfer allegiance from Peugeot to Citroën; Peugeot had confirmed an earlier 2004 announcement that it was to abandon the sport as a works team in favour of its (corporate) colleagues at Citroën. Hearing this, Malcolm Wilson made haste to raise funds to meet Grönholm's high fees (having the BP sponsorship deal helped enormously), and the resulting deal bore immediate fruit in the next two seasons. Grönholm would win twelve WRC events in the Focus WRC, and finished second in the World Rally Championship for Drivers in each of those years.

As noted in the main text (page 134), the announcement in September 2007 of his decision to retire from rallying was an unwelcome surprise to all, but it was not to be the end of his involvement in motorsport. He sat out the 2008 season, except for a few international rallycross events, and turned down a series of potentially lucrative offers from Ford, Citroën, and Subaru. Apart from the very occasional 'celebrity' appearance for one or other of these teams, he made no attempt to get back into mainstream rallying.

Grönholm retired in 2007, at 39 years old. He was still quick enough, and still much in demand, but he insisted that he wanted to stop there and then: while, as he said, he "still had the speed to win rallies …"

battle between Grönholm and Loeb in his Citroën went on for most of the year. Ultimately, though, because Loeb won eight events, he also took the World Rally Championship for Drivers by a single point.

The season started in a manner that M-Sport surely hoped would continue. The Rallye Automobile Monte Carlo, in January, had Marcus Grönholm driving a car so new that his own preferred seat was not even fitted until 'shakedown day.' Nevertheless, he was settled happily into second place behind – guess who – Sébastien Loeb, until the Frenchman went off the road. Loeb remained stuck for several minutes before a patriotic display of spectator-power restored his unfamiliarly-

liveried blue Citroën back on the stage. Grönholm was now in the lead, and the lanky Finn made no mistakes, winning with a margin of just 62 seconds. Team-mate Hirvonen was more circumspect in the new car, but still managed seventh place.

Then – miracle of miracles – M-Sport took the same two cars up to Sweden, slightly refreshed and carefully prepared, where Grönholm beat Sébastien Loeb yet again. Both suffered the kind of problems that would force you or me to visit a garage. In its case, however, all that was needed was a visit to the cold mechanics, in Swedish midwinter, to rectify the problem in minutes. For Grönholm's, there was a difficulty in starting from parc fermé in the bitter cold, and later a hydraulic

This was the 'Class of 2006,' as the drivers lined up in Monte Carlo for the start of the year. Marcus Grönholm, who would win seven WRC events that year, is third from the left in the front row.

Marcus Grönholm and his Focus WRC EU55 BMV, on the start line of the 2006 Swedish Rally, which he won outright.

Marcus Grönholm drove EU55 BMV eight times in 2006, winning four of those outings. Here, he's on his way to victory in the Acropolis Rally, with the car looking a bit battered and scraped by the rough conditions.

Marcus Grönholm celebrates his fourth victory of 2006, this time in his native Finland.

Once again driving 'BMV,' Grönholm won the Rally of Turkey in October 2006, his fifth of a phenomenally successful season.

Grönholm won the 2006 Rally New Zealand very comfortably in EU55 CNN, with team-mate Mikko Hirvonen close behind him in second place.

In a hurry, as usual; Marcus Grönholm and his Focus WRC, on his way to a time control on Wales Rally GB. This would signal his seventh victory in a single season, and helped Ford secure the World Rally Championship for Manufacturers.

leak plastered the windscreen and nearly immobilised the car. Even so, Grönholm set more fastest stage times than any of his rivals, and team-mate Hirvonen might even have joined him on the podium if the engine alternator belt (which also drove the water pump) had not broken. As it was, the breakage caused overheating and almost immediate retirement.

This run of good fortune could not last, even with drivers of the calibre of Grönholm and Hirvonen on board. Sure enough, in Mexico the streak of good luck finally came to an end. Starting at the front of the field on the first day, Grönholm had to act as the 'road sweeper' for everyone else. He struggled to produce times on par with Petter Solberg's Subaru and Sébastien Loeb's Citroën behind him, then put his Focus off the road where there were no spectators to help him get back on track. The regulations allowed him to restart on day two, after which he struggled up to eighth place at

Service – cold but calm – for Marcus Grönholm's new car on the 2006 Rallye Automobile Monte Carlo.

Ford top management in Monte Carlo. Left to right: Ian Slater, John Fleming and Jost Capito.

Marcus Grönholm on his way to victory on 'home snow' in Sweden, February 2006.

Mikko Hirvonen hard at work in Spain, with no time to look at the view.

the finish, though without recording a single fastest time. Hirvonen, similarly, went off the road while fighting for a place in the top five. He could not be retrieved until the end of the day, but eventually rejoined and took 14th place. This, in other words, was an event to forget, though both cars had to face expensive rebuilds and would not be used again until the Rally Argentina, seven weeks down the line.

Loeb was expected to set most – if not all – the fastest times in the Spanish RallyRACC Catalunya. In the event, however, Marcus Grönholm found his ex-Monte-winning Focus set up to be exactly to his liking and stormed off into the distance in first place. Unfortunately, on the fifth stage both of M-Sport's Focus WRCs suddenly shed the turbocharger wastegate of their engines, later found to be a classic failure of the holding down bolts. This had never happened before, and totally mystified technical chief Christian Loriaux. Regardless, the delay caused by the cars staggering into service and having new parts installed

meant that the damage was done. Grönholm lost the lead, Hirvonen slipped off the leaderboard, and a struggle for credibility ensued.

The fight back began on the second morning, from tenth and 14th places for Grönholm and Hirvonen respectively. Grönholm was so dominant (and perhaps inspired by his misfortune) that he had pulled back to fourth place by the end of day two, and was fastest on every one of the four Sunday stages. This cemented him in third place, though he was not quite able to catch the leading Citroëns.

Encouraged by this rather startling performance, M-Sport sent the same two refreshed cars to contest the Tour de Corse just two weeks later, where both came astonishingly close to outright victory on the serpentine tarmac roads of the Mediterranean island. Grönholm fought tooth and nail with Loeb's Citroën right from the start, holding second place at the end of the first day, and continuing to hold it convincingly until the end of the event. Grönholm set five fastest stage

Mikko Hirvonen and Phil Short talk tactics on Corsica.

times and achieved five other 'podium' placings. Hirvonen, for his part, soon settled into fourth, which he held comfortably until the end of the event.

The euphoria stemming form the early season Monte Carlo and Sweden victories had somehow already evaporated, and matters weren't helped when the long trip to Argentina for late April soon proved to be a waste of time. To begin with, on the first day, Grönholm's car stuttered to a halt with a totally seized transmission, but thanks to the odd rules governing WRC competition, he was allowed to 'retire' on the first day, have his car repaired overnight, and restart on day two. Accordingly, at the end of the event he was credited with tenth place, and had no fewer than seven fastest and seven second-fastest times credited to him. Team-mate Hirvonen was less lucky,

Mikko Hirvonen taking a tight tarmac hairpin in a picturesque old village, Corsica 2006.

when his engine expired after eight stages, with no hope of an overnight repair.

Even more frustrating was the team's disappointment in Rally d'Italia Sardegna (Sardinia, Italy). Grönholm stepped into his Monte-winning car (EU55 BMV) expecting the event to be a hot, gusty, loose-surfaced race where the Focus WRC would be ideal. And so it was, for just seven stages. On the eighth stage (on day two), the Focus jumped high and landed with a crunch. The engine sump shield bent, which in turn smashed the engine oil cooler; in an instant it was game over.

Technical chief Christian Loriaux blamed himself for this, as the car had been running with a thicker sump shield at first, but a thinner and lighter version had been substituted for the Saturday and Sunday stages: "Everything we'd heard pointed to it being smoother and faster on leg two. You can't say this definitely wouldn't have happened with the thicker guard on, but it would have been more protection … We were just unlucky here."

Hirvonen, on the other hand, was lucky, if not quite lucky enough. He took second place behind the dominant Loeb, with five fastest times to his credit. Even with Mikko Hirvonen putting up this excellent performance, however, M-Sport was extremely unhappy about the whole weekend …

Finally, though, the tide seemed to turn for M-Sport. Grönholm produced an absolutely sparkling performance to win in the Acropolis Rally of Greece, claimed a close third place in Germany's Rallye Deutschland, and then took another victory in the Neste Rally Finland. In a way, M-Sport was expected to win in Greece, having claimed the event four times in the last six outings. Doubtless with this in mind, Grönholm put up a really splendid show (he beat Loeb's Citroën, if not decisively, then comfortably), and set no fewer that 11 fastest stage times in the 18 competitive sections of this rough and demanding event. Perhaps, though, he should have expected this, for the Focus he was driving (EU55 BMV) was the self-same machine that had already helped him deliver two wins in 2006, in Monte Carlo and Sweden.

For M-Sport, one of the high points in Greece was the attendance of Ford 'top brass,' including John Fleming, Steve Odell, Ian Slater and Ingvar Sviggum who, between them, controlled Ford of Europe's decisions over money and marketing; hence Malcolm Wilson's anxiety for his team to put on a good show for them, which it duly did. The other highlight was the holding of the original super special stage

in the modern Olympic stadium, which attracted tens of thousands of spectators. The fact that Hirvonen took third place overall was a real bonus.

A nine week gap then gave the hard-pressed mechanics a chance to reintroduce themselves to their families, though this did not stop the ceaseless building, testing, repairing, and development of the Focus WRC for future events. Perhaps pessimistically, M-Sport did not expect to beat the flying Citroëns on the all-tarmac Rallye Deutschland, which was what one media cynic described as "ideal Loeb country …" Nor did it, in the end, but Marcus Grönholm still took a sturdy third place behind two Citroëns, with two fastest and six second-fastest stage times. Mikko Hirvonen, in his sister car, was settled into fifth place until the last hours, where he suffered first from an engine pipe that came loose, and then finally from a failed alternator that left the Focus stranded a the side of a public road.

Just seven days later (lunatic pre-season planning by the authorities had made for a very tight schedule) the entire WRC circus had to transplant itself from West Germany to Jyväskylä, in central Finland. There, it had to repair and freshen up the same cars that had just competed in Germany, before tackling the high-speed gravel stages of the Neste Rally Finland, where average speeds were in the region of 80mph.

Both Grönholm and Hirvonen, of course, loved every minute of it; this was their home turf, and since Grönholm himself had won the event five out of the last six occasions (in Peugeots), he was expected to shine. He did not disappoint, setting fastest time on 12 of the 21 stages, and second fastest on six more. That he 'only' managed to beat Loeb by 67 seconds (Loeb was fastest five times) was a measure of just how determined the Frenchman was to match him, metre for metre.

More good news for M-Sport came from the fact that Hirvonen set four fastest times himself, finishing third overall and well ahead of the rest of the field. This meant that Ford was now steadily closing the gap on Citroën for the World Rally Championship for Manufacturers, an accolade it had not won since 1979.

In the meantime, two 'rough road' cars (EU55 CNF and EU55 CNJ, which had already been globe-trotting to Mexico and Argentina) had been flown back to Cumbria, completely refurbished, and were then flown half-way round the world to compete in Japan in September. Because of the distances

Marcus Grönholm for the high jump, in Japan 2006. He would finish second overall.

Co-ordinator John Millington and the two Finnish co-drivers working on the service plan before Japan in 2006.

Is this rallying, or show business? Downtown Kita Aikoku before the start of the 2006 Rally Japan.

involved, this was not one of the more popular events in the calendar, but as Marcus Grönholm had won the event in 2005 (in a Peugeot) there were high hopes.

In the end, it was a case of 'nearly, but not quite.' Although Grönholm set no fewer than 15 fastest stage times (out of 27 stages), he made two slight errors on the second day of the rally that cost him more than a minute. The result, hotly contested until the end, was that Grönholm finished second overall, just 5.6 seconds behind Loeb's Citroën. Mikko Hirvonen, fast becoming a very definite world-beating prospect in Ford's

M-Sport's spacious service park on the Rally of Turkey 2006.

future, again took third place, and the gap separating Ford and Citroën in the World Rally Championship for Manufacturers was cut to a mere 11 points.

Three weeks later, the WRC circus was back in Europe for the low-speed, rough and ready stages of Cyprus. Looking at the results table, it was very much a case of deja vu; not only did Loeb win once again, but Grönholm and Hirvonen also took second and third places. More than this was the fact that Grönholm led for the first one and a half days, setting nine fastest stage times, and the winning gap was a mere 21 seconds. The World Rally Championship for Manufacturers lead was now only seven points away.

Throughout the season, the Loeb vs Grönholm duel never looked like it would end. As Grönholm once commented in his (ghosted) column for *Autosport*: "It's amazing to think that, despite the fact Seb and I have different cars and different driving styles, we end up just a tenth of a second apart after a 30 kilometre stage …"

The rest of the season seemed to bunch together, giving the WRC teams a real sense of urgency and leaving all the team managers, planners, and co-ordinators quite out of breath. Not only would there be four WRC rounds in the next two months (Rally of Turkey, Rally Australia, Rally New Zealand,

and Wales Rally GB), but championship leader Sébastien Loeb was sidelined with a broken arm following a mountain bike accident on 26 September. It was soon clear that he would not be back behind the wheel for at last the rest of the calendar year. Everyone in rallying naturally felt sympathy for the unfortunate Frenchman. For Grönholm, though, the news meant that Loeb's lead in the World Rally Championship for Drivers might be surpassed, while M-Sport now looked certain to win the equivalent for Manufacturers.

For M-Sport at least, events would transpire in its favour. In the final four events, M-Sport cars won every time. One victory went to Hirvonen (his maiden win), while the other three were claimed by Grönholm; it was only his accident in Australia that stopped him winning the World Rally Championship for Drivers.

In Turkey, the Ford team put on a textbook performance, setting ten fastest stage times and 12 other podium times between it, and finishing first and second without drama and with no suggestion of team orders being applied. Just two weeks later – in Perth, Australia – it all went wrong for Grönholm. Leading the event at first, his front suspension hit a rock on a stage, causing the car to roll, and dropping him to dead last by the time he recovered the car (in all, he lost well over ten minutes in the incident). Undeterred, however,

A proud moment for M-Sport in Turkey,
where it celebrated a first and second place finish.

Grönholm began the long fight back up the leaderboard. By the end of the event he had set no fewer than ten fastest stage times, but ultimately remained 12 minutes behind event winner Mikko Hirvonen. His final result of fifth place put Loeb's championship lead just barely out of grasp.

Then came New Zealand, three weeks after Australia. Here, naturally, M-Sport used the same two cars that had performed so well in the previous event. There was ample time for the cars to be refreshed in the interim (Grönholm's car was actually flown back from Australia to Cumbria for work to be done, before being returned to New Zealand less than a week later). All the effort was clearly worthwhile; not only did Marcus Grönholm win yet another round of the

Four M-Sport-built Focus WRCs line up for Rally Australia. Left to right: Luís Pérez Companc's Stobart-entered car, the two official
M-Sport entries, and Matthew Wilson's leading Stobart car.

There was a totally unofficial – but fierce – competition to jump highest and longest at this point in Australia in 2006. Pictured is Mikko Hirvonen on his way to a fine outright victory.

Richard Parry-Jones, Ford's worldwide technical chief, and Malcolm Wilson celebrate the winning of the 2006 World Rally Championship for Manufacturers, in New Zealand 2006.

2006 series, but Mikko Hirvonen took second place, just 56 seconds behind him. Grönholm totally dominated the event, taking 13 fastest stage times, and only narrowly beaten on the other four stages.

Ford had won in New Zealand for the first time in many years (this was Grönholm's fourth victory in the event, the other occasions in Peugeots). The icing on the cake, however, was that with the win Ford had cemented its victory in the World Rally Championship for Manufacturers, eight seasons after the Focus WRC had started its glittering career. This was an outstanding performance all around, and M-Sport had made it into an even more special occasion by ensuring that Ford's worldwide technical chief, Richard Parry-Jones was present for the great day. It was Richard who, along with Martin Whitaker, had originally approved M-Sport's plans to develop the Focus

WRC. In New Zealand, his joy (captured on film while holding the trophy) was obvious to all.

This left only the Wales Rally GB event, based in Cardiff, to round off what had been a great season (Marcus Grönholm's failure to win the World Rally Championship for Drivers from Loeb – by a single point – was the only thing to mar the results). This final outing was not a stroll for Grönholm, but he led every single one of the 17 stages and won the event quite comfortably.

It was not quite the same happy season ending for Mikko Hirvonen, for although he was second fastest to Grönholm

The instant Marcus Grönholm crossed the final line of the final stage in the 2006 Rally of New Zealand, the management team erupted. Left to right: Phil Short, Jost Capito, Malcolm Wilson and John Millington.

on each of the first three stages, he slid off a track on the third, thumped the side of the Focus quite severely on his side of the bodyshell, and damaged the roll cage so badly that the scrutineers felt that they had no alternative but to disqualify him from making any further progress. Hirvonen was philosophical about all this and, knowing that he had already secured his team place for 2007, vowed to win the event himself next year.

M-Sport, therefore, was happy to face the 2007 season with real confidence. It clearly had a totally competitive rally car that could win events on tarmac, snow, and gravel stages, and its newly-won World Rally Championship crown gave it a certain serenity of approach to the future. With Marcus Grönholm clearly among the best of the best drivers, with Mikko Hirvonen growing in confidence and achieving greater results by the month, and with what now seemed like unrestrained backing from Ford Motor Co, even better fortunes were hoped for in the coming season.

The only cloud on the horizon was that Sébastien Loeb had recovered from his broken arm and hoped to come to terms with the new Citroën C4 SRC, in order to match Grönholm second-by-second, stage-by-stage. This would inevitably mean a return to ferociously competitive battles for outright victories between the two drivers.

As usual, the Ford vs Citroën rivalry kicked off in Monte Carlo where, this year, there was virtually no snow. As was almost expected by now, the French company took the

The triumphant end of a triumphant season: with Marcus Grönholm, Timo Rautiainen, and EU55 CNF on the podium at Cardiff, after Wales Rally GB in December 2006. It was Ford's first World Rally Championship for Manufacturers victory since 1979.

Although he usually had a smile on his face, John Millington's task as team manager/co-ordinator was very demanding.

M-Sport's workshops are vast but, as this 2006 study confirms, there was always plenty of activity at every work station. Some of the cars in this group, of course, are Fiestas being built for other rally categories.

honours on its home ground, but its victory was short-lived after Grönholm thrashed Loeb in the following Swedish Rally event. At the time, one had to wonder whether it was going to be like this all year. With the benefit of hindsight, it can be confirmed that yes, it would be.

Rallye Automobile Monte Carlo boasted 15 stages of mainly well-gritted tarmac roads, and Loeb was fastest on almost half of them. Grönholm, meanwhile, was unable to set a single fastest time, and suffered an unspecified Ricardo transmission problem mid-event, which almost caused his retirement. Finally, he had to settle for third place, while Mikko Hirvonen placed fifth.

In Sweden, where the snow lay deep and crisp and even, it was a different story. In the two weeks between events, the same two Focus WRCs had been trucked back to Dovenby Hall from Monte Carlo, where they were rebuilt and once again made ready, then shipped on to Karlstad via a North Sea ferry. What followed could never be described as a walkover: such events never were with Sébastien Loeb in opposition with a competitive car. Nevertheless, Marcus Grönholm's victory over Loeb by just 54 seconds also included no fewer than 11 fastest event times, as well as seven other podium times, in the 20-stage event. Hirvonen took third place overall, and Henning Solberg's fourth place in his Stobart VK Ford Rally Team Focus WRC rounded off a great weekend for Ford.

After this, the WRC teams had just five days to pack up in Karlstad and drive briskly across the border to Norway. There they needed to reach Hamar, north of Oslo, before setting up shop again ready to tackle the Rally Norway. M-Sport again used the same cars that had already competed in Monte Carlo and Sweden. This time, however, the cars had time for little more than the equivalent of an overnight 'wash and brush-up,' but the result of this rush was highly satisfactory.

Although Loeb was as rapid as expected, it did not help the Citroën team that the Frenchman went off on several stages. In the process, Loeb picked up considerable penalties, ruining his chances at taking the event, and finally ending up 18 minutes off the pace. This was a big surprise, but an even bigger one developed within M-Sport where, in the absence of any team orders to the contrary, Hirvonen won the event. He defeated Grönholm by just nine seconds, with both achieving about the same number of fastest, and near-fastest, times throughout the event. This was Hirvonen's second WRC event victory, and the general feeling was that it would not be the last.

By 2007 Mikko Hirvonen was enjoying himself, and almost matching Grönholm with his stage times: who needs contact with the track?

Mikko Hirvonen was rapidly reaching maturity as a driver in 2007, and was always likely to snatch a victory if Marcus Grönholm's car faltered.

Not only did M-Sport take first and second places in Norway, but Henning Solberg also notched up third in one of the Stobart Fords. The result was the first ever 'lock out' of the podium for the Ford Focus WRC, and Ford's first in general since Rally New Zealand in 1979.

Three weeks later, across the Atlantic and the Caribbean, Rally Mexico told a different story. Not only was the event to be a gravel rally, but it was to be held at a significantly high altitude too. Marcus Grönholm nevertheless fought it out, stage by stage and second by second, with Sébastien Loeb, the result being that Grönholm had to settle (most reluctantly) for second place. His final result put him just 56 seconds behind Loeb after 20 special stages, with the two notching up six fastest times each. Mikko Hirvonen, proving himself once again, placed third.

The WRC 'circus' returned to Europe, and the Rally de Portugal, where unseemly – even seemingly seedy at first –

Marcus Grönholm jumping high towards his victory in Sweden 2007.

Service in Sweden 2007, and a view of the massive under-engine skid shield carried by the M-Sport Focus of that period.

Mikko Hirvonen notched up his first WRC victory of 2007 in Norway, using the same car which he had already driven in Monte Carlo and Sweden.

events transpired. The usual battle between Ford and Citroën took everyone's attention for the entire weekend, but the focus was shifted when FIA officials stepped in to penalise both Fords (which were again the hard-working ex-Monte/Sweden/Norway cars). To quote rallying's senior historical doyen, Martin Holmes:

"Sébastien Loeb drove impeccably … he finished the rally less than a minute ahead of the Ford of Marcus Grönholm with Mikko Hirvonen nearly two minutes further behind. Six

A proud moment for M-Sport, Ford and the Focus WRC, with a complete 'lock-out' of results in Norway, 2007. From left to right: the top drivers were Marcus Grönholm (second), Mikko Hirvonen (winner), and Henning Solberg (Stobart car – third).

hours after the finish, however, all six '06 model Focus WRCs were given a five minute penalty for being fitted with too-thin rear side windows. This dropped Grönholm to fourth and Hirvonen to fifth … The spate of stewards' decisions dated 1st April seemed initially like an annual joke, but this was for real."

This overnight sensation caused several thoughts to spring forth. Was this caused by cheating, or by an accident in manufacture of the panes? How was the discrepancy discovered? How much advantage did Ford gain – if any – by running undersized and, one assumes, lighter windows? Team boss Malcolm Wilson was adamant that nothing underhand had been involved, and that the windows had come from a regular supplier. The stewards, meanwhile, made sure that the thickness of the panes was accurately measured with micrometers. It was later suggested that samples had somehow been stolen from M-Sport's spares stocks in the service park in Portugal, but who was the individual who had read tea leaves, and bothered to measure the thickness of them?

Whatever the case, the damage was done. For a short time there was a hunt for perpetrators, but the end result was that this was an unhappy, rigidly-applied use of regulations, and one that resulted in Grönholm losing his lead in the World Rally Championship for Drivers. It was with great relief for the team that, within a month, the WRC competition moved on. This time it was yet another trip across the Atlantic, to compete in Argentina (where the Focus had previously been victorious in 2002, piloted by Carlos Sainz).

Sensibly, M-Sport had left the Mexico cars on that side of the world, knowing that they would be competing in Argentina six weeks later. It had then flown out mechanics and new parts well in advance, so that much time could be spent in preparing the cars for the gravel stages of Argentina. Grönholm and Hirvonen took second and third places, behind the inevitable Loeb; "Second again," Grönholm was later quoted as saying, "I f*****g hate being second …"

The rally itself centred around Villa Carlos Paz, some 700km kilometres from Buenos Aires, but first there was a super special in the capital city, followed by a transporter transit for all the cars to the rest of the event. "Never Again," was the universal reaction from every European participant, and they got their way.

Two weeks later, and the world of rallying was back in a familiar environment. The Rally d'Italia Sardegna (taking part on the Italian island of Sardinia) operated on a sensible time schedule, on typical gravel tracks, and with an organisation that worked well. Not only that, but for M-Sport there was the delightful result that Grönholm and Hirvonen took first and second places (with Henning Solberg's Stobart car in fourth).

The Focus cars used in Sardinia were the very same as those that had already been seen in 2007's Rallye Automobile Monte Carlo, Swedish Rally, and Rally de Portugal. This speaks volumes for the rugged, near bomb-proof, manner in which the Focus WRCs were habitually being prepared at this time. Not that the drivers were ever soft on them: Grönholm, for

*Marcus Grönholm hurries towards
victory in the Rally of Italy – held on
the island of Sardinia – in 2007.*

*The Acropolis Rally of Greece had
always been one of Ford's most
successful events. Marcus Grönholm
won in 2007: the fifth such victory for
Ford in the 2000s.*

instance, damaged one suspension corner of his car at one stage, before shunting and losing his spare wheel at another. He did, however, have the relief of seeing Loeb crash his Citroën. Suddenly, miraculously, it seemed the lead in the World Rally Championship for Drivers had changed again … Would it last?

Grönholm had clearly decided that it should, because the Acropolis Rally of Greece – another Mediterranean event, with the same temperatures, dust, and atmosphere as Sardinia – was to be another triumph for the lanky Finn. Since this was Ford's sixth win at the event in eight years, and Grönholm's second (having won the previous year), there was a definite lift in the team's morale.

There was more to come, much more. The entire organisation could now look forward to something approaching a summer holiday, with no fewer than eight whole weeks between the Acropolis Rally of Greece and the next event, the Neste Rally Finland.

M-Sport was delighted to announce, at the beginning of July, a new sponsorship deal with the Abu Dhabi Tourism Authority. The link-up came into effect at once, but from the beginning of 2008 the team was to be known as – deep breath time – the 'BP Ford Abu Dhabi World Rally Team'. The car liveries would gradually change to make the most of the new sponsor, and a third regular driver – Sheikh Khalid Al Qassimi – would join Grönholm and Hirvonen in the team's line-up.

Malcolm Wilson and Jost Capito stand proudly in front of all eleven Focus WRCs that lined up on the Neste Rally Finland in 2007 (the front pair are official M-Sport cars). This was a new world record for the number of WRC-specification cars that had started any rally up to this point.

Once it took effect, the Abu Dhabi sponsorship of M-Sport cars became very emphatic!

This was an enormous leap forward for Malcolm Wilson, M-Sport, and the Focus WRC programme in general. This deal would underpin the entire programme for a five year period (thought, potentially, to be worth more than £20 million). Cynically, perhaps, one could see this as a great

relief for Ford, as its current relationship with M-Sport was due to come to a close at the end of 2008, and the possibility remained that the factory deal would not be renewed. What's more, although we did not know it in 2007, by that time Ford's finances, alongside the world's economy, would be trembling.

Back to mid-2007, and Ford of Europe's President, John Fleming (who had already been seen on several WRC events, enjoying the successes of the Focus) commented: "Ford is delighted to welcome Abu Dhabi into the WRC. This is a major boost for the sport."

As ever, there was more to the deal than meets the eye, and it soon became known that Abu Dhabi and M-Sport had been talking about such a partnership since February 2007, and the government of Abu Dhabi had been in detailed discussion with both Subaru and Mitsubishi before that.

That was the good news that came out over the 'holiday' period. More worrying was the news that Marcus Grönholm was still undecided as to his future in the sport. At 39 years of age, he admitted that he was beginning to feel the strain. He

Marcus Grönholm at his best in the Neste Rally: in front of an adoring crowd, on his way to his seventh Finnish victory.

The substantial Abu Dhabi sponsorship deal was announced in mid-2007, with the original layout of the decals on the Focus WRC shown here.

Malcolm Wilson, the Abu Dhabi banner, and Sheikh Khalid Al Qassimi, making the sponsorship message very clear!

insisted that he was still totally happy with Ford and the Focus, but mentioned that he might retire completely at the end of 2007.

The engineering team, meanwhile, had a lot with which to occupy itself over the break. Not only was it engaged in normal preparation for the Neste Rally Finland, but it was also working on the newly-homologated 2007/2008 specification of the Focus WRC cars. This was more of a major rethink of the

Not much spare space in the engine bay of the 2007 Focus WRC.

New M-Sport recruit Khalid Al Qassimi getting used to European rallying conditions on tarmac, this being the Rallye Deutschland in 2007. All his previous outings in other makes of car had been on gravel rallies.

car's details, and was certainly not a brand new car. For the rest of the season, these updated cars would only be available to Grönholm and Hirvonen.

Work on the engine had resulted in some additional weight being pared off, with unnecessary parts of the block being machined away, lighter internal components, and a lighter one-piece exhaust manifold. At the same time, continued development work by Pipo Moteurs was claimed to have culminated in more low-speed torque.

The new version of the car was revealed at the same time as the Abu Dhabi sponsorship was announced, so one saw prominent Abu Dhabi logos on all corners of the car. There were changes to the front bumper moulding (the static ground clearance was raised a little to reduce the possible damage of 'nose-diving' on bumpy ground), as well as adjustments to the mounting of the rear spoiler. All-in-all, though, this was an update that mainly proved just how good the existing car had actually been.

Immediately after this development became known, Marcus Grönholm tackled the blisteringly fast stages of Finland. There he found that, for once, the car completely blew the Loeb/Citroën opposition out of the water, and won the Neste Rally Finland very convincingly. How convincingly? Well, there were 23 special stages, over which Grönholm set no fewer than 17 fastest and five second-fastest times. Whenever he didn't quite make it in front, his team-mate Mikko Hirvonen stepped in, setting five fastest times in his place. More than that, though, was the fact that this was Grönholm's seventh victory in the Neste Rally Finland: a new rallying world record in many categories.

Although M-Sport had given the Citroëns a sound thrashing in Finland, the situation was quickly reversed two weeks later; Rallye Deutschland – in Trier, Germany – offered tarmac stages upon which the French crews seemed to be quite unbeatable. Based west of Frankfurt and close to the border with Luxembourg, the event was very familiar to Loeb, who led the event almost from start to finish. Grönholm's Focus was always in contention, remaining in close pursuit until literally the final stage. There, he apparently flinched upon seeing an approaching cow that might have been trying to cross the unpoliced road. His reaction caused him to crash off the road, smash the rear of his Focus, and drop to fourth place.

Two weeks later, happily, it was a different story. Rally New Zealand saw Grönholm adjudged as the outright

Marcus Grönholm recorded his fifth outright WRC event victory of 2007 in New Zealand in September.

winner, but only by the record-setting margin of 0.3 seconds. This success – the second successive Focus win in New Zealand – was fought over 18 gravel stages, second for second, with Grönholm leading three times and Loeb twice. Another statistic emphasises just how close the event was: Grönholm set eight fastest stage time to Loeb's nine, while Loeb was second fastest eight times, but Grönholm nine times. After the first day Grönholm led by 13 seconds, but then Loeb was ahead by 1.7 seconds after day two. On the very last stage of all (a super special round on a manufactured stage near Hamilton), Loeb cut Grönholm's already-tiny lead by 0.4 seconds. The world's media was exhausted and exhilarated by this duel, so the effect on the drivers can only be imagined.

For M-Sport, Citroën, and world rallying in general, it was a real relief to have four weeks to return from Down Under, and build up new cars. For M-Sport this meant repreparing the Rallye Deutschland machines, though in the case of EU07 SSX

– the car in which Grönholm had 'flinched' at a cow – more than just cosmetic work was required.

In the meantime, Marcus Grönholm had finally decided that he was going to quit rallying at the end of 2007. At that point – mid-September 2007 – he still led Loeb for the World Rally Championship for Drivers, but had decided that enough was enough. In truly gentlemanly fashion, he had taken the decision in time for Malcolm Wilson and M-Sport to plan ahead for the after-Grönholm period.

Marcus himself had no doubt as to what should follow, urging Malcolm Wilson to 'promote' Jari-Matti Latvala, and give M-Sport an all-Finnish driving team:

"Mikko [Hirvonen] will replace me," Marcus commented, "and I think Jari-Matti definitely has the speed. Maybe he needs a couple more years to be perfect, but he is ready for number two."

There were to be no surprises in Spain, for the RallyRACC Catalunya. Although Grönholm's Focus set more fastest stage

Khalid Al Qassimi and Malcolm Wilson discuss the Focus, and tarmac rallying, in Spain in 2007.

Khalid Al Qassimi at speed in Spain, demonstrating the incredibly low tarmac 'stance' of the latest Focus WRC.

Mikko Hirvonen, on his way to fourth overall in Catalunya, in front of a large crowd.

Service under canvas – a long way from the scrappy side-of-the-road servicing of decades earlier.

times than Loeb's Citroën – eight against five – it was the Frenchman who was almost always in the overall lead, and who ultimately won by just 14 seconds. It was one particular stage – number six, in the rain – that made his point; Loeb's tyre choice eclipsed that of his Ford rival, so much so that in 26 kilometres he claimed a further quarter minute against his rival's time.

It was not all bad news for Ford, however, as the team was now in an almost unassailable position in the World Rally Championship for Manufacturers. Grönholm still led Loeb by six points in the drivers' counterpart, Mikko Hirvonen picked up fourth place overall, and no fewer than 12 Focus WRCs (all of which had originally been built at Dovenby Hall, of course) turned up at the start.

With the rallying season now sprinting towards an exciting climax – five WRC events were scheduled for the final eight weeks, and both major championships still had to be settled – the scene moved swiftly across the Mediterranean, to the island of Corsica. The Tour de Corse was another all-tarmac event where the Citroën/Loeb combination was expected to set all the standards. Sure enough, this was exactly what happened.

Marcus Grönholm on his way to a spirited second place in Corsica in 2007, just 24 seconds behind the winning Citroën.

This was the frenetic pre-rally signing session in Japan, in 2007.

The Focus WRC in Japan, showing off the very obvious Abu Dhabi support that M-Sport cars now carried.

A determined but happy Mikko Hirvonen in Japanese dust, on his way to victory.

Using the same cars as had just been driven in Spain, the M-Sport drivers tried their absolute utmost to keep abreast of the Citroën, but Grönholm could set only two fastest times in comparison with the nine set by Loeb. Once again the Finn finished second overall (this time by 24 seconds over 15 special stages). M-Sport retained a healthy lead in the Championship for Manufacturers, while Grönholm's lead over Loeb in the Championship for Drivers slipped to a mere four points.

Unhappily for Mikko Hirvonen, his event lasted just two stages. On the second, his Focus WRC slipped off the road, wiped off the right-hand rear wheel and much of the suspension, mangling the bodywork around it in the process, and ensuring that EO56 TZR would need a major rebuild before it looked rally-ready again for Ireland.

In the meantime, the entire 'circus' made its reluctant way around the world once again, returning to the unpopular venue of Kita Aikoku in Japan. By the end of Rally Japan both the leading contenders must have wished they had stayed in Europe, as both crashed out of the event. The end of Grönholm's event came on the fifth stage, where his accident

Celebrations at Rally Japan in 2007, for the Focus WRC's first success in that nation.

The ceremonial hand-over of duties as Ford's motorsport director, from Jost Capito (right) to Mark Deans.

Legends of a previous rallying age met contemporary legends in Ireland in 2007. Left to right: Timo Rautiainen, Michèle Mouton, Paddy Hopkirk and Marcus Grönholm.

Before the start of the 2007 Rally of Ireland, Marcus Grönholm was presented to HRH Princess Anne, whose chosen spectator sports are usually equine, or rugby union.

damaged the roll cage. This, according to the FIA's rigorously applied rules, meant that the car had to be withdrawn.

"I went off into a straw bale on the right-hander," Grönholm commented, "that span me round and threw the car off the road on the next left. The car dropped and landed on some trees. The sill next to me was pushed up ..."

Loeb, for his part, could never quite benefit from this mishap, and settled into second place before crashing badly in the middle of the second day. He only returned to set a series of fast times under meaningless 'SuperRally' conditions for the final day. Loeb's crash was explained when co-driver Daniel Elena admitted to reading out a false pacenote description, claiming that this was the first time he had ever committed this sin.

Where was M-Sport's Mikko Hirvonen while all this carnage unfolding? Serenely in the lead, it seemed; he took up the first place position before the end of the first day, and never let it slip thereafter. This was EJ56 FXA's first success (after three consecutive third places), and it would triumph yet again after returning to contest the Wales Rally GB a few weeks later.

This was for real: Grönholm's M-Sport Focus WRC racing past the front entrance to Belfast's seat of government, Stormont Castle, on the opening stage of Rally Ireland in 2007.

Then came a real novelty. Rally Ireland, which promised no fewer than 20 all-tarmac special stages, was competing in the WRC series for the very first time. What's more, there was a real quirk to the proceedings: whereas the event was to be based in Sligo, on the north west coast of the Republic of Ireland, the very first stage was held in and around the magnificent buildings of Stormont Castle in Belfast (this was the administrative head of the Northern Ireland government). A flight was organised between these two locations for the crews, while the rally cars had a leisurely transporter run.

For M-Sport, Rally Ireland brought mixed fortunes. On the one hand, Ford and M-Sport clinched the World Rally Championship for Manufacturers (this being back-to-back with the 2006 victory), but on the other hand Marcus Grönholm crashed out on the Lough Gill stage, leaving EU07 SSX badly crumpled against a stout stone wall. At first there

The Irish are incredibly enthusiastic about rallying, as is clear from this picture of Mikko Hirvonen tackling a hairpin junction in the peaceful countryside close to the West Coast.

In a change of personnel at the top, Jost Capito was promoted within Ford and Mark Deans (ex-Boreham) took over as motorsport director in late 2007.

2007's grand finale took place in Wales, based around Swansea and Cardiff, where what seemed like every rallying enthusiast in the country was out rooting for M-Sport and, in particular, Marcus Grönholm. The World Rally Championship for Drivers now stood with Loeb leading Grönholm by six points; even if Grönholm won the event outright, Loeb just had to finish fifth or higher to stay ahead of him in the rankings.

In the end, it was as if a Hollywood scriptwriter had prepared the scene for what happened over the three days. All except the Epynt stage were on gravel, and every driver was out to win, not just to count points. Ford elected to retrieve the cars that had competed in Japan, and give them a thorough rebuild at Dovenby Hall before transporting them down to Wales. M-Sport also prepared to give an emotional farewell to Grönholm, and Mikko Hirvonen was able to unleash the most dazzling of smiles to the media when it was confirmed that he would be leading the team in 2008.

Even with such a dramatic stage set, there was a real surprise as the event unfolded. It was Stobart-driver Jari-Matti Latvala, driving EJ56 FZB (starting its 12th event of 2007), who set no fewer than ten fastest times on the 17 stages in the event. The event had started badly for him, as his car's windscreen wipers had failed on an early stage while he was far from service support. From stage seven to the finish, however, he was continually fastest except for the rather pointless Cardiff-based super special, where Grönholm put in a sparkling encore. In the end, he finished in tenth place.

were worries for Grönholm himself, as the impact came on his side of the car, and he was knocked unconscious in the accident. After a brief stay in the local hospital in Sligo, however, he was released to make – he hoped – a full recovery and to prepare for the last event: both of the rally season, and of his career.

Hirvonen, meanwhile, struggled to keep on terms with the flying Citroëns. The rival cars having benefited from Loeb travelling to compete in an earlier event in the country, and he was only able to achieve fourth place overall. Jari-Matti Latvala put up a sparkling performance of his own in the leading Stobart Focus, managing to outpace Hirvonen and take third place overall: the highest finish a Stobart car had so far achieved. Grönholm's DNF (or Did Not Finish) meant that he had ceded the lead in the World Rally Championship for Drivers. It would now be all to play for in the Wales Rally GB, in two weeks' time.

A poignant but sad occasion, as Marcus Grönholm prepares to retire from rallying at the end of 2007. Malcolm Wilson presents him with a souvenir, showing rally plates from all his successes in M-Sport cars.

In the fog of 2007's Wales Rally GB, but this Focus WRC doesn't let that hinder its progress.

Rally GB winners in 2007 – Mikko Hirvonen and Jarmo Lehtinen holding the magnificent trophy which goes with that achievement.

Lewis Booth of Ford congratulates Marcus Grönholm with a handshake, on the occasion of the Finn's retirement from WRC competition.

Where were the principal protagonists while all this was going on? Loeb admitted that he was going rather cautiously, knowing that he could not match the Focus WRC drivers on British soil, while Marcus Grönholm – on his last-ever M-Sport outing – was always among the leaders, eventually finishing in second place. The winner, no question, was Mikko Hirvonen. His Focus WRC took the lead on the very first special stage, and never faltered. Ahead of Grönholm by nearly 40 seconds after day one, 36 seconds after day two, and 44 seconds at the end, this was a consistent, spectacular even, performance.

At the end of the year, therefore, M-Sport Focus WRCs had recorded eight outright wins, while Grönholm's final tally was five victories, as well as ending five events in second place and two in third. For everyone connected with this effort, it had been a remarkable year.

Could 2008 even be the equal of this?

THE STOBART VK M-SPORT FORD RALLY TEAM

Was this a works team or not? How closely were its fortunes, and its cars, related to the official BP Ford World Rally Team? This was something of a puzzle, and one that set the media to thinking in 2006. The fact is that, for 2006 and beyond, a second seriously-professional Focus WRC team was developed, also based at Dovenby Hall. The Stobart operation might have been separately administered (though Malcolm Wilson was still called 'team principal'), the cars were separate from those of the official BP Ford effort, and the mechanics separately employed, but there was one other extremely strong link: the Wilson name showed how close the relationship actually was.

Although Malcolm Wilson's son Matthew was only 18 years old, he was to be the regular team leader. He had started rallying as soon as he received his driving licence, had already won events in the UK, and even already suffered his first rallying injury (he broke his forearm on the Trackrod rally). Towards the end of 2005, he had won the Rally Ireland outright, making the otherwise cynical media sit up and take notice. Other drivers, it was suggested, would perform in some of the events, and would bring their own support (ie, finance) to make this possible.

By this stage a major sponsor – Eddie Stobart Trucks – had also become associated with rallying, and with M-Sport cars. Founded by the eponymous Eddie Stobart in Carlisle, this concern had grown into a massive haulage company, and was already supplying truck transportation for the M-Sport team. Stobart's first direct link with the WRC came in 2005, with entries in Rally d'Italia Sardegna, the Acropolis Rally of Greece, and Wales Rally GB, but, for 2006, efforts were to be ramped up. There was to be a two – or even three – car team entered into almost all the events in the calendar, and the team's name had expanded to The Stobart VK M-Sport Ford Rally Team, where VK stood for Vodka Kick, a co-sponsor company owned by rally enthusiast Steve Perez.

Throughout the year, Matthew Wilson was joined variously, and in many cases regularly, by Peter Tsjoen, Kosti Katajamäki, Luís Pérez Companc, Jari-Matti Latvala, Juan Pablo Raies and Andreas Mikkelsen. This team was more modestly set up, financed, and crewed than the front-line BP Ford team – and enjoyed modest success during the season, finishing a distant fifth in the World Rally Championship for Manufacturers – but certainly merits coverage of what was achieved.

It was usual to see two, or sometimes three, Stobart cars starting in every WRC event. Matthew Wilson started and finished in every event (his best result being eighth in Argentina), while the team's most outstanding finish was Jari-Matti Latvala taking fourth place in Wales Rally GB. For Matthew Wilson himself, to set a fastest stage time in Argentina was a real bonus.

For 2007, Stobart became even more ambitious, and used a series of close-to-current works-specification Focus WRCs. It now seemed to be very much the 'back-up' works (or M-Sport) team. Team leader, as before, was Matthew Wilson – still only 20 years old – who started all 16 WRC events, finishing 14 times and suffering not a single accident. His best result was sixth overall in Rally Wales GB, where he was beaten only by two 'official' BP Fords, two works Citroën C4s, and by Petter Solberg's Subaru Impreza. During the season Matthew was joined by Henning Solberg (who started and finished every one of the events, and recorded two third places in Norway and Japan), and Jari-Matti Latvala (similarly started all events, with a best of third in Ireland, and fourth places in Argentina and Corsica). Andreas Mikkelsen, Gareth Jones, and Alessandro Bettega also occasionally appeared on a one off-basis, sometimes with a financial helping hand from their personal sponsors.

As in 2006, the Stobart cars were as reasonably up-to-date, from a technical standpoint, as could be arranged at all times. They did not share any sponsorship or fuel/oil supplies with the 'official' M-Sport cars, nor did they enjoy any support from

Abu Dhabi when the Tourism Authority joined forces with BP for the official-sponsored team in mid-season. By the close of the season it was fairly clear that Malcolm Wilson and M-Sport were looking favourably on the development of Wilson's son, and were also impressed by the progress Latvala (who was still only 22 years old at the end of the 2007 season) was making. Time would prove that in both cases such judgement was well-founded.

NEW REGULATIONS IN 2006, AND A NEW FOCUS WRC TO MATCH THEM

As has already been noted in a previous chapter, M-Sport began lobbying Ford for the finance needed to help it develop a new-generation Focus WRC before the end of 2004. Approval for this was gained during the winter, and work began in early 2005. Although he was already happy to finally tackle an all-new car, technical chief Christian Loriaux was doubly delighted with the wider bodywork provision that would apply, and of which he intended to take full advantage.

It was Loriaux and M-Sport, in fact, that had started the move to legitimise wider-track rally cars in the first place. Up until this point, WRC regulations had limited the overall width of eligible cars to 1770mm/69.7in, but when Ford announced the new-generation Focus – on which a new model would have to be based – the width was already in excess of that figure.

It was therefore made clear to the FIA that unless it would authorise wider cars, M-Sport would have to withdraw from the World Rally Championship. When rival manufacturers, and the authorities, considered the implications of such a major participant having to withdraw from the sport, it was agreed to authorise a change. Widths of up to 1800mm/70.9in were to be allowed, but only for cars that were longer than 4200mm/165.4in. Soon after this, however, M-Sport clouded the horizon by stating that it might have to withdraw from rallying on financial grounds, and would not need the allowance for a wider-width car after all!

To quote a rival technical director, who by this point had already authorised a significant amount of money on making changes, "It was quite a silly situation, and sense only returned when Ford finally decided that it would come back and develop its new Focus after all."

Other wide-ranging changes to WRC regulations were also imposed. The FIA made it clear that only eight new chassis could be constructed by a team, with permission to "construct two extra chassis in case of 'complete destruction.'" Active front and rear differentials were banned, as was water injection into the engines, and water cooling sprays on the intercoolers.

Design work – starting from renderings on the team's computers – began just before the end of 2004, with detail design following in January 2005. Because the new-generation Focus road car was originally a five-door car, and

Christian Loriaux's neatly-engineered layout of the Focus WRC of the mid-2000s included upward facing cooling fans, and much neat but effective electronic wiring.

a three-door ST version was not scheduled to appear for some time, M-Sport gained another concession from the FIA so that it could start work on that three-door type. Each of the new shells, incidentally, would take up to 12 weeks to construct.

Apart from the fact that the new Focus would take shape around a new bodyshell, the most important innovation was that Loriaux had decided to ditch the existing Xtrac longitudinal transmission in favour of a totally fresh five-speed Ricardo system. The main gearbox was to be mounted alongside the engine in such a way that would be totally familiar to millions of users throughout the world. Ricardo, of course, was a larger concern than Xtrac, and came with the added bonus of its transmission division being based close to Coventry.

For some context, Harry Ferguson Research had been set up in the 1950s in order to develop a four-wheel drive 'peoples' car.' This project was later abandoned, and the company pivoted to become FF Developments, a true four-wheel drive specialist. Over time, the company progressed to designing four-wheel drive systems for several Ford cars, such as the Sierra, Granada, Escort (both the RS Cosworth and Escort WRC), and RS200 models. During this period, the company was sold to Ricardo, in 1994, continuing to operate under the name FFD-Ricardo. It would be this talent that would lend itself to the new Focus transmission.

In later years, Christian Loriaux made his reasoning for the move to Ricardo very clear:

"The original Focus WRC had a longitudinal gearbox, which in my opinion was wrong … you were moving the centre of gravity of the box backwards by about 40cm/16in, but you were also making it 30kg/66lb heavier. If we could make the transmission a normal layout, you might save all that, and your weight distribution would be much better. We reviewed that layout, saved a lot of weight, and saved on 90-degree turns of torque too. On tarmac too; we were running a trick centre differential, so that we had permanent drive to the rear wheels. On tarmac we could use rear-wheel drive only, but clutching drive to the front wheels when we wanted."

In the Mk2 Focus production car, the latest-generation 2-litre engine featured an aluminium cylinder block. Rally car development work (M-Sport and Pipo Moteurs, in France, were jointly responsible, with Cosworth no longer

involved) began before the end of 2004, with the first examples ready by May/June 2005. Assembly of the first car began during the summer, and the very first tests of the car were carried out as late as October, just in time to gain sporting homologation, and the chance to enter Rally Australia in November. At this point, new-signing Marcus Grönholm had seen the car, but hadn't had a chance to drive it.

The suspension of the new car was a lineal development from that of the 2005 car. There was initial excitement among the media that the tyres were now quoted as being 'BF Goodrich,' but this was primarily a marketing decision by Michelin (who owned the once-independent American brand) to restate its priorities.

Changes to the 2006 machines came regularly, and were mainly confined to improvements to the reliability and durability of the cars. This was due to the latest changes in regulations, limiting the amount of new chassis that could be constructed. Each car, as a result, was having to be used more frequently – and more intensively – than ever before. Clearly the basic specification was a success, with Marcus Grönholm in particular either winning or finishing very close behind the winner (usually Sébastien Loeb) in most events. Even when the car let him down, or was crashed, he still contended for a top placing. During the season there were seven outright victories in 16 rallies, which compared with the eight outright victories (all by Sébastien Loeb) recorded by Citroën.

For the start of the 2007 season, with new homologation regulations promised but not yet enacted by the FIA, M-Sport pushed on into the WRC series with only minor changes from 2006. While it was known 'in the business' (though not announced in advance) that a major sponsor would soon join forces with M-Sport, the pause in technical change was much more widely known. Happily, of course, the towering talents of Marcus Grönholm ensured that the victories continued to flow even in absence of substantial technical changes. Before the Rallye Automobile Monte Carlo, Malcolm Wilson confirmed that he did not expect the new batch of changes to be introduced before mid-season, starting with the Neste Rally Finland. These, when they came, were not announced in detail, and were quite overshadowed by the big news of sponsorship by the Abu Dhabi Tourism Authority.

WORKS M-SPORT CARS USED – 2006 AND 2007
2006

Amazingly, M-Sport's front-runners, Marcus Grönholm and Mikko Hirvonen, used only six different cars during the intensive 16-event 2006 World Rally Championship series (thanks to the rigid rules prohibiting the use of what we might once have called 'cloned' cars, this was a genuine tally). Grönholm started an incredible eight events in EU55 BMV, winning on four of those occasions; not even Colin McRae had been able to achieve that.

These were the six cars:

EU55 BMV
EU55 BNA
EU55 CNF
EU55 CNJ
EU55 CNN
EU55 CNX

EU55 BMY and EU55 BMZ, the two original second-generation cars that had been used in only one event in 2005 (Rally Australia), were not seen in events at all during 2006. They were instead relegated to the important task of being test cars.

None of the original cars from 2006 were ever to be used in 2007 by the official M-Sport team.

2007

EU55 CNV
EJ56 FXA
EJ56 FZB
EJ56 FZV
EO56 TZR
EU07 SSX
EU07 STX

FOCUS WRC CARS USED BY THE STOBART TEAM – 2006 AND 2007
2006

S568 RHH
EK52 NWN
EG53 AVD
1 ES*
EF04 VVB
EF04 WBW
EU55 BNA**
EU55 CNK
EU55 CNV

* usually hiding another identity, mainly S568 RHH
** ex-BP-Ford team used for one event only

Except for EU55 BNA, which was used under Stobart colours by Jari-Matti Latvala, the Stobart and M-Sport team cars were not swapped about during the year. Even that one-off use can be explained by the fact that Latvala had just been signed up by the Stobart team for 2007, so this effectively qualified as a 'test run.' In M-Sport hands, earlier in 2006, EU55 BNA had already competed (and finished, with honour) eight times in Mikko Hirvonen's hands – and after the Stobart run on Wales Rally GB, it was permanently taken over by the Stobart team for 2007.

2007

1 ES
S568 RHH
EG53 CCN
EU55 BMZ
EU55 BNA
EU55 CNF
EU55 CNJ
EU55 CNK
EU55 CNX
EJ56 FZB
EJ56 FZV

CHAPTER **SEVEN**
2008-2010 – Winning to the end

S ettling on an M-Sport driver line-up for 2008 had taken up some time in the last few months of 2007. Marcus Grönholm had given Malcolm Wilson a lot of notice of his intention to retire from the sport, but to attract someone of similar talent was always going to be impossible.

In the end, Mikko Hirvonen moved up to become the 'number one,' and as early as September 2007 names such as Petter Solberg (unhappy with his lot at Subaru) and Markko Märtin (who was officially still 'retired') were being mooted in the press. Even François Duval was considered for a time. Finally, just before Christmas 2007, Malcolm Wilson happily welcomed Jari-Matti Latvala to the regular M-Sport driving roster (there was never any inference, or intention, of painting him as a 'second driver' to Hirvonen, for he had already shown impressive pace in the Stobart cars during 2007). At the same time, it was confirmed that Sheikh Khalid Al Qassimi (who hailed from the UAE, of course) would also compete in ten of the 15 rounds.

Once the Abu Dhabi sponsorship deal was signed in 2007, Khalid Al Qassimi joined the M-Sport driving team.

After observing the 2006 and 2007 seasons, where Marcus Grönholm had won no fewer than 11 WRC events for M-Sport, it was accepted that 2008 might not be so startlingly successful for the Focus. Nevertheless, the season turned out to be very successful for the team, with four further outright victories (in 15 starts), and M-Sport finishing a close second to Citroën in the World Rally Championship for Manufacturers.

The season started in fine style with two brand new cars (EU07 SSZ and EU07 SUF), both of which would complete nine WRC events during the year, securing an outstanding 12 podium positions between them. Not many enthusiasts realise just how hard such cars were being worked in the early 2000s; an average works Escort of the 1970s or 1990s, for comparison, tended to tackle no more than four or five events before being pensioned off as a test and practice machine.

The Focus WRC was clearly still competitive as it took to the stages of the Rallye Automobile Monte Carlo, and likely to win events. However, the persistent problem of the last few seasons (rarely uttered out loud, but realised by all) continued into the new year; namely, the growing dominance of Citroën and Sébastien Loeb as major competition. Hirvonen was more competitive than ever during the event, but could not quite keep up with the flying Citroëns (the roads were almost completely clear of snow and ice, a situation that did not favour the Finn). Latvala was hampered by punctures that arose after he veered slightly off the line and broke an alloy wheel on two occasions, as well as his car suffering a broken rear suspension arm in one of those incidents.

Incidentally, if there was anything likely to bring a bit of cheer to Ford after this event, it was that François Duval – in a 'guest appearance' for the Stobart team – finished fourth overall, a mere 1.1 seconds away from a podium finish.

Just two weeks later the professional teams had all packed up and transported their cars, personnel, and kit to Karlstad, setting up shop for the Swedish Rally. In an event where there was far less snow and ice than usual for Sweden in February, Jari-Matti Latvala – Ford's new recruit – took the overall lead on the second of 18 special stages, and held it to the end. This was a wonderful boost for him, and for the team, as it was his very first WRC victory (many more would follow, but not in 2008). Mikko Hirvonen came in behind Latvala, placing second. Among the many records set by Latvala at this time was one that marked him as the youngest-ever driver to win a WRC event.

Jari-Matti Latvala won his first WRC rally for M-Sport in Sweden in 2008.

Jari-Matti Latvala enjoying the adulation of a large Scandinavian crowd in the 2008 Swedish Rally, on his way to his first-ever WRC event victory.

Mark Deans, once a junior member of the Boreham hierarchy, became the motorsport director at Ford in the late 2000s, supervising the company's involvement in the World Rally Championship scene.

Rallying isn't always glamorous: this was Latvala's passage through thick, choking, dust in Mexico in 2008.

For once, the Citroëns had failed to shine, with Loeb actually retiring after leaving the road. The M-Sport team thought, justifiably, that it deserved a bit of good luck, and it enjoyed it throughout the event. Not only that, but the Stobart team provided Gianluigi Galli with third place. This was great news to M-Sport, as the result meant that the Ford Focus WRC had a lock-out on the podium positions of this prestigious event.

The same two M-Sport cars were speedily brought back to the UK, completely refreshed at Dovenby Hall, and flown out to Mexico for the third event of the year. Rally Mexico – with its warm, dry, conditions, and often considerable altitudes – saw the team cars take third and fourth places. It was now abundantly clear that Latvala could generally maintain the

Jordan is beautiful, but mainly a Middle Eastern wilderness, as Mikko Hirvonen discovered on his way to victory in 2008.

same pace as Mikko Hirvonen. In fact, Latvala led the rally for nine stages, before his engine unhappily suffered from a high-pressure turbo pipe failure. The pipe leaked air in precisely the worst location, completely upsetting the engine tune until the car reached service, and costing him more than two minutes and two places on the leaderboard. Hirvonen had seemingly drawn the 'unlucky straw' before the event, and his car suffered from various punctures throughout, which in the end meant that he was a full two minutes behind team-mate Latvala.

Rally Argentina – an event that M-Sport had not won since Carlos Sainz's swansong victory in 2002 – then followed, but proved an expensive waste of time. Although both team cars led to begin with, Latvala put his Focus off the road on the first day and lost several minutes before it could be retrieved, and just one stage later Hirvonen's car suffered suspension damage. On day two Latvala came off the road again, then discovered a broken electrical connexion meant that the engine could not be started after it had stalled.

To the amusement of the official WRC TV camera crew, Jari-Matti Latvala proved that human beings really do float in the waters of the Dead Sea in Jordan, in 2008.

In earlier days, final retirement would have been inevitable for both machines, but in 2008 cars were allowed to be classified at the end – because of the byzantine way in which retired cars were allowed to be rebuilt overnight – and compete in the final stages, albeit taking significant penalties. Over the course of the event, Hirvonen and Latvala set eight fastest stages times (and ten other podium times) between them. However, since they were respectively 25 minutes (minutes, not seconds) and 50 minutes behind Loeb's winning pace by the end of the event, this was a real humiliation: the first that M-Sport had suffered for a very long time indeed.

A brief stint back home followed, before moving on to the Middle East for the Jordan Rally. M-Sport was using the totally refreshed Monte Carlo/Sweden/Mexico cars, and there was an immediate – and very welcome – change of fortune for the team. The WRC cavalcade had descended on Jordan for the very first time, finding a beautiful country in which 22 (sometimes remote) gravel stages were located. For Mikko Hirvonen, in complete contrast with his recent unhappy visit to Argentina, this was a truly triumphant outing. Not only did he drive in contention throughout, but he took and held the lead towards the end. Along the way he set four fastest stage times, as well as three second-fastest and no fewer than ten third-fastest times.

The Jordan Rally made much of the locale's heritage, placing the ceremonial start amid the Roman ruins of Alwadi on the shores of the Dead Sea. Ford's much-respected third driver, Sheikh Khalid Al Qassimi, was the only works pilot with any previous experience of rallying in this part of the world. All three M-Sport Focus WRCs reached the finish, after some carefully choreographed strategic driving allowed them to start the final day behind Dani Sordo's Citroën, which was acting as an unwilling 'sand sweeper' for the stage (the seasoned strategist Phil Short was behind this manoeuvre), the result being that Latvala and Hirvonen were only 8.5 seconds and10.4 seconds adrift at that point.

All would have been well if Latvala had not then gone off the road and damaged his suspension in an incident that cost him more than ten minutes and six places. The more seasoned Hirvonen swept smoothly along, pushing Sordo down to second place, and won outright by 76 seconds. Henning Solberg's Stobart-supported Focus WRC put in another seasoned performance, taking fourth place, and

Mikko Hirvonen flying high, on his way to second place in Sardinia in 2008.

Matthew Wilson came in at fifth. With seven Focus WRCs finishing in the top ten, it had been a good weekend for M-Sport, and for Ford.

In the next four events – from the Rally d'Italia Sardegna in mid-May to the Neste Rally Finland at the end of July – M-Sport had a very hectic time in keeping its cars fresh and competitive. Solace could be taken, at least, in the fact that three of those events were around the Mediterranean, and the fourth was in Finland. All of the events were familiar to the team and its drivers, and all were likely to be good for the versatile and still-improving Focus WRC.

Before these events, the results stood with Ford just barely leading both the World Rally Championship for Manufacturers *and* the World Rally Championship for Drivers. It seemed ungracious, therefore, that Ford (via its motorsport director, Mark Deans) commented publicly that it thought the World Rally Championship was under-promoted, and that there might be a change in the company's relationship with M-Sport at the end of the season.

M-Sport's immediate reaction to this blast from its paymaster was to guide its drivers to finish second and third on the gravel stages of Sardinia. Jari-Matti Latvala set no fewer than ten fastest stage times (of the total 17 stages), only failing to win the event outright after coming off the track at one point. The incident punctured one of his tyres

Jari-Matti Latvala, sideways in the dust, in the 2008 Acropolis, where he set five fastest special stage times.

and cost him up to two minutes, leaving him languishing in seventh place before climbing back up to third by the end of the event. Hirvonen, who was never quite as astonishingly fast as his team-mate this weekend, finally took second place overall. He ended immediately behind – who else – Loeb's Citroën. Once again there was a distinguished performance from a Stobart car, with Gianluigi Galli taking fourth place behind Hirvonen.

Just two weeks later it was almost the same story in Greece, where the Acropolis Rally had reverted to its traditional 'showpiece' start beneath the Parthenon itself. Unfortunately for BP Ultimate, the main sponsors of the event, M-Sport (its principal rallying clients) could not quite finish at the top of the podium. Mikko Hirvonen ended with third place, just two minutes behind the winning Citroën in a 20-stage event. At one point the M-Sport cars had been in second and third places, but both went off the road briefly at the same spot, hitting the same unforgiving part of the Greek landscape in the process. More dramas followed – including a high-pressure turbocharger pipe failure, and

a broken suspension link following another excursion – leaving neither car able to approach a win, and scuppering the chance to make it seven Focus WRC successes in Greece since 2000.

The mood suddenly changed when the team migrated to Turkey in June. The two ex-Acropolis cars were once again painstakingly rebuilt, freshened up and placed on the starting line. This was an event that Marcus Grönholm's Focus WRC had won in 2007, so there were hopes among the M-Sport personnel for a repeat performance, and to everyone's delight this is precisely what happened. There followed a titanic battle for victory, in hot and dry conditions and across all 19 gravel stages. Not only was the competition fierce between the two M-Sport drivers, but Sébastien Loeb was ever-present and trying to muscle in too. The lead changed no fewer than five times, with Hirvonen and Latvala setting fastest times on eight stages between them. When the end came in Kemer, Hirvonen had beaten team-mate (and, in this instance, rival) Latvala by just eight seconds, with Loeb's Citroën another 16 seconds further back.

Mikko Hirvonen's second Focus WRC victory of 2008 came in Turkey, his team-mate Latvala taking second place behind him. Together they dominated the fastest stage times during the event.

This staged group celebration in the finishing area of the 2008 Rally of Turkey emphasised that the Focus WRC had notched up its one hundredth consecutive points score in a WRC event.

There was great joy at M-Sport over this achievement, as the result marked the 100th consecutive points-scoring outing for the Focus. Not only that, but Phil Short's crafty 'rallymanship' gave the team perfectly rally-legal ways of making sure that the two M-Sport cars were not running as 'sweepers' at the front of the field. This even went so far as having in-car electronics to tell the crews to slow down by a few seconds (or not, as the case might be) to make such scheming possible. In his authoritative end-of-season rally annual, Martin Holmes summed it up perfectly: "So, when Ford's competition managers not only planned but pulled off the most stunning and precise tactical manoeuvre in rallying, it was breathtaking …"

M-Sport did not enjoy as much outright good fortune on the Neste Rally Finland, which followed in August, where its cars were reassuringly competitive until problems struck. Between them, Hirvonen and Latvala took 11 fastest times on the 24 special stages, and Hirvonen was often within a few seconds of taking outright victory from Loeb's Citroën. Latvala crashed on the third stage, and unfortunately had to miss nine later stages to stay within the event. The event ended with Hirvonen in second, Al Qassimi in 11th, and Latvala down at 38th place.

At this point in the season the M-Sport team seemed to lose its edge. It only achieved one further victory in the final six events of 2008, slipped from the lead in the World Rally Championship for Manufacturers, and saw Mikko Hirvonen struggling to hold on to his second place in the drivers' equivalent. Although no fewer than 13 Focus WRCs started the Rallye Deutschland in August, none of them seemed to enjoy this all-tarmac event – not even the new-for-rallying 2008-specification factory team cars – and neither of the M-Sport drivers achieved a fastest stage time. The star performance for the cars was actually set by François Duval, who managed third overall in a Stobart car. This was the first all-tarmac WRC event of the year – eight months into the season – and the conditions clearly did not suit Jari-Matti Latvala, who suffered several off-road excursions over the weekend. He finished nearly five minutes adrift of Mikko Hirvonen, and could only take ninth place to Hirvonen's fourth.

Two weeks later the entire WRC 'family' flew half way round the world to compete in New Zealand, where M-Sport was faced with defending two recent victories (by Marcus Grönholm in 2006 and 2007). Even though M-Sport used the same two faithful cars that had started the season in Monte Carlo, they didn't bring much luck to the team. Both drivers led the event from time to time, and after two days, they were installed in first and second place. However, Hirvonen suffered punctures, went off the road at one point, and could only take third place overall, while Latvala suffered a big accident on the last day, and was forced to retire.

As 2008 rushed towards its climax in the Wales Rally GB, it didn't look like M-Sport's luck would change. Spain's Rallye Catalunya, in October, saw Hirvonen trade fastest times on tarmac against his arch-rival Sébastien Loeb, but finishing just a minute – and two places – behind him. For tactical reasons (and because Duval was thought to be slightly faster on tarmac stages), Latvala and François Duval changed places for Catalunya and the following event. This meant Duval was driving an M-Sport car, and Latvala one run by the Stobart team. Clearly this move paid off, as while Hirvonen finished third overall, Duval was just eight seconds behind, in fourth. The duo took six stage fastest times between them.

Just seven days after this (thankfully only a trek along the south coast of France, and a ferry to Ajaccio) came the Tour de Corse tarmac event. Barring the fact that one of the leading Citroëns fell by the wayside, the result was very much as before, this time Hirvonen taking second place and Duval right behind him, only seven seconds adrift! Once again, team

Three state-of-the-art Focus WRCs lined up ready to tackle the 2008 Rally of Spain: the two official M-Sport entries, and Henning Solberg's Stobart-entered car.

Mikko Hirvonen won his third victory of 2008 in Japan.

tactics and team orders had an important part to play here, but punctures and off-road excursions made the calculations of Phil Short and Malcolm Wilson difficult to put into practice!

After all this coming and going on tarmac, it was surely a relief for M-Sport to go off to Japan at the very end of October. Hirvonen and (restored to M-Sport) Latvala once again met up with the cars that had been used in New Zealand several weeks earlier; both of these hard-working machines were starting their eighth event of 2008, and would not only tackle Japan, but would also be returned to the UK for Wales Rally GB. Finally, after the traumas of the late summer, everything in

An enthusiastic British crowd watches, despite cold and muddy conditions; Jari-Matti Latvala makes his way to second place in the Wales Rally of Great Britain in 2008, setting five fastest stage times along the way.

Japan worked out perfectly. Mikko Hirvonen led throughout, and Latvala followed closely behind. To great relief, there was never any unexpected drama, underlined by Hirvonen setting fastest times on 11 of the 26 stages. For M-Sport, the fate of the World Rally Championship for Manufacturers had still not been settled. As it stood Citroën led it by just 12 points, and Wales Rally GB was still to come.

Four weeks later, with plans for 2009 already being laid and several existing Focus WRCs being completely rebuilt and refurbished, the 15th and last championship round of the 2008 season took place: the Wales Rally GB, based in Swansea, but culminating in Cardiff. While the World Rally Championship for Drivers was already settled – Mikko Hirvonen was placed second – the fate for Manufacturers was not yet written. From Dovenby Hall, M-Sport entered its usual three drivers – Hirvonen, Latvala, and Sheikh Khalid Al Qassimi – while the Stobart team lined up Matthew Wilson, François Duval, Henning Solberg, and Barry Clark. On top of this line-up,

the world-famous motorcycle champion Valentino Rossi was entered in another Stobart car.

In the end, and after 17 special stages (just two of them on the super special tarmac of the Millennium Stadium in Cardiff), it was Jari-Matti Latvala who finished second overall. Latvala led narrowly until three stages from the end of the event, only to be overhauled by Loeb's Citroën, which finally won the event by 13 seconds. As for Hirvonen, having set one fastest stage time, he then attacked the spectacular Sweet Lamb stage. Several thousand spectators were gathered, only to watch Hirvonen invert his Focus WRC in front of them, and lose several minutes putting everything to rights. At a stroke, the World Rally Championship for Manufacturers title was gifted to Citroën, and Hirvonen continued 'down among the dead men' for the rest of the event. He would finally struggle back up to take eighth place overall. To his great credit, Valentino Rossi, who admitted to being a complete novice at rallying on gravel stages, kept on going, and finally finished 12th.

Mikko Hirvonen, on his way to third place in the 2009 Rally Ireland, drifts round a hairpin bend in front of a large crowd.

So, what happened next? Although Ford was no doubt impressed with M-Sport's four outright victories in 2008, as a self-avowed 'winner' it was disappointed that M-Sport had not completed a hat-trick of World Rally Championship for Manufacturers titles. The company was also suffering financially because of the general worldwide economic downturn, and it was announced by Ford's motorsport supremo Mark Deans that the company's financial support to the WRC team was to be sharply reduced for 2009.

2009

The Focus was now entering its 11th season in the WRC, and although it was still as demonstrably competitive as ever, much seemed to have changed for the sport in which it had become so famous. To an almost audible sigh of relief from those who had to control the team's tightly-stretched finances, the number of qualifying events had been reduced sharply to 12 (Monte Carlo, Sweden, and Mexico had temporarily disappeared from the calendar). Even so, the year still held much dithering from the FIA as to the way that the sport would be controlled from 2011 onwards. The main competition, as it had been for several recent years, was between M-Sport's Focus WRCs and Citroën's formidable C4s. As in several other seasons, M-Sport seemed to start the year relatively slowly, but built up towards a crescendo as the months passed by. Towards the end of the year, the M-Sport cars would win rallies outright on five consecutive occasions.

Phil Short was an important member of M-Sport's strategic operations until the winter of 2008/2009.

Even with a reduced event calendar, M-Sport had to struggle with a sharp reduction in its operating budget compared with previous years. To stretch finances further, the team also knew full well that the Focus WRC could not be used after the end of 2010. One consequence of this financial cut was that Phil Short – the hugely respected 'sporting advisor' who had been Malcolm Wilson's principal strategist – left the team in January. He was thankfully not lost to the sport, being almost immediately appointed manager of the new Pirelli Star Driver programme that was due to start up shortly.

At the end of January 2009 the make-up of the M-Sport operation, and of the Stobart team that shared many of its facilities, looked very familiar. The financial strain, allied to sheer hard-nosed planning, would see M-Sport use only six cars during the season, of which three had already featured in 2008. All these cars carried the flamboyant blue/green/red livery that played up the major sponsorship/support from the BP/Castrol giant and the Abu Dhabi Tourism Authority.

As in 2008, the driver line-up looked formidable. Mikko Hirvonen and Jari-Matti Latvala continued as before, while Sheikh Khalid Al Qassimi participated in a third car on no fewer than nine occasions. Pirelli provided 'control' tyres throughout (as it did to the other major teams), and for the first time new regulations ensured that the team was obliged to use Carless 'control' fuel (doing nothing for BP's morale and attitude to the sport that it was supporting so strongly).

Even so, the season started off at the end of January on unfamiliar ground. The first event took place in the Irish town of Sligo, instead of in the glamorous Casino Square of Monte Carlo, and there would be 17 tarmac stages with not a sign of snow and ice. This time around, however, Rally Ireland did without the politically-conscious super special in Northern Ireland, followed by the ludicrous wholesale trucking of all the cars across the island and into the Republic. This time all was compact, and felt all the better for it.

Although the event started brightly for M-Sport, with Latvala setting fastest time on the very first (very wet) stage by no less than 17.6 seconds, that later developed into what some cynics described as the 'usual' Hirvonen-Loeb battle. The French driver gradually drew away from the Finnish hero, as Hirvonen's fortunes took a knock on the first day when his auxiliary driving lamp pod came loose. Before this, however, Latvala bravely and rather recklessly went too fast on flooded roads, aquaplaning in a deep puddle at one point, and sliding off the road. The car suffered a damaged front suspension, two punctures, and a broken driveshaft, all of which put him out of the event for the rest of the first day. It clearly wasn't his weekend, having already suffered a road accident in pre-event testing too!

The weather continued to be discouragingly wet for the rest of the event, with stages being cancelled because of flooding. No matter how he tried, Hirvonen could not quite get back on terms with Loeb, though he set five fastest stage times before the close of the event. On the other hand, Sheikh Al Qassimi (aided, no doubt, by the presence of his regular Irish co-driver Michael Orr) took eighth place, remarkable on an event with unfamiliar road conditions. Then, the day after the event finished, it snowed …

In February, however, the WRC turned to the predictably cold, crisp, and very white Rally Norway. This truly Scandinavian three day event smoothly took over from the Swedish Rally, and resulted in the expected M-Sport/Citroën battle, with the resulting honours just about even. Although Loeb ultimately won, he was only ahead of Hirvonen's Focus WRC by ten seconds, and the Finn set eight fastest, six second-fastest, and five third-fastest stage times. His team-mate Latvala came in just behind in third place. Perhaps the most meritorious result was that of the Stobart team, with Henning Solberg arriving fourth in his orange-hued car, and the other two cars seventh (Matthew Wilson) and eighth (Urmo Aava).

Mikko Hirvonen, second overall in Norway in 2009, jumping high in a snowy stage.

Who said that rallying wasn't popular with spectators? Jari-Matti Latvala on the super special stage at the Algarve stadium, near Faro, in 2009.

The Cyprus Rally came next: a mostly dry and sunny event, with rough and slow stages, where Ford cars had often won in the past. M-Sport thought that this could potentially mark its first win of 2009, sending the ex-Norway cars – carefully reprepared – and added Sheikh Al Qassimi to the team's strength. As it transpired, this was yet another case of 'so near and yet so far,' for although Hirvonen set three fastest stage times, and Latvala two more, the Citroën was just able to squeak past them. It wasn't a simple story, as although Hirvonen, was safe, secure, and consistent throughout, the youthful Latvala again suffered a big accident that ruined his chances. On this occasion he slid off the road and remained off for more than 20 minutes, only managing to finish 12th, no less than 22 minutes behind his team-mate. Some stern talking followed the event, and it was hoped that he would be more fortunate in the future. Unhappily, he suffered two more big accidents later in the year, and just a single outright victory did little to rescue his 2009 reputation; some thought he was fortunate to retain his position into 2010.

Events in the Rally de Portugal almost mirrored what had transpired in Cyprus. Once again it was Hirvonen who finished second, Sheikh Al Qassimi who took a consistent eighth place, and Latvala who suffered yet another enormous shunt. The gap between Hirvonen winning outright and having to settle for second place was a mere 24 seconds (over 18 stages), and he took three fastest stage times and another ten podium times in what was a neat and very professional performance. Jari-Matti Latvala, on the other hand, was fastest on the first two gravel stages before crashing his Focus WRC heavily on the very next one. This car – PX08 AXD – suffered from the high-speed accident, rolling a long way off the track (the damage was so great that it ended up appearing to make love to a stout tree). According to footage shot while this was all happening, the car rolled 17 times, and a much-shaken Latvala later admitted that he thought he was going to die.

As already noted, WRC regulations would not allow this car to be totally recreated from all-new parts, and so some engineers forecast that it would be written-off. In the

'How am I going to tell Malcolm Wilson that I've lost a bit of my Focus?' This was Latvala's dilemma at one point during the 2009 Rally Argentina.

end, a shortage of 'oven-ready' cars at Dovenby Hall saw a monumental rebuild being tackled, the result being that it would not be used again until 2010 (but included a victory for Latvala in Finland).

Three weeks later M-Sport tackled Rally Argentina with cars that had already competed in Ireland, Sweden, and Cyprus. No better luck in store, however, for although Latvala partly redeemed his 'crasher' reputation by finishing in sixth place. Even so, he found it difficult to stay out of the limelight, with the Focus' bonnet becoming detached at one point and disappearing into the Pampas, which left the car looking very bare, and a little slower than before. It hardly needs saying that the resourceful M-Sport mechanics fitted a fully-liveried replacement just as soon as they were allowed to get their hands on it. Mikko Hirvonen's Focus, meanwhile, suffered sudden engine expiration mid-stage and took several minutes to be persuaded to restart.

Jari-Matti Latvala's first victory with the BP-Abu Dhabi team came in Sardinia in May 2009.

Left to right: Jari-Matti Latvala, Mikko Hirvonen, along with their co-drivers Miikka Anttila and Jarmo Lehtinen, celebrate a stunning first and second place win in Sardinia, in 2009.

With Latvala down to sixth place after the bonnet episode, and Hirvonen out of the event (ending a streak of 35 consecutive WRC rallies without retirement), this was almost a humiliation for the team. The fact that Stobart cars, driven by Henning Solberg and Matthew Wilson, finished third and fifth was little consolation.

It is hard to see how things could have been worse for M-Sport. Citroën was leading the World Rally Championship for Manufacturers by a huge margin, with twice as many points as M-Sport, and the Drivers standings were just as emphatic in Loeb's favour.

Sardinia, in May, finally signalled a turn-around. In the next three months, M-Sport WRCs won not one, not two, but five events on the trot. Considering that this achieved using just five different cars (PX08 AXD was back at Dovenby Hall, crumpled and awaiting its rebuild), and that Citroën was making every effort to stop M-Sport, this was remarkable. It helped, of course, that these five events included two of M-Sport's favourite locations: the Acropolis Rally of Greece and Neste Rally Finland. The team was also delighted to win once again in Australia, which had often been such a disappointing outing in the past.

Sardinia (or the Rally d'Italia Sardegna, as it was officially called) was a beautiful, hot and sunny location in the Mediterranean, with all its special stages on gravel. This was a combination that had previously appealed so much to Marcus Grönholm, where his Focus WRC had won in 2007. 2009's

outing proved just as successful, with not only Jari-Matti Latvala winning convincingly, but a composed and seemingly consistent Mikko Hirvonen also taking second place. The stats made for very satisfying reading, as Latvala set more fastest stage times than anyone else in the event (six out of the 17 stages), and Hirvonen was consistently in the top three.

This was a huge relief to M-Sport, having not won a WRC event since Japan in the autumn of 2008. Phil Short's absence was felt among the strategists as they considered the relevant factors of who should run ahead, who should stay clear of marbles and dust clouds, and who might have to deal with 'team orders.' Nevertheless, the event went well for M-Sport, while things did not go so well for its rivals. Latvala led the entire event from start to finish – never looking stressed – providing a good portent for the future, and a huge relief to Latvala after the previous events!

Only three weeks later, the entirety of the WRC shipped itself across the Mediterranean to Greece, to tackle the Acropolis (though M-Sport opted to use different cars to tackle the event itself). The team drivers used the 'other' three well-prepared cars, two of which had just been trucked out, after being flown home from Argentina and rebuilt in Cumbria!

By this time, incidentally, there was considerable controversy brewing back in the UK. With basic financial reasons at the heart of it all, the Welsh Legislative Assembly – the title sponsor of the Wales Rally GB – proposed to drop

Ford simply loved competing in the Acropolis rally, and Mikko Hirvonen added to the victory roll in 2009.

its support at the end of the year. The MSA's subsidiary, International Motor Sports Limited, pointed out that there was a legal and binding agreement in place stretching to the end of 2011, and a promise of a messy legal dispute concerning 'Breach of Contract' helped to settle matters.

The potential tragedy of all this was that although many individual members supported the continuation of the sponsorship, the all-powerful (and stone-hearted) Welsh Treasury officials did not trade in sentiment. For a time, therefore, it looked as the 2010 event might find itself based in Newcastle-on-Tyne, with much of its stage mileage concentrated in the legendary Keilder Forest complex (a prospect that caused a stir in the hearts of every British rally enthusiast). In the end the dispute was partially resolved; the word 'Wales' was removed from the event's title for the 2009 event, but all ruffled feathers had been smoothed over, and financial support was restored for 2010!

Back on the WRC circuit, M-Sport's revival continued apace. Not only did Hirvonen and Latvala take first and third places at the Acropolis Rally of Greece, but Sheikh Khalid Al Qassimi also fought hard against the hot and dusty conditions and took a sturdy sixth place. Ford's new motorsport boss, Gerard Quinn (taking over at very short notice from Mark Deans, who retired from the company to take up a new non-Ford business appointment), was delighted. This was despite Latvala giving him the now-usual Latvala welcome by leading for five stages, before crashing off for a considerable period, dropping down to 11th, and having to struggle back to a podium position. Citroën's Sébastien Loeb also crashed heavily in mid-event (not that M-Sport was complaining), and failed for finish for the first time in two whole seasons.

The teams were then allocated just 11 days to get their cars, personnel, and all their hardware across the crowded highways of south and central Europe, before being faced with Rally Poland, a new event that was celebrating its arrival in the World Rally Championship. The Focus WRC proved itself to be the 'class of the field' on this gravel event, where Hirvonen won once again (using the same car in which he had just triumphed

Gerard Quinn replaced Mark Deans as Ford's top man in charge of motorsport policy, in June 2009.

Only two weeks after triumphing in Greece, Mikko Hirvonen repeated the trick by winning the 2009 Rally Poland.

Mikko Hirvonen well above 'home territory,' and watched by a large crowd of spectators, on his way to winning the 2009 Neste Rally Finland.

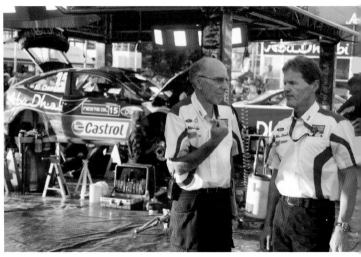

Team manager John Millington and Malcolm Wilson in discussion about the Neste Rally, with Khalid Al Qassimi's car receiving service in the background.

in Greece), while he and Latvala also took seven fastest stage times (of 18 in all). Following his severe crash in Greece, Loeb was further demoralised when he suffered another accident on the very first day, and having to claw his way back into the charts under 'SuperRally' regulations.

By this time in the season, the media was waiting for Jari-Matti Latvala to do something unusual, and he did not disappoint. Settled in second overall on the very last (super special) stage in Mikołajki, he slid off the track and hit a barrier in the full view of thousands of Poles, and was unable to finish the event. This would be the very last time that Latvala was

entrusted with AG57 CKA – he had already treated it roughly on six events during 2009 – but it was not the end of that car's M-Sport career, as Sheikh Al Qassimi would use it for much of the 2009 and 2010 seasons that followed.

More positively, however, following the Polish visit, Hirvonen had taken a narrow lead over Loeb in the World Rally Championship for Drivers, and the mood at Dovenby Hall had definitely lightened. There was good reason, because, after a short four-week break, the WRC circus then moved on to Finland, where both Hirvonen and Latvala were hoping to win (if only to match Marcus Grönholm's double victories in

2006 and 2007). As the WRC rallying expert Martin Holmes later wrote: "The others were nowhere! The four official Ford and Citroën crews completely dominated the Neste Oil Rally Finland, leaving the others straggling behind. Mikko Hirvonen gained his third successive WRC victory …"

Little more needed to be said, except that both teams produced cars capable of providing many fastest stage times. In the case of M-Sport, ten went to Hirvonen and six to Latvala. At the end of the event in Jyväskylä just 67 seconds separated the top four drivers on the leaderboard.

After all this head-to-head Scandinavian combat, it was time to travel half way round the world to compete in Australia. The event was based in Kingscliff, on the coast of New South Wales, where the weather was fine, and where several stages were completed in darkness (a very rare occurrence at this time in the WRC's history). M-Sport had enough to time to get the winning Neste Rally Finland cars back to Dovenby Hall, get them thoroughly refreshed, and to transport them back to Australia with a plan to repeat Hirvonen's 2006 victory (his very first in the WRC).

As expected, this was another titanic battle between M-Sport and Citroën, with all four cars setting fastest times, and all four having near-faultless runs. This ensured that after no fewer than 33 special stages, the gap between first and fourth was only 112 seconds. The stats, of course, only tell part of the story; in fact no fewer than five drivers held the lead at one time or another. Hirvonen led briefly on day two, but was elevated to ultimate victory on the very last special stage, where every C4 in the Citroën team was penalised one minute by the scrutineers on the grounds that they were carrying non-standard front suspension links.

Pandemonium ensued, of course. At least one pundit was heard to claim the result as payback against Citroën, 43 years after the Mini Coopers were turfed out of the 1966 Rallye Automobile de Monte-Carlo. The result stood regardless, and the consequence was that at this point, with just two more events to be held in 2009, Hirvonen now led the World Rally Championship for Drivers by five points (above Loeb), and M-Sport had closed the gap in the Manufacturers leaderboard to just 13 points.

With such tiny gaps now separating the two manufacturers and drivers towards the end of the season, the last two events of the year were bound to be of vital importance. These final events were to be Spain's RallyRACC Catalunya, starting on

Great publicity shot! Mikko Hirvonen in Sydney, Australia before the 2009 rally, with the famous Harbour Bridge, and the Opera House in the background.

SA09 VHR was the only '09' registered Focus ever used by the official M-Sport team – and here it was, on the way to victory in Australia in 2009, with Mikko Hirvonen at the wheel.

2 October, and the Rally of Great Britain on 23 October. For M-Sport, the intention was to run all three front-line team crews on both occasions. Amazingly (and this emphasised the shortage of individual cars available), those three crews would again use the same cars that had just completed the Neste Rally Finland and the Rally of Australia. They would therefore complete the season having enjoyed a very busy life.

Citroën started the Catalunya event as favourites – it had won the event for the previous four years – and as it transpired these forecasts were upheld. Although Mikko Hirvonen managed to finish third, he could not set a single fastest stage time on this all-tarmac event. With Loeb returning his first victory since Argentina in April, this left the championship finely poised. Hirvonen was just a single point ahead of Loeb and there was all to play for in the Rally of Great Britain that followed. Jari-Matti Latvala finished sixth and avoided damaging his car (to Malcolm Wilson's great relief), and the only real disappointment was that Khalid Al Qassimi had to miss two special stages after his Focus WRC suffered an under-bonnet engine fire caused by a leaking oil tank.

Now it was time for the final showdown, and the culmination of what had been a coruscating 12-event season. As expected, the Rally of Great Britain was based in Cardiff, held completely within the bounds of south and central Wales. The event was comprised of 16 gravel stages, most of them very wet and often muddy, and not even a super special to confuse the casual spectators. M-Sport entered its usual three crews – Hirvonen, Latvala and Sheikh Al Qassimi – and was also backed up by two formidably competitive Stobart cars (driven by Matthew Wilson and Henning Solberg). Citroën faced it with C4s driven by Sébastien Loeb, Danny Sordo, Sébastien Ogier, and (as a one-off) Petter Solberg.

From Friday morning to Sunday afternoon, with a return to Cardiff each evening, there rarely seemed to be a pause for rest. The result was that the expected head-to-head between the Focus WRC and the C4 took everyone's attention. Loeb set nine fastest and five second-fastest times, with Hirvonen and his Focus WRC being fastest seven times, and second-fastest four times. Technically speaking, the M-Sport cars were as competitive as usual, but all three cars suffered from a spate of broken driveshaft couplings. Hirvonen's car fortunately only suffered from this on the public highway, on its way back to the end-of-day service halt in Cardiff.

At the end of day one, Hirvonen was just 5.3 seconds off the pace, but two hiccups caused that gap to increase markedly the following day. On consecutive stages the engine seemed to falter, with Hirvonen unable to do anything to restore it to health. Just as suddenly, however, it recovered and carried on serenely to the close. Even so, with just one day to go, the gap had increased to 30.2 seconds.

Then came day three, with four stages – totalling just 50 miles – remaining. On the penultimate stage, in Margam Park,

the Focus WRC leapt up high over a bump, and landed heavily. The lightweight bonnet made a bid for freedom, flying up and obscuring the Finn's vision to such an extent that the crew had to stop, wrench the panel free, and carry on with a naked engine bay.

And that was that. As soon as the result became clear, it showed that Hirvonen had finish second – by just a single point – to Loeb in the World Rally Championship for Drivers, and – as expected – M-Sport also ended up as runners-up in the Manufacturers yet again. This had been a season in which the Focus WRC notched up five victories (in 12 starts), and in which Hirvonen had excelled (four wins, second place five times, and third place twice).

Although there is no such thing as a happy second-place finisher, Malcolm Wilson was still delighted to see how competitive Mikko Hirvonen had been throughout the year and forecast that he would become World Rally Champion soon. He was demonstrably less happy, however, with Jari-Matti Latvala's fortunes during a tempestuous year.

Perhaps this was best summed up by *Autosport*'s David Evans who, in his end of season survey, commented that:

"Latvala is coming. And when he gets where he's going, he'll probably look back at this year, and wonder how on earth he kept his job. Latvala tried the patience of every Ford worker to the maximum this year. Just when it seemed it couldn't get any worse, he crashed again … On the other hand, Hirvonen collected 11 podium finishes from 12 starts and came within a point of the title. And the Finn did it off his own bat. He's getting better and better …"

2010

Because the 2009 season had ended remarkably early – a full two months before Christmas – and the 2010 season was not scheduled to begin until mid-February in Sweden, M-Sport had more than three months to settle back at Dovenby Hall. It could use this time to recover from the drama of the last few weeks of the 2009 season, and to start to prepare its strategy for 2011, when 1.6-litre Fiestas would take centre stage.

Despite the financial purse-strings being drawn as tight as ever, the team was looking to wring the very best out of the dear old Focus WRC for 2010, which was to be the car's 12th and final year. Those financial constraints, however, meant that five of the six cars that M-Sport had committed to the 2010 Championship had already been used in 2009.

Mikko Hirvonen on to M-Sport's first victory of 2010 – the Swedish rally – with a crowd of people braving the bitter cold.

Mikko Hirvonen, with Jari-Matti Latvala behind him, ready to take the start of Rally Jordan from the Roman remains arena at Jerash.

As ever, M-Sport's principal objective was to contest, and ideally to win, the World Rally Championships – both of them, Manufacturers and Drivers – while developing its Fiesta programmes as smoothly as possible, for it hoped to build and sell at least 50 such cars during the year. Not only was the S2000 project to continue, but work on the 2011 Fiesta WRC would intensify as the season progressed.

Few technical changes were forecast for the last of the Focus WRCs, but this comment also applied to every other

team contesting the 2010 series: the FIA had placed a ban on new homologations in this 'old' formula. Early in the year M-Sport confirmed that Mikko Hirvonen and Jari-Matti Latvala would continue to be the team's two principal drivers and, for the first time, made it clear that Hirvonen was to be the 'number one' driver. Latvala would be expected to support him in any way specified, while Sheikh Khalid Al Qassimi would continue as the team's third driver. He was scheduled to contest only eight of the 13 WRC rounds, and so would find time to contest some of the Middle East Rally Championship events in the newly-developed Fiesta S2000.

The season opened with Rally Sweden in mid-February, where there was much consistent snow and ice, and where four stages were tackled in darkness. For M-Sport, the good news was that it started the year with a great result: outright victory for Mikko Hirvonen in BK08 LCW. This was the very last Focus WRC to be commissioned, and would be used by him on no fewer than six events during the season, though with no further victories. As ever, Citroën's Sébastien Loeb always looked ready to take the victory should Hirvonen even so much as flinch. The Finn's final winning margin was 42 seconds. Latvala fought hard and finished third, while Sheikh Al Qassimi took a sturdy 13th. Hirvonen, Latvala and Loeb shared almost all the fastest times on the stages, where their performance was often determined by the condition of the well-worn studded tyres they had to use between visits to the service park in Hagfors. This, incidentally, was the fourth successive time that a Focus WRC had won the Swedish Rally …

Circumstances were entirely different for the WRC circus in Mexico three weeks later: different cars to use, altitude adding to the engine settings conundrums, and mainly warm and dry stages for everyone to enjoy. For reasons that no-one at M-Sport seemed able to solve at the time, the Focus WRCs were utterly uncompetitive on this event, for they did not manage to set a single fastest stage times, nor did they finish in any of the top three positions. Although M-Sport had four weeks to delve into the problems before travelling to Jordan, by this point in the car's career it was decided to leave them gently to rest. However, to add to the mysteries, the same two cars were eventually transported to New Zealand for the May-scheduled rally, where they were more than competitive, and won!

Back in April, though, the WRC scenario returned to normal for the Jordan Rally. Although Hirvonen was in fifth place at the

Malcolm Wilson and Gerard Quinn welcome FIA President Jean Todt to the M-Sport nerve-centre.

end of the first day (those running near the front of the event had more sweeping problems than usual), his Focus suffered major suspension damage after an excursion on day two, and resulted in his missing no fewer than six special stages. Plunged right out of the running, Hirvonen was eventually classified 20th, nearly 47 minutes off the pace! Latvala, on the other hand, was as competitive as could be hoped, setting the fastest time on five stages, and achieving nine other podium times before finishing second behind Loeb's Citroën.

Amazingly, Hirvonen's chassis-battered car from Jordan was repaired for The Rally of Turkey (based in Pendik, south east of Istanbul), which followed just two weeks (and a couple of countries) away. The car was obviously so well-repaired that it was competitive again, and Hirvonen battled away in the top positions for the whole weekend. Clearly this mixed event – five tarmac stages out of the 21 stage total – suited the opposition as well, as the Citroën finally squeezed ahead of the Focus with a small margin. Unhappily, Latvala went off the road for a time on the second day (losing nearly 20 minutes, but finally being retrieved and struggling to the finish). Hirvonen's spirited fight was similarly harmed on the final day when – just 15 seconds adrift of Loeb's Citroën – he slid off on one stage, suffering a puncture, and losing both a minute and a place on the leaderboard, having to settle for third overall instead.

Although M-Sport was now trailing Citroën in the World Rally Championship for Manufacturers, it could at least hope

for an improvement in New Zealand. This was a geographically far-flung event that had not always been kind to the team. For a time, too, it looked as if none of the European-based WRC teams would be able to get to New Zealand at all, 2010 being the year in which a massive volcanic explosion in Iceland led to masses of ash entering the atmosphere, causing wholesale delays to the world's aircraft. Two weeks before the event was due to start, both Ford and Citroën warned that they might have to cancel as they could not get assured aircraft bookings for their precious cars and equipment. Just in time, though, the crisis eased, aircraft once again became available, and the team travelled to Auckland as planned.

The result was an astonishing success for M-Sport and for Jari-Matti Latvala. Not only did a Focus WRC win the event, but (barring a single occasion on day one) it did not lead the event at all until the final moment. The final winning margin over Sébastien Ogier's Citroën C4 was a meagre 2.4 seconds! Until the very end, any one of five drivers – two in Focus WRCs – might have thought they could win the event: it was as close-fought as that. Latvala, in fact, did not take the lead until three corners – *corners*, not stages – from the end of the final special stage, when he encountered Ogier's Citroën bumper lying in the road as a result of *his* final excursion!

Latvala also achieved the victory without setting a single fastest special stage time (but was never outside the top few), all of which gave the sport's number-crunchers cause for a great deal of thought. With Mikko Hirvonen in fourth place,

Jari-Matti Latvala enjoying himself on the super special stage of Rally New Zealand in downtown Auckland. He would go on to win the event outright.

but a mere 22 seconds behind the winning Focus WRC, one can immediately see how close this 21-stage event had been. Ford and M-Sport were delighted to point out that with this result Ford had now overtaken Lancia as the 'winningest' brand in WRC competition.

Now it was back to Europe, to the Rally de Portugal, and back to what had become Ford's normal rallying situation. Its French rivals were once again just – but only just – likely to beat it on the Iberian peninsula. Disappointingly, events played out as expected, and although there would be four Focus WRCs in the final top ten, it was Citroën who just made it to the finishing banner ahead of them. Mikko Hirvonen finished fourth – using SA09 VHR, the most recently registered Focus – while Al Qassimi took ninth. Latvala returned to form, and not in a positive sense, when he crashed early on the second day, and the team did not think it possible to get him back under 'SuperRally' conditions.

This, incidentally, where Sébastien Ogier won a WRC event for the very first time, and it can be no coincidence that within

weeks of this Malcolm Wilson apparently proposed that he join the M-Sport team for 2011! As the history books now confirm, Sébastien refused this offer at the time, but finally arrived to lead the M-Sport/Fiesta WRC team in 2017.

There was no improvement in fortune for Rally Bulgaria (the first time that the WRC had visited the country), where the 13 all-tarmac special stages (some wet, some dry) proved to be ideal for the opposition. Looking back, this was probably M-Sport's most disappointing outing of the season, as the two team drivers could only finish fifth and sixth behind a veritable phalanx of Citroëns, and neither Hirvonen nor Latvala took any top three stage times.

Ford desperately needed a boost to its fortunes. In Finland, three weeks later, it found one in the form of Jari-Matti Latvala winning the event outright (though his margin over Ogier's Citroën was a mere ten seconds). Three Focus WRCs ended up battered and broken after accidents (two of them being official M-Sport entries, the other being Henning Solberg's Stobart machine). No matter, however, as

Rallying was an incredibly popular spectator sport in Finland in the 2000s: there were thousands watching Mikko Hirvonen jump his way through a special stage in the Neste Rally.

Jari-Matti Latvala gave the Focus WRC its final victory, in Finland, July 2010. He set five fastest stage times, and twelve other podium positions along the way.

'Yes! We did it in our own country in 2010.' Jari-Matti Latvala celebrating success with his co-driver Miikka Anttila in the Neste Rally Finland.

A technical detail of the aero arrangements in the final version of the Focus WRC, showing how the hot air from the twin-cooling fans exited the bonnet area.

this the 44th outright World Rally Championship victory for the Focus WRC

Mikko Hirvonen had led the high-speed Neste Rally Finland outright after three stages, with two fastest and one second-fastest time, before he had a high-speed accident. He rolled the car (SA09 VHR) after a jump, crashing into the trees, and resulting in a car that looked as if it could never possibly be used again.

To quote Hirvonen immediately afterwards: "The accident happened at a jump immediately after a fast right bend. The car landed on the road, but started to roll, and it went over three or

four times. It was certainly the biggest accident I've had …" His co-driver Jarmo Lehtinen had similar memories, but was sure that something had broken on the chassis as the car landed from the first jump, and was uncontrollable thereafter.

Amazingly, it took M-Sport's incredibly talented mechanics only six weeks to get the wreck back to Dovenby Hall, rebuild it, and to get it out to Japan for another outing!

This must not detract, however, from Latvala's remarkably assured performance in PX08 AXD, where he took over the lead almost as soon as Hirvonen's Focus WRC ended up in the trees, and never let it slip thereafter. That car and the

This atmospheric evening shot of the M-Sport service area shows how there was space for all three works cars to be fettled at the same time.

A proud moment for Malcolm Wilson in Spain, in 2010. He and his long-time friend – and world-class driver – Carlos Sainz pose with a poster commemorating M-Sport's 200th start in a WRC event rally.

speedily recreated SA09 VHR were both made ready to tackle Rally Japan in September, where M-Sport hoped to restore its fortunes even further.

In the meantime, the all-tarmac-stages of Rallye Deutschland, where a Focus WRC had never previously shone. Not to put too fine a point on it, but in the past this had always seemed to be a Citroën-benefit (Sébastien Loeb had won it seven times previously), and there was no discernible change in 2010. Neither Hirvonen nor Latvala could set fastest times, and Hirvonen's BK08 LCW hit a series of transmission problems. Let us just say that Latvala tried his hardest for three days, eventually finishing fourth.

M-Sport's efforts on the last of the Focus WRCs never flagged, and nor did the drivers' spirits. By this time, however, it was clear that there was no more to come from the car. It was finally reaching the end of its 12-year rallying career. Just four events, and the use of all six of the official works cars remaining in active service, separated the car from retirement.

Jari-Matti Latvala, deep in a Welsh water splash, on his way to taking third place in the Rally of Great Britain 2010, along with second in the World Rally Championship for Drivers.

It was therefore a somewhat downbeat approach to the car's final retirement. In Japan, three cars started and two finished (Sheikh Al Qassimi's machine had an accident and had to withdraw), with M-Sport's regular drivers sharing seven fastest stage times between them, and with Jari-Matti Latvala finishing third overall. Three weeks later, on the twisty tarmac of the Alsace mountains for the Rallye de France (replacing the Tour de Corse in the calendar), Sébastien Loeb excelled on what was virtually his home doorstep, though Hirvonen and Latvala took fourth and fifth places. The penultimate Focus appearance, then, followed in Spain's RallyRACC Catalunya. Here, M-Sport used the same two cars as had recently appeared in France, and the result was exactly the same as before.

SWANSONG

And so the Focus World Rally car came to the end of its magnificent 12-season front-line career, ending with a

On his way through the Margam Park stage of the 2010 Rally of Great Britain, Mikko Hirvonen knew full well that this was the last time he would go rallying in the charismatic Focus WRC.

This nostalgic shot was posed as the Focus WRC came to the end of its WRC career at Wales Rally GB in 2010, with a preserved 1999 example nestling close to one of the very last Focus WRCs ever built. S9 FMC recorded the M-Sport team's first victory – the Safari of 1999 – while SA09 VHR was the last new Focus WRC ever to be registered at Dovenby Hall. Mikko Hirvonen drove it to fourth place in the Wales Rally GB of 2010, the last event to be tackled by an M-Sport Focus WRC car.

nostalgic and very appropriate showing in the Wales Rally GB of November 2010. There were sparkling works-built cars on the start line, three of them entered by the official BP Ford Abu Dhabi WRT, and three more entered by the Stobart M-Sport Ford RT.

Nor was this just an appearance for show, with two of the official cars – driven by Latvala and Hirvonen – taking third and fourth places, and Latvala himself setting fastest stage times on four of the event's 20 special stages. All but one of the Focus WRCs – the exemption being the Stobart car driven by the Chinese pilot Liu Caodong – reached the finish.

By this time, M-Sport was heavily committed to design, development, and manufacture of its new-generation 1.6-litre Ford Fiesta WRC cars. As such there were no technical novelties on this final event, and nor were any of the cars new. Latvala's third-place machine, in fact, was already two years old, and was on its seventh WRC event of 2010.

It was a sturdy, if not sensational, way to bring this model's career to an end, and a brief summary of that must be:

First event:	1999 Rallye Automobile Monte Carlo
Last event:	2010 Wales Rally GB
Cars built:	97
WRC outright victories:	44

And a final thought: will any other Ford car ever achieve so much again?

THE STOBART VK M-SPORT FORD RALLY TEAM – 2008 TO 2010

As in 2006 and 2007, the Stobart Focus team operated as a thoroughly professional operation. It was not officially a works team, but worked with Focus WRCs that were as close as possible to the latest M-Sport specification, and with drivers who were definitely of very high class. Anyone privileged enough to visit the main assembly/maintenance workshops at Dovenby Hall would soon see that the Stobart cars (visually different in every way from the M-Sport cars) had their own dedicated team of mechanics, but would be set up to the same ultra-high standards.

As in previous years, the nominal 'team leader' in 2008 was Matthew Wilson (though this was never spelt out). Wilson celebrated his 21st birthday immediately after the end of the Rallye Automobile Monte Carlo (in which he finished tenth), and competed in all 15 World Rally Championship rounds. He suffered only two retirements over the season, both due to technical malfunctions. He regularly finished in the top ten, his best overall placing being fifth in the Jordan Rally, and sixth both in the Rally Mexico, and in the Acropolis Rally. The Stobart team came fourth in the overall World Rally Championship for Manufacturers of that year.

Stobart usually entered at least three – occasionally four – cars in most events, and several drivers made up the roster. Henning Solberg started all events, taking fourth in Jordan, and three fifth places. Gianluigi Galli started ten times (third in the Swedish Rally, and fourth in the Rally d'Italia Sardegna), while François Duval started seven times and took third overall in the Rallye Deutschland and the Tour de Corse). Jari-Matti Latvala, who had a troubled year in the official M-Sport team, was briefly rested from M-Sport's official team in mid-season, and appeared in a Stobart car in RallyRACC Catalunya.

In 2009 the Stobart VK M-Sport World Rally Team – to give out its full title, and illustrate that it really was the close back-up, or auxiliary, to BP Ford Abu Dhabi WRT – was as active, professional, and resourceful as ever, tackling all 12 of the WRC events of that year. Apart from occasional guest appearances from drivers like Urmo Aava and Krzysztof Hołowczyc (the latter being a Pole, rallying in his own country), it was always Matthew Wilson and Henning Solberg who rallied the Stobart cars all round the world.

Although the team was never quite strong or lucky enough to break through to the top of the podium, it was Henning Solberg who not only took two third places overall – in Argentina and Poland – but backed these up with fourth place results in Ireland and Norway. Matthew Wilson's best showings were both in fifth place, in Cyprus and in Poland. All in all, the Stobart team thoroughly deserved its third place in the World Rally Championship for Manufacturers, behind the might of Citroën and the 'official' M-Sport team.

Although the team carried on throughout the 2010 season, it was clear that the effort behind the Focus WRC was slowly running down, and the team did not enjoy quite as much success as it had in 2009. Throughout the season, the team relied on the expertise of the same experienced drivers

CARS USED BY THE STOBART TEAM – 2008 TO 2010
2008
1 ES
EJ56 FXA
EO56 TZR
EA07 RGZ
EU07 TSX
EU07 SSX
EU07 STX
EU07 SUH
EU07 SUO
EU07 SUV
EU07 TZR
2009
1 ES
EU07 SUA
EU07 SUF
EU07 SUO
EU07 SUV
PX08 AXC
2010
1 ES
EA07 RGZ
EU07 SSZ
EU07 SUF
AG57 CKA
PX08 AXC
MM59 ORT

as the previous year: Matthew Wilson and Henning Solberg. Matthew started all 13 WRC events in Focus WRCs, while Henning started nine times in a Focus WRC, along with four times in Fiesta S2000s in a different category.

Financial details were never publicised, of course, but it seemed fairly certain that the appearance of no fewer than six other drivers on a one-off basis must have involved support for the Stobart team in one way or another. Among those drivers, it was Marcus Grönholm, Juha Kankkunen, and François Duval who provided most of the media talking points, though none of them (not even the recently-retired Grönholm) provided any unexpected high results.

Of the regular drivers, Matthew Wilson took fifth on one occasion (Jordan), backing this up with five other sixth place results, while Henning Solberg achieved sixth place three times in Sweden, Mexico, and Wales Rally GB. The Stobart team took fourth in the World Rally Championship for Manufacturers.

M-SPORT FOCUS WRC – TECHNICAL CHANGES FROM 2008 TO 2010

A series of outwardly minor, but significant, development changes took place in 2008. However, nothing major was planned, or executed, for the car that had proven to be so successful in previous seasons. As one cynic commented: "The only important change was to the driving seat: Marcus Grönholm was no longer in it!"

Because of new WRC regulations, all cars in the WRC series now used a (large choice) of Pirelli control tyres, so M-Sport spent much time testing the various types to find which best suited the latest Focus WRC. One should note that this move came at the same time as the use of mousse within the tyres was banned.

Effective from August 2008, a new version of the car's homologation was incorporated into the Focus WRCs, partly to keep abreast of style changes introduced on the Focus road cars of the period. These involved slight changes to the front end of the bodyshell, including a reprofiled headlamp aperture and slight changes around the front air intake. There were no changes to the basic chassis and running gear, though inside the engine there was a new and lighter crankshaft, and modifications were made to the turbocharger and to the electronic mapping of the engine itself. This was done without affecting the quoted peak horsepower, which remained listed (publicly, at least) as 300bhp at 6000rpm.

It was a similar story in 2009, where changes incorporated in an updated homologation – dated April 2009 – were mainly developmental, and not fundamental to the layout, operation, or performance of the machine itself. Changes to the power unit and installation included the use of a lighter-weight flywheel and an electrically-driven, rather than belt-driven, water pump, these first being seen in Portugal. Since the disqualification of the very first Focus WRC, from the Rallye Automobile Monte Carlo of 1999 for having an illegal water pump (see Chapter 3), the regulations had changed, making

this driver-controlled, switchable, electrically-driven pump completely acceptable.

By the autumn of 2009, and with the major changeover to 1.6-litre engined WRC cars in mind, the FIA decreed that no further major homologation changes would be allowed. For 2010, therefore, the only advance allowed (and this only for the M-Sport cars, not even to the works-assisted Stobart cars) was the use of fast-adjustment devices for altering the suspension ride heights. This would make each car more suitable for events where tarmac stages and gravel stages might be encountered without it being possible to visit a scheduled service point.

WORKS M-SPORT CARS USED – 2008 TO 2010

By 2008, the Focus WRC was well on its way to having what the military would call a 'mature' specification. The previous major change had been unveiled at the end of 2005, and the road car on which the Focus WRC was based was not due to be replaced before the end of the decade. What's more, it was already thought that a totally different basic WRC specification (involving specially-developed, bespoke, direct-injection 1.6-litre engines) would be enforced in manufacturers after the 2010 season.

Accordingly, the cars listed below looked very similar to the 2006 and 2007 types. These were are follows:

2008

None of the works cars that had been used by M-Sport in 2007 were rallied by the team again in 2008, some being sold off to other individuals/organisations, or transferred to the Stobart organisation (where they could still be seen in the same Dovenby Hall workshops).

These were the eight 2008 M-Sport World Championship rally cars:

EA07 RGZ
EA07 PXN
EU07 SSZ
EU07 STZ
EU07 SUA
EU07 SUF
PX08 AXC
PX08 AXD

Getting the sponsor's message across: this was the rear end of a 2010 M-Sport Focus WRC.

2009

In a change of policy, brought about not only by the imminence of the complete change in WRC regulations for 2011, but also major financial budget restrictions, M-Sport continued to use three of the 2008 team cars again in 2009, these being marked below by an asterisk (*), along with just three new identities:

AG57 CKA
EU07 SSZ *
PX08 AXB
PX08AXC *
PX08 AXD *
SA09 VHR

2010

Since M-Sport knew full well that 2010 would be the last season in which the Focus WRC could be used at the WRC level, the company decided to refurbish the best of its existing stock of works rally cars, and use them all over the course of the season before selling most of them off to private owners.

Only one all-new car – BK08 LCW – was commissioned during the year. For number-crunchers, the slight confusion here is that it carried a mid-2008 registration plate, even though it had not been put on the road for two more years! Cars used in previous seasons are once again identified with an asterisk (*).

AK57 CKA *
EU07 SUF *
BK08 LCW
PX08 AXB *
PX08 AXD *
SA09 VHR *

NOSTALGIA

M-Sport organised a function to celebrate the end of the Focus WRC's great career, at Cardiff during Wales Rally GB. When it did so, it made sure that many of the personalities of the Focus WRC's recent past were present. A group photograph was taken around two of the cars. One was S9 FMC, the very early example with which Colin McRae had won the Safari Rally of 1999 (and achieved the Focus WRC's first victory). The other was SA09 VHR, the only 09-registered Focus WRC ever produced, which was about to end its busy career by taking Mikko Hirvonen to fourth place in the Wales Rally GB.

As the previous chapters have already made clear, by the end of the 2000s a change in World Rally Car format was becoming inevitable, if only because of the steadily reducing number of different manufacturers that could afford to go on competing at this level. The figures for teams entering genuine works cars were stark indeed: in 2007 there were three (Ford, Citroën, and Subaru), in 2008 there were four (Suzuki joined in, briefly), and in 2009 and 2010 there were just two, as Ford competed head-to-head with Citroën.

Accordingly, the FIA's decision to impose a new format in 2011 was welcomed, with several other manufacturers (most notably VW and BMW/Mini) forecast to join the fray. Effectively there was to be a completely new WRC formula, centring on the use of special 1.6-litre engines (a connection with a corporate engine was not required), for which direct fuel-injection was to be compulsory. M-Sport had therefore virtually frozen the Focus WRC specification before the end of 2009, while it moved on with a new project based on the smaller, lighter, 1.6-litre Ford Fiesta.

The change, long forecast and much discussed, came about for several good – and even several bad – reasons. One, for sure, was to pay lip service to the latest technical trends, one of which (according to the FIA) was the gradual downsizing of production car engine sizes. This would effectively mean that original WRC engines would come to be seen as old-fashioned dinosaurs, and specially-designed turbocharged 1.6-litre engines – with direct fuel-injection and a 33mm diameter inlet restrictor – should take over instead. This, it was thought, would still allow teams to have 300bhp-plus power units, and make the rallying no less exciting than before.

The rest of the chassis would, in essence, be based on regulations that already applied to the existing lower-division Super 2000 cars, but with more freedom to use special aerodynamic features, and lighter materials.

As M-Sport had already completed a Super 2000 Fiesta prototype in 2009 (using a normally-aspirated version of the existing Focus WRC 2-litre power unit), Christian Loriaux's

Because the World Rally Championship regulations had changed, M-Sport had to develop new-generation 1.6-litre Fiesta World Rally Cars for 2011. These were immediately successful, and Mikko Hirvonen won the Rally Sweden in February 2011 …

… with his team-mate Jari-Matti Latvala in third place. The tradition continues …

WORLD RALLY CHAMPIONSHIP COMPETITION IN 2011

M-Sport (and, therefore, Ford) had a great deal of warning about a major change to the regulations that would govern the World Rally Championship from 1 January 2011, but although the FIA's proposals were presented, modified and re-modified in 2008/2009, it was clear that the Focus WRC would no longer be eligible for use after the end of 2010.

In December 2008 the FIA concluded that to reduce the cost and performance of competing cars, the top division of the World Rally Championship should be for 2-litre engined four-wheel drive cars, broadly based on the current 'division two' Super 2000 category.

This was emphasised in March 2009, when it was stated that turbocharged cars would not be eligible for WRC points: a point that led to much resistance from the manufacturers and teams who might be tempted to compete. An FIA statement that turbocharged 1.6-litre engines might be allowed from 2013 onwards was met with derision and disbelief.

The situation was partly resolved in July 2009 when the FIA buckled under pressure from the manufacturers, and decided that the WRC of 2011 would be for turbocharged 1.6-litre engined cars which would be smaller and could be lighter than the existing crop. This finally convinced M-Sport that there would have to be life after the Focus, and all development work on that car virtually ceased from that point.

engineering team enjoyed a flying start when considering the new formula. The car was well-established in a testing programme before the new WRC regulations were finally settled. Dedicated work on a Fiesta WRC began in May 2009, and the very first prototype car ran in September 2009, with the Focus WRC still having more than a full season left to run.

As we now know, Pipo Moteurs designed a brand-new 1.6-litre engine for the Fiesta WRC. The first test car began evaluation in June 2010 (still well before the end of the Focus WRC's final season), and the first all-new, definitive Fiesta WRC ran in October 2010. The cars were on the start line for Rally Sweden in February 2011.

As already noted in the previous chapter, the Focus WRC's career came to a sudden, if expected, close on 14 November 2010 in Cardiff, where the BP Ford Abu Dhabi WRT works entries took third and fourth place in the Wales Rally GB. Four of the top seven finishers were Focus WRCs: a good, if not sensational, way to end a 12-year front-line career.

Ford Focus WRC specifications, 1999-2010

FORD FOCUS WRC - ORIGINAL STYLE, 1999-2004

This was the basic specification of the original generation of Focus World Rally Cars, as originally engineered in 1998, and that evolved, gradually, over the next six seasons:

○ **Engine**
Ford Zetec-M, developed first by Mountune, then from 1999 by Cosworth.
4-cylinder aluminium cylinder head, cast iron cylinder block, 2ohc, 1988cc, bore x stroke 84.8mm x 88mm.
Turbocharged with Garrett turbo, a 34mm turbo inlet passage restrictor, and with Pectel – later Cosworth-developed – engine management system.
Peak power (nominal): 300bhp at 6500rpm.
Peak Torque: 405lb-ft/56kg-m at 4000rpm.

○ **Transmission**
Transverse engine, with longitudinal main gearbox, allied to four-wheel drive. Engineering and manufacture by Xtrac.
6 forward ratios, with sequential change.

○ **Brakes**
Four-wheel disc brakes, by Brembo.
Front disc diameter: 300mm (gravel)/380mm (tarmac).
Rear disc diameter: 300mm (gravel)/300mm (tarmac).

○ **Dimensions**

Wheelbase:	102.95in	2615mm
Overall length:	163.5in	4152mm
Overall width:	69.7in	1770mm
Overall height:	55.9in	1420mm
Unladen weight:	2712lb	1230kg

FORD FOCUS WRC - REVISED STYLE/ SECOND-GENERATION, 2005-2010

The basic specification of the second-generation Focus World Rally Cars, as originally built around the alloy Duratec-R engine, first used in 2005. It then evolved over the next six seasons:

○ **Engine**
Ford Duratec-R, developed originally by Cosworth, then manufactured by M-Sport/Pipo Moteurs.
4-cylinder, aluminium cylinder head, aluminium cylinder block, 2ohc, 1998cc, bore x stroke 85 x 88mm.
Turbocharged with Garrett turbo, a 34mm turbo inlet passage restrictor, and with Pi/Cosworth-developed engine management system.
Peak power (nominal): 300bhp at 6000rpm.
Peak Torque: 405lb-ft/56kg-m at 4000rpm.

○ **Transmission**
Transverse engine, with transversely-mounted main gearbox, allied to four-wheel drive. Engineering and manufacture by Ricardo.
6 forward ratios, with sequential change.

○ **Brakes**
Four-wheel disc brakes, by Brembo.
Front disc diameter: 300mm (gravel)/370mm (tarmac).
Rear disc diameter: 300mm (gravel)/370mm (tarmac).

○ **Dimensions**

Wheelbase	103.9in	2640mm
Overall length	171.7in	4362mm
Overall width	70.9in	1800mm
Unladen weight	2712lb	1230kg

World Rally Championship record, 1999 to 2010

Year	World Rally Championship for Manufacturers	World Rally Championship for Drivers
1999	4th	6th (Colin McRae)
2000	2nd	4th (Colin McRae)
2001	2nd	2nd (Colin McRae)
2002	2nd	3rd (Carlos Sainz)
2003	4th	5th (Markko Märtin)
2004	2nd	3rd (Markko Märtin)
2005	3rd	4th (Toni Gardemeister)
2006	1st	2nd (Marcus Grönholm)
2007	1st	2nd (Marcus Grönholm)
2008	2nd	2nd (Mikko Hirvonen)
2009	2nd	2nd (Mikko Hirvonen)
2010	2nd	2nd (Jari-Matti Latvala)

Works Focus WRC rally highlights, 1999-2010

[World Rally Championship. First, second and third place results quoted.]

Event	Result/Driver	Comment
1999		
Rallye Monte Carlo	3rd (disq)/Colin McRae	Disqualified due to alleged homologation mistake
Swedish Rally	3rd/Thomas Rådström	
Safari Rally	1st/Colin McRae	S9 FMC. Focus' first victory
Rallye de Portugal	1st/Colin McRae	S7 FMC
2000		
Rallye Monte Carlo	2nd/Carlos Sainz	
Swedish Rally	3rd/Colin McRae	
Rallye de Portugal	3rd/Carlos Sainz	
Rallye Catalunya/Spain	1st/Colin McRae 3rd/Carlos Sainz	V5 FMC
Rally Argentina	1st/Colin McRae 2nd/Carlos Sainz	V5 FMC
Rally of New Zealand	2nd/Colin McRae 3rd/Carlos Sainz	
Neste Rally Finland	2nd/Colin McRae	
Cyprus Rally	1st/Carlos Sainz 2nd/Colin McRae	V6 FMC
Tour de Corse	3rd/Carlos Sainz	
2001		
Rallye Monte Carlo	2nd/Carlos Sainz 3rd/François Delecour	
Swedish Rally	3rd/Carlos Sainz	
Rallye de Portugal	2nd/Carlos Sainz	
Rally Argentina	1st/Colin McRae 3rd/Carlos Sainz	X5 FMC
Cyprus Rally	1st/Colin McRae 3rd/Carlos Sainz	X7 FMC
Acropolis Rally	1st/Colin McRae	Y4 FMC
Neste Rally Finland	3rd/Colin McRae	
Rally of New Zealand	2nd/Colin McRae	
2002		
Rallye Monte Carlo	3rd/Carlos Sainz	

Event	Result/Driver	Comment
Swedish Rally	3rd/Carlos Sainz	
Rally Argentina	1st/Carlos Sainz 3rd/Colin McRae	EX02 OBC
Acropolis Rally	1st/Colin McRae 3rd/Carlos Sainz	X7 FMC 9
Safari Rally	1st/Colin McRae	EK51 HYB Colin McRae's 10th
Rally of Great Britain	2nd/Colin McRae 3rd/Carlos Sainz	
2003		
Rally of Turkey	3rd/François Duval	
Acropolis Rally	1st/Markko Märtin	EO03 YRJ
Neste Rally Finland	1st/Markko Märtin	EO03 YRJ
Rallye Sanremo	3rd/Markko Märtin	
Tour de Corse	3rd/François Duval	
Rallye Catalunya/Spain	3rd/Markko Märtin	
2004		
Rallye Monte Carlo	2nd/Markko Märtin 3rd/François Duval	
Rally Mexico	1st/Markko Märtin 2nd/François Duval	ET53 URO
Rally of New Zealand	3rd/Markko Märtin	
Cyprus Rally	2nd/Markko Märtin	
Rally Argentina	3rd/François Duval	
Neste Rally Finland	2nd/Markko Märtin	
Rallye Deutschland	2nd/François Duval	
Rally Japan	3rd/Markko Märtin	
Rally of Great Britain	3rd/Markko Märtin	
Tour de Corse	1st/Markko Märtin	ET53 UJP
Rallye Catalunya/Spain	1st/Markko Märtin	ET53 UJP
Rally Australia	3rd/François Duval	
2005		
Rallye Monte Carlo	2nd/Toni Gardemeister	
Swedish Rally	3rd/Toni Gardemeister	
Acropolis Rally	2nd/Toni Gardemeister	

Event	Result/Driver	Comment
Tour de Corse	2nd/Toni Gardemeister	
2006		
Rallye Monte Carlo	1st/Marcus Grönholm	EU55 BMV
Swedish Rally	1st/Marcus Grönholm	EU55 BMV
Rallye Catalunya/Spain	3rd/Marcus Grönholm	
Tour de Corse	2nd/Marcus Grönholm	
Rally d'Italia Sardegna	2nd/Mikko Hirvonen	
Acropolis Rally	1st/Marcus Grönholm	EU55 BMV
Rallye Deutschland	3rd/Marcus Grönholm	
Neste Rally Finland	1st/Marcus Grönholm	EU55 CNN
Rally Japan	2nd/Marcus Grönholm 3rd/Mikko Hirvonen	
Cyprus Rally	2nd/Marcus Grönholm 3rd/Mikko Hirvonen	
Rally of Turkey	1st/Marcus Grönholm 2nd/Mikko Hirvonen	EU55 BMV
Rally Australia	1st/Mikko Hirvonen	EU55 CNX
Rally of New Zealand	1st/Marcus Grönholm 2nd/Mikko Hirvonen	EU55 CNN
Rally of Great Britain	1st/Marcus Grönholm	EDU55 CNF
2007		
Rallye Monte Carlo	3rd/Marcus Grönholm	
Swedish Rally	1st/Marcus Grönholm 3rd/Mikko Hirvonen	EJ56 FZV
Rally Norway	1st/Mikko Hirvonen 2nd/Marcus Grönholm	EJ56 FZB
Rally Mexico	2nd/Marcus Grönholm 3rd/Mikko Hirvonen	
Rally Argentina	2nd/Marcus Grönholm 3rd/Mikko Hirvonen	
Rally d'Italia Sardegna	1st/Marcus Grönholm 2nd/Mikko Hirvonen	EJ56 FZV
Acropolis Rally	1st/Marcus Grönholm	EJ56 FZV`
Neste Rally Finland	1st/Marcus Grönholm 2nd/Mikko Hirvonen	EU07SSX
Rallye Deutschland	3rd/Mikko Hirvonen	
Rally of New Zealand	1st/Marcus Grönholm 3rd/Mikko Hirvonen	EU07 STX
Rallye Catalunya/Spain	3rd/Marcus Grönholm	
Tour de Corse	2nd/Marcus Grönholm	
Rally Japan	1st/Mikko Hirvonen	EJ56 FXA
Rally of Great Britain	1st/Mikko Hirvonen 2nd/Marcus Grönholm	EJ56 FXA
2008		
Rallye Monte Carlo	2nd/Mikko Hirvonen	
Swedish Rally	1st/Jari-Matti Latvala 2nd/Mikko Hirvonen	EU07 SUF

Event	Result/Driver	Comment
Rally Mexico	3rd/Jari-Matti Latvala	
Jordan Rally	1st/Mikko Hirvonen	EU07 SSZ
Rally d'Italia Sardegna	2nd/Mikko Hirvonen 3rd/Jari-Matti Latvala	
Acropolis Rally	3rd/Mikko Hirvonen	
Rally of Turkey	1st/Mikko Hirvonen 2nd/Jari-Matti Latvala	EU07 SUA
Neste Rally Finland	2nd/Mikko Hirvonen	
Rally of New Zealand	3rd/Mikko Hirvonen	
Rallye Catalunya/Spain	3rd/Mikko Hirvonen	
Tour de Corse	2nd/Mikko Hirvonen 3rd/François Duval	
Rally Japan	1st/Mikko Hirvonen 2nd/Jari-Matti Latvala	EU07 SSZ
Rally of Great Britain	2nd/Jari-Matti Latvala	
2009		
Rally Ireland	3rd/Mikko Hirvonen	
Rally Norway	2nd/Mikko Hirvonen 3rd/Jari-Matti Latvala	
Cyprus Rally	2nd/Mikko Hirvonen	
Rallye de Portugal	2nd/Mikko Hirvonen	
Rally d'Italia Sardegna	1st/Jari-Matti Latvala 2nd/Mikko Hirvonen	PX08 AXC
Acropolis Rally	1st/Mikko Hirvonen 3rd/Jari-Matti Latvala	PX08 AXB
Rally Poland	1st/Mikko Hirvonen	PX08 AXB
Neste Rally Finland	1st/Mikko Hirvonen 3rd/Jari-Matti Latvala	SA09 VHR
Rally Australia	1st/Mikko Hirvonen	SA09 VHR
Rallye Catalunya/Spain	3rd/Mikko Hirvonen	
Rally of Great Britain	2nd/Mikko Hirvonen	
2010		
Swedish Rally	1st/Mikko Hirvonen 3rd/Jari-Matti Latvala	BK08 LCW
Jordan Rally	2nd/Jari-Matti Latvala	
Rally of Turkey	3rd/Mikko Hirvonen	
Rally of New Zealand	1st/Jari-Matti Latvala	PX08 AXB
Neste Rally Finland	1st/Jari-Matti Latvala	PX08 AXD
Rally Japan	3rd/Jari-Matti Latvala	
Rally of Great Britain	3rd/Jari-Matti Latvala	

In summary, in that successful twelve-year period, the official works team recorded:

- 44 outright victories
- 44 second place results
- 52 third place results

Works Focus cars used in WRC events

My friend and colleague Martin Holmes, who probably knows more about rallying than anyone on the planet, often commented succinctly on the Focus' career in his authoritative annual, *World Rallying*.

With his gracious permission, I now quote an extract he once wrote:

"A total of 97 Focus World Rally Cars were built in the 12 years they were used in world championship competition, starting at Monte Carlo 1999. During the lifetime of the Focus there were two major design upgrades, for the 2003 and then the 2006 season … The final appearance of a new Focus was 'SA09 VHR', Hirvonen's car in Sardinia 2009. The most successful Focus in the WRC was 'EU55 BMV', which won four events in 2006 …"

To make Martin's comment even more clear, according to this author 84 of those cars were used or started events as official works machines, and are listed below. The remainder were built and allocated to entrants such as the Eddie Stobart team, whose cars should be best described as 'works-assisted' machines.

All these cars were built, prepared, and maintained at M-Sport's HQ at Dovenby Hall, in Cumbria.

This is when each of the official works cars first appeared in public, to be campaigned, in the Focus WRC's long career:

1998
S16 FMC*

* Original test/prototype car

1999

S6 FMC	S7 FMC	S8 FMC	S9 FMC	S10 FMC
S11 FMC	S12 FMC	S14 FMC	S15 FMC*	S16 FMC**

* Original test/practice car
** First appearance as a rally car

2000

V2 FMC	V3 VMC	V4 FMC	V5 FMC	V6 FMC
V7 FMC	V8 FMC	V9 FMC	V10 FMC	

2001

X3 FMC	X4 FMC	X5 FMC	X6 FMC	X7 FMC
X8 FMC	Y3 FMC	Y4 FMC	Y5 FMC	Y6 FMC
Y128 XEV	Y129 XEV			

2002

X493 YOO	Y129 XEV	EK51 HYA	EK51 HYB	EX51 UAA
EX51 UAB	EX51 HXZ	EX02 OBB	EX02 OBC	EX02 OBD
EX02 OBE				

2003

EJ02 KMU	EJ02 KMV	EO03 XYG	R55 OTH	EO03YWC
EO03 YRJ	EK52 LNP	EK52 NWN		

2004

EF04 VVB	EG53BDU	EG53 CCN	EN02 UCT	ET53 UJP
ET53 UNY	ET53 URO			

2005

EF04WBW	EG53 AVD	EO03 XYG	EU55 BMY	EU55 BMZ

2006

EU55 BMV	EU55 BNA	EU55 CNF	EU55 CNJ	EU55 CNK
EU55 CNN	EU55 CNV	EU55 CNX		

2007

EJ56 FXA	EJ56 FZB	EJ56 FZV	EO56 TZR	EU07SSX
EU07STX				

2008

EA07 PXN	EA07 SSZ	EU07 STX	EU07 STZ	EU07 SUA
EU07 SUF	EU07 SUH			

2009

AG57 CKA	PX08 AXB	PX08 AXC	PX08 AXD	SA09 VHR

2010
BK08 LCW

These were the cars used by the closely-related 'Stobart' team between 2005 and 2010, some of which were originally used by the 'official' works team:

2005

1ES	EK52 LNF

2006

S568 RHH	EK52 NWN	EG53 AVD	EF04 VVB	EF04 WBW
EU55 BNA	EU55 CNK	EU55 CNV		

2007

EG53 CCN	EU55 BMZ	EU55 CNF	EU55 CNJ	EU55 CNX
EJ56 FZB				

2008

EJ56 FXA	EO56 TZR	EU07 RGZ	EU07 SSX	EU07 SUH
EU07 STX	EU07 SUO	EU07 SUV		

2009

EU07 SUA	EU07 SUF	PXO8 AXC

2010

AG57 CKA	EU07 SSZ

APPENDIX **V**
Works drivers, 1999-2010

	Victories	2nds & 3rds
1999		
Simon Jean-Joseph		
Colin McRae	2	
Thomas Rådström	1	
Petter Solberg		
2000		
Tapio Laukkanen		
Piero Liatti		
Colin McRae	2	4
Carlos Sainz	1	6
Petter Solberg		
2001		
François Delecour	1	
Mark Higgins		
Colin McRae	3	2
Carlos Sainz	5	
2002		
François Duval		
Mark Higgins		
Markko Märtin	1	
Colin McRae	2	1
Carlos Sainz	1	4
2003		
François Duval	2	
Mikko Hirvonen		
Jari-Matti Latvala		
Markko Märtin	2	2
2004		
François Duval	5	
Markko Märtin	3	6
Janne Tuohino		
Antony Warmbold		
2005		
Luís Pérez Companc		

	Victories	2nds & 3rds
Toni Gardemeister	4	
Mikko Hirvonen		
Roman Kresta		
Daniel Solà		
Henning Solberg		
Antony Warmbold		
2006		
Marcus Grönholm	7	5
Mikko Hirvonen	1	7
2007		
Khalid Al Qassimi		
Marcus Grönholm	5	7
Mikko Hirvonen	3	7
2008		
Khalid Al Qassimi		
François Duval	1	
Mikko Hirvonen	3	8
Jari-Matti Latvala	1	6
2009		
Mikko Hirvonen	4	7
Khalid Al Qassimi		
Jari-Matti Latvala	1	3
2010		
Mikko Hirvonen	1	1
Khalid Al Qassimi		
Jari-Matti Latvala	2	4

Stobart team drivers - effectively the back-up works team:

	Victories	2nds & 3rds
2005		
Mark Higgins		
Matthew Wilson		

	Victories	2nds & 3rds
2006		
Luís Pérez Companc		
Kosti Katajamäki		
Jari-Matti Latvala		
Pieter Tsjoen		
Matthew Wilson		
2007		
Alessandro Bettega		
Gareth Jones		
Jari-Matti Latvala	1	
Andreas Mikkelsen		
Henning Solberg	2	
Matthew Wilson		
2008		
Barry Clark		
François Duval	1	
Gianluigi Galli	1	
Henning Solberg		
Matthew Wilson		
2009		
Urmo Aava		
Krzysztof Hołowczyc		
Henning Solberg	2	
Matthew Wilson		
2010		
Per-Gunnar Andersson		
Ken Block		
Liu Caodong		
François Duval		
Marcus Grönholm		
Henning Solberg		
Matthew Wilson		

World Rally Car regulations, as launched in 1997

When the FIA introduced a new top-level homologation category to head up World Rally Championship events in 1997, this signalled yet another a complete upheaval in the sport. Instead of the Group A category that had dominated the sport for some time, an entirely new grouping – World Rally Cars – would take over. The FIA's objective was to encourage more manufacturers to enter a sport that had come to be dominated by Lancia, Ford, Mitsubishi, Subaru and Toyota. It was a misguided policy, but it would take a few years to prove to be so.

When the World Rally Championship was first set up in 1973, the honours were originally shared by the two-wheel drive FIA Group 2 (1000 cars had to be built) and Group 4 (400-off) machines, while four-wheel drive cars became eligible from 1979. Then, from 1982, a major change took place with the introduction of Group A (5000-off) and Group B (400-off) to take over their place. It was at this time that newly-designed and extremely fast Group B cars, such as the Peugeot 205 T16 and the Lancia Delta S4, led to many pundits calling the sport too dangerous to carry on in its current form.

Following several harrowing accidents in 1986 (reaching a sickening climax with the death of Henri Toivonen in a fiery crash during the Tour de Corse), the major part of WRC participation was restricted to Group A cars from 1987, and (after the cars required to be built per year being reduced to 2500) so it remained until the end of 1996.

In that decade the peak power output of a Group A car's 2-litre engine was progressively stifled by tightening the regulations concerning the turbocharger inlet orifice via a restrictor. This was balanced, however, by advances made in the braking, tyre performance, transmission, and engine torque delivery departments. Not only that, but the development of projects such as the Ford Escort RS Cosworth, Toyota Celica GT4, and Lancia Delta Integrale types (all of which were effectively 'homologation specials,' built in sufficient quantities to ensure Group A homologation) meant that other 'fringe' manufacturers were clearly discouraged from trying to break into this rather settled grouping.

Accordingly, in the mid-1990s, the FIA decided to make an important move that in its view would make it possible for new makers to get involved. Effective 1 January 1997, the World Rally Championship was to be contested by a new type of car called a 'World Rally Car.' Homologation was made much easier (and with much reduced investment costs), because teams only had to present the makings of just 20 sets of new cars.

Specifically, they would have to show only: one complete road car on which the WRC was based; one prepared WRC body-in-white; one complete WRC vehicle; and one complete set of components, including engine, transmission, chassis parts (suspension, brakes, and steering gear), and control systems. The engine was to be a turbocharged two-litre unit.

A study of the basic regulations that applied to these cars shows that the FIA was determined to keep the cars' straight-line performance at the existing (mid-1990s) Group A levels. It would, however, allow an engineering team to have considerably more technical freedom as to how this was to be achieved.

The car's structure had to be based on that of an existing model of which at least 25,000 units were being produced every year. Despite this, there was freedom to convert two-wheel drive cars to four-wheel drive, and to add turbochargers to otherwise normally-aspirated engines, all allied to totally special transmission systems. It was also possible to design and fit different suspension systems, though the front suspension had to be 'of the same type' as the chosen donor car.

To allow the most suitable wheels and tyres to be used in this exciting sport, a WRC's bodywork (specifically the wheelarches) could be widened to 1770mm/69.7in. Not only that, but – within certain specified limits – the bodywork of WRC cars could be treated to a new breed of aerodynamic add-ons, specifically transverse spoilers to help produce downforce at high road speeds. The most significant change regarding the structure, however, was that it was no longer permitted to ever have a WRC car re-shelled: each car had to have a stamped non-transferable identity in the structure itself. Post-crash, if a car still had an undamaged roll cage, the shell could be rebuilt around it. On the other hand, if a roll cage was damaged/distorted in the crash, restoration was not permitted, and the car would have to be written-off.

In some ways, this was meant to produce a new breed of 'silhouette' cars: models that bore superficial resemblance to their road car counterparts, but that were quite different mechanically. Because of the need to invest in only twenty such cars – all without even a nodding acquaintance of accepted ride, handling, comfort, and convenience standards – it was thought that hitherto uninterested manufacturers might have a change of heart.

This was a total change from previous practice. Thousands of enthusiastic private owners, for instance, had bought, driven, and habitually used road car versions of the latest 1990s Group A cars. Now it was simply not possible, let alone unlikely, that a WRC would attract the same sort of clientele. In the case of the front-line Ford cars, there had been well over 5000 Sierra Cosworth 4x4s, and more than 7000 Escort RS Cosworths. In comparison, only a mere 50 Escort World Rally Cars (none of them Type Approved for normal road use), and precisely 97 Focus WRCs (all solely for competition use) were ever built.

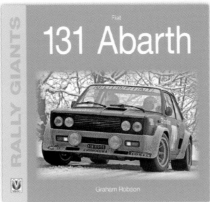
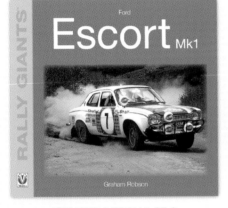

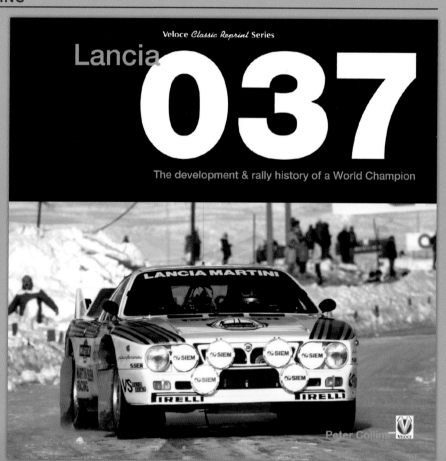

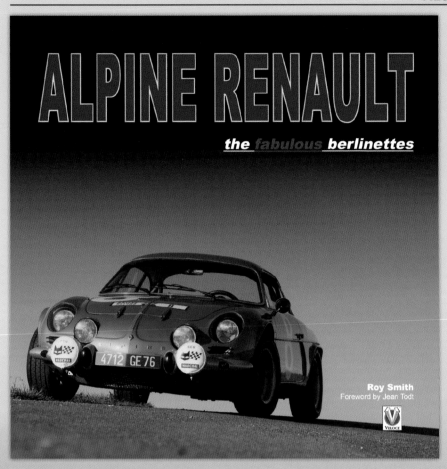

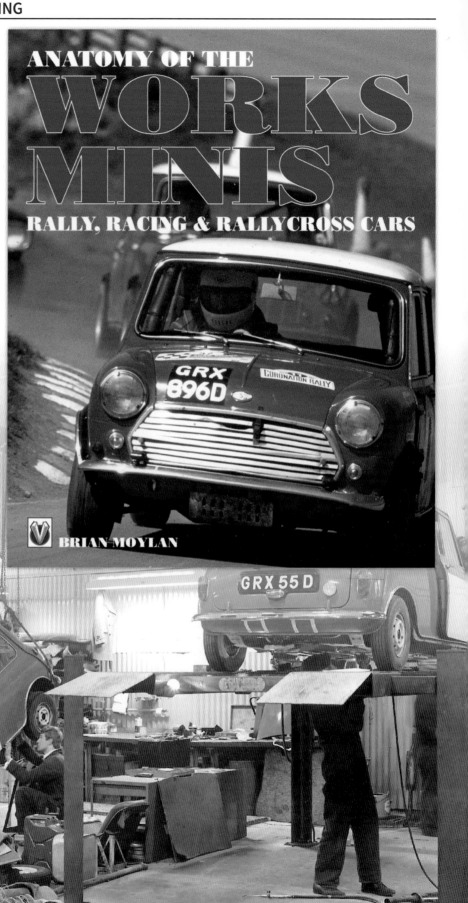

Index

Please note: Because frequent mentions of Malcolm Wilson, M-Sport, Dovenby Hall, and World Rally cars – along with their sponsors – occur throughout this book, no attempt has been made to provide individual references.